SECOND LANGUAGE WRITING
Series Editor, Paul Kei Matsuda

Second language writing emerged in the late twentieth century as an interdisciplinary field of inquiry, and an increasing number of researchers from various related fields—including applied linguistics, communication, composition studies, and education—have come to identify themselves as second language writing specialists. The Second Language Writing series aims to facilitate the advancement of knowledge in the field of second language writing by publishing scholarly and research-based monographs and edited collections that provide significant new insights into central topics and issues in the field.

Books in the Series

The Politics of Second Language Writing: In Search of the Promised Land, edited by Paul Kei Matsuda, Christina Ortmeier-Hooper, and Xiaoye You (2006)
Building Genre Knowledge, Christine M. Tardy (2009)
Practicing Theory in Second Language Writing, edited by Tony Silva and Paul Kei Matsuda (2010)

Practicing Theory in Second Language Writing

Edited by
Tony Silva and Paul Kei Matsuda

Parlor Press
West Lafayette, Indiana
www.parlorpress.com

For Gus Entler

Parlor Press LLC, West Lafayette, Indiana 47906

S A N: 2 5 4 - 8 8 7 9

Library of Congress Cataloging-in-Publication Data

Practicing theory in second language writing / edited by Tony Silva and Paul Kei Matsuda.
   p. cm.
 Includes bibliographical references and index.
 ISBN 978-1-60235-138-7 (pbk. : alk. paper) -- ISBN 978-1-60235-139-4 (hardcover : alk. paper) -- ISBN 978-1-60235-140-0 (adobe ebook : alk. paper)
 1. Language and languages--Study and teaching--Research. 2. Rhetoric--Study and teaching--Research. 3. Second language acquisition--Research.
I. Silva, Tony. II. Matsuda, Paul Kei.
 P53.27.P73 2009
 418.0071--dc22
                          2009043991

Cover design by Paul Kei Matsuda and David Blakesley
Printed on acid-free paper.

Parlor Press, LLC is an independent publisher of scholarly and trade titles in print and multimedia formats. This book is available in paper, hardcover, and Adobe eBook formats from Parlor Press on the World Wide Web at http://www.parlorpress.com or through online and brick-and mortar bookstores. For submission information or to find out about Parlor Press publications, write to Parlor Press, 816 Robinson St., West Lafayette, Indiana, 47906, or e-mail editor@parlorpress.com.

Contents

Introduction

Tony Silva and Paul Kei Matsuda

THE ISSUES

Theory is a term that has been used widely in the field of second language writing. Yet, partly due to the interdisciplinary nature of the field, the term often means different things to different people. Second language writing specialists—teachers, researchers and administrators—have yet to have an open and sustained conversation about what theory is, how it works, and, more important, how to *practice* theory.

This collection will feature fifteen chapters by distinguished scholars in second language writing who will explore various aspects of theoretical work that goes on in the field. The authors of the first four chapters address the nature and role of theory in second language writing. The authors of the next nine chapters reflect on their own theoretical practices. The authors of the final chapter take up the issue of theory in writing dissertations on second language writing.

Some of the key questions explored in this collection include the following:

- *The Nature of Theory.* What is the nature of theory in second language writing? What role does theory play in second language writing research, instruction, and administration? Is it possible (or even desirable) to develop a comprehensive theory or theories of second language writing?
- *Applied Theories.* How do various theories from other areas of inquiry inform second language writing research, instruction, and assessment? What are some of the advantages of using theories from other fields? What are some of the limitations? How can the value of new theoretical perspectives be assessed?

- *Theorizing and Theory Building.* How do second language writing teachers, researchers, and administrators develop theories of second language writing? What might a theory of second language writing look like? What is the relationship between the conceptual work of theorizing and data-driven theory building?

- *Practicing Theory.* How might second language writing teachers, researchers, and administrators deal with theory? What are some of the practical issues that arise in working with various types of theory? How do second language writing specialists learn to work with theory? How does theory inform instruction and administration as well as materials development?

THE CHAPTERS

PART I. THE NATURE AND ROLE OF THEORY IN SECOND LANGUAGE WRITING

In "Between Theory with a Big 'T' and Practice with a Small 'p': Why Theory Matters," Dwight Atkinson attempts to clarify relationships between theory and practice in L2 writing. Suggesting that a simple theory-practice distinction is not a productive way to think about L2 writing, he asserts that it is the speculative and thoughtful nature of theory *combined* with practice that gives them an important role in helping teachers and researchers do what they do. Atkinson then distinguishes between different forms of theory and practice in L2 writing. The first, *Theory with a big T,* refers to a system of principles, ideas, and concepts used to explain, understand, or predict phenomena. Atkinson posits two kinds of *Theory with a big T:* scientific theory, from the natural sciences—exceptionless, objective, truthful, and empirically confirmed accounts of some part of the natural world—and social macro-theory, representing grand attempts to explain how the human world works. *Theory with a small t* is described as a speculative approach, the opposite of *Theory with a big T. practice with a small p* is described as customary or habitual action, assuming a common-sense view of reality. *Practice with a big P* is characterized as outward-looking, reflective, and open to reformulation and has the potential to dialogue with, inform, and even instigate or upset theory. Atkinson contends that what is at stake is understanding one's own place and the place of others in local and global systems, in helping people understand the effects of their actions.

In "Theories, Frameworks, and Heuristics: Some Reflections on Inquiry and Second language Writing," Alister Cumming considers the nature of theory in second language writing research by reflecting on the place of theory in his own data-based descriptive research. He starts by relating two stories of his childhood explorations, one involving no theoretical framework and the other guided by theoretical assumptions and procedures. He then considers his experience as a student of biology and of literature, both of which made use of different sets of conceptual and descriptive frameworks as well as discovery procedures (or heuristics). Through these stories, he not only illustrates how theory informs the process of knowledge construction but also demonstrates how theory provides a context that gives a sense of purpose to research activities. He further considers his insights in the context of second language writing research and argues for the importance of theory—or theories—as frameworks for describing and conceptualizing second language writing as well as heuristics for making pedagogical and policy decisions.

In "Multicompetence, Social Context, and L2 Writing Research Praxis," Lourdes Ortega and Joan Carson concern themselves with the congruence between theory and research practices in work that explores interfaces between second language writing and second language acquisition. Using disciplinary insights about multicompetence and social context, they explore four ways in which current research praxis can be made to better match current theoretical understandings of second language writing. These ways include: (1) studying multicompetence via within-writer designs, (2) developing analytical systems to study other languages vis-à-vis English, (3) judging the quality of multicompetent writing through a bilingual lens, and (4) grounding theoretical models in a variety of social contexts. The authors maintain that a reorientation of research praxis in these directions could have two beneficial consequences. It could enable L2 writing researchers to better capture what multicompetent writers can do, as opposed to only understanding what they cannot or wish not to do in their L2, English. Additionally, they suggest that the changes they discuss would by necessity lead to a healthy increase of dialogue and collaboration among L2 writing researchers (where *L2 writing* is often associated with English writing exclusively) and researchers working on

L2 writing within the perspectives of foreign and heritage language education.

Lynn M. Goldstein's chapter, "Finding 'Theory' in the Particular: An 'Autobiography' of What I Learned and How about Teacher Feedback," presents an autobiographical account of her research career, focusing on the evolution of her understanding (i.e., theory) as she engaged in ongoing research on teacher feedback and student revisions. She does not see her research stemming from a theoretical perspective; instead, she characterizes her research as a cycle starting with questions that arise in her teaching practices, which then leads to research that generates an understanding about the phenomenon. She begins by contrasting her earlier and simpler conception of teacher feedback to the most recent and more dynamic conception. She then articulates six principles that helped her develop a more sophisticated understanding of teacher feedback that is grounded in the classroom reality. The six guiding principles of her research practice include: (1) understandings come not only from formal research but also from the classroom, (2) let the data speak for itself, (3) use multiple data sources, (4) be open to alternative analyses and interpretations of the data, (5) step back and take a second look after a period of time, and (6) look at each student as an individual rather than focusing only on the aggregate data. While she acknowledges that her research is not atheoretical, she emphasizes the importance of grounding her research in the reality of classroom practice, and calls for more research that tests current theories against the actual lived experience of teachers and students in the classroom.

Part II. Reflections on Theoretical Practices

Theory and Qualitative Research

In "Practicing Theory in Qualitative Research on Second Language Writing," Linda Harklau and Gwendolyn Williams take up the question of whether and to what extent theoretical perspectives are articulated in qualitative studies focusing on second language writing. Emphasizing the centrality of theory in qualitative research—and the importance of explicitly addressing theory in conducting qualitative research—they review how the research literature in second language writing between 2001 and 2006 engages theory and report that the existing literature does not articulate its theoretical and methodological assumptions explicitly. They discuss two possible reasons for this tendency: (1) the dichotomy between positivism and post-positivism has masked the complexity and diversity of perspectives among post-positivist approaches, and (2) the false sense of shared assumptions and theoretical orientations. They conclude by pointing out the centrality of theory of method (i.e., methodology), the diversity of methodological perspectives within qualitative research, the importance of continued efforts in methodological innovations, and the need for multiple theories for second language writing research.

In "Cleaning up the Mess: Perspectives from a Novice Theory Builder," Christine Tardy shares the perspective of someone who describes herself as a relative novice in theory building—though certainly a highly successful one. While she initially found the prospect of engaging with theory—"research-driven explanations of complex phenomena"—rather intimidating, she gradually began to see her work as building theory as she gained experience and confidence. She starts by describing her early training in quantitative research and describes how she came to see qualitative research as a viable means of addressing *hows* and *whys* of genre knowledge development. She then traces the process of her qualitative research projects— a pilot study, a dissertation, and a book, *Building Genre Knowledge* (Parlor Press, 2009) that helped her see her work as building theory.

Theory and Quantitative Research

In "A Reconsideration of Contents of Pedagogical Implications and Further Research Needed) Moves in the Reporting of Second Language Writing Research and Their Roles in Theory Building," Doug Flahive argues for the need for change in conventions used to report research in L2 writing and offers specific suggestions regarding the nature of these conventions. His focus is on two moves which have become ritualized in the reporting of L2 studies: Pedagogical Implications (PIs) and Further Research Needed (FRN). His focus on the need for revision in the contents of these moves is motivated by his role as a teacher-educator and his desire to see the field of L2 writing mature in ways consistent with sound principles of social science inquiry. He begins by describing activities he uses to nurture a spirit of critical inquiry in his students. Next, he presents summaries of his professional experiences and research projects that shaped his current views on the role of theory, research, and practice. He then provides a check-list to assess research studies. Finally, he looks critically at a corpus of studies in which examples of PIs and FRN are found. Overall, his objective is to make L2 writing researchers more aware of how altering the contents of these Moves can make their research more pedagogically relevant and more useful to researchers and theorists.

Dudley W. Reynolds, in "Beyond Texts: A Research Agenda for Quantitative Research on Second Language Writers and Readers," argues the importance of representing complex phenomena such as second language writing as they are—as complex phenomena—especially at this historical juncture in which the public is looking to scientifically based research to guide educational policies. To examine how the phenomenon of second language writing is represented in the literature, he presents a survey of research studies published in major journals in applied linguistics and composition studies between 2001 and 2005. He found that there is a balance between quantitative and qualitative studies, although relatively few studies combine quantitative and qualitative perspectives. He also found that quantitative studies tend to focus on textual issues rather than issues related to the writer, reader or interaction among them. Based on these findings, he emphasizes the importance of resisting designs that oversimplify the meaning-making process or trivialize the significance of individual differences.

Theory and Ideology in L2 Writing

A. Suresh Canagarajah's "Ideology and Theory in Second Language Writing: A Dialogical Treatment" is a multivocal essay involving a writing teacher (Min-Zhan Lu, here reconstructed), the author (Canagarajah), and a straw man critic. In this piece, he addresses the charge that ideologies are an imposition on writing practice. He narrates the experience of a multilingual student and a writing teacher to show how ideological explanations provide an important orientation toward understanding textual conflicts and creative options. In order to develop this perspective, he challenges other stereotypes about ideologies (i.e., that they are deliberately constructed for purposes of social control and that they inculcate an illusory view of social life). He demonstrates how ideologies are always already there in social practice, that their manifestation is both unconscious and material, and that they can enable a deeper understanding of social life and human agency for textual/discursive change. Canagarajah's chapter includes five parts: a description of the writing teacher's dilemma, a response to this dilemma, professional implications growing out this response, the theory/ideology connection, and a reflexive conclusion. He concludes with a description of his tool box approach to writing theories, wherein he picks and chooses theories to explain specific areas of writing practice but is not fully committed to any of them and has the detachment necessary to critique and reconstruct them if the complexities of practice demand a different theory.

In "Critical Approaches to Theory in Second Language Writing: A Case of Critical Contrastive Rhetoric," Ryuko Kubota explores how conceptual principles of what is critical within applied linguistics can apply to contrastive rhetoric. She argues that the area would benefit from the application of critical applied linguistics to an inquiry into cultural difference in rhetorical organization for several reasons: (1) classification and descriptions of rhetoric based on cultural differences tend to produce and reinforce cultural stereotypes or essentialism, (2) such cultural essentialism directly affects teachers and learners not only in classroom instruction but also on wider issues of text production and curriculum development, (3) the discourse of cultural difference in rhetoric persists in both academic and public spheres, and (4) the poststructuralist plurality of meanings and postcolonial appropriation of language as resistance can provide a different perspective on the cultural uniqueness of rhetoric. She argues that these trends justify the application of critical applied linguistics to contrastive rhetoric research. Kubota concludes that critical contrastive rhetoric affirms the plurality of rhetorical forms and students' identities in L1 and L2 writing, problematizes the taken-for-granted cultural knowledge about rhetorical norms, and allows writing teachers to recognize the complex web of rhetoric, culture, power, discourse, and resistance within which they conduct classroom instruction and respond to student writing.

Theory and L2 Writing Instruction

"Theory and Practice in Second Language Writing: How and Where Do They Meet?" by Wei Zhu addresses the relationship between theory and instructional practice in second language writing. First, the author provides an overview of different conceptions of theory in relation to second language writing research. Next, she discusses second language writing instruction and assessment as a situated practice. She then explores the interaction between the two, emphasizing the bidirectional, interdependent, dynamic, and reciprocal nature of the relationship. She concludes the chapter with a discussion of the implications of various conceptions of theory and practice as well as their relationship. She also considers the implications for the preparation of future second language writing teachers.

In "Theory-and-Practice and Other Questionable Dualisms in L2 Writing," John Hedgcock explores the complexity of the relationship between practice and theory in second language writing by examining operational definitions of theory and practice, the distribution of labor with regard to theory and practice, the reification of a unidirectional theory-to-practice relationship, the practice-theory separations in the rhetoric of the field's canonical texts, and the pervasiveness of practice. Hedgcock also looks at the epistemological landscape of this topic—its theoretical catalogues and methodological taxonomies—via the relevant work of scholars in both first and second language writing. He then turns to the current situation in the field, noting the interdependent connections among theory-building, research, and instructional practices. Hedgcock also touches upon the promise of praxis (i.e., theories of practice) and offers his personal thoughts on the reductive and misleading nature of the theory/practice dualism; the congruence (or lack thereof) of portrayals of theory-building, research, and models of practice; the degree to which a coherent epistemology is truly necessary; the questions, frameworks, and methods of inquiry coincident with/propelled by pedagogical paradigm shifts; reciprocity (or lack thereof) in the relationship between the first and second language writing communities; and the relationship among theory, empirical research, and instructional practice in the second language writing community.

Theory and L2 Writing Assessment

In "Assess Thyself Lest Others Assess Thee," Deborah Crusan examines the division in writing assessment between theorists and large scale test developers and discusses how mandated transfer of responsibility from locally developed assessment to one-size-fits-all state and federal standards runs counter to writing assessment theory. She considers the politics of writing assessment, looking at how assessment drives instruction, how what does not appear on tests tends to disappear from classrooms, and how politics affects pedagogy. Crusan does not call for the abolition of standardized testing. Her concern is the protection of the kind of writing assessment teachers do at their institutions; the prevention of intrusion and exclusive use of standardized tests when assessing for placement, diagnosis, and achievement; and the need for a re-examination of the use standardized tests scores as the sole criteria upon which to base critical decisions about students. Crusan recognizes the importance of being accountable to outside forces and public agencies that fund education while helping ensure that these programs are true to assessment theorists' philosophies of education, theories of language, and pedagogies. She believes it vital that teachers become involved in the design and implementation of writing assessment and illustrates how this can be done by offering an example of how assessment professionals can retain control of assessment at their institutions.

Theory and Dissertation Research

In the final chapter, "'Do I Need a Theoretical Framework?' Doctoral Students' Perspectives on the Role of Theory in Dissertation Research and Writing," Diane Belcher and Alan Hirvela address the issue of theory for doctoral students who are completing their dissertations. Among the many topics these students must negotiate during the dissertation experience—from the development of the proposal to the writing of the final draft of the completed dissertation—is the role of theory in a particular study. How important is the theoretical framework? Where should it be included in the dissertation? What are its functions? What are the student's responsibilities in the construction and application of the theoretical framework? This chapter addresses these and related questions by presenting a qualitative study of doctoral dissertation writers' experiences with theory in research related to second language writing. Based on the study, the authors present guidelines for future dissertation writers offered by the informants themselves, all of whom have successfully completed their own theoretically informed dissertations.

Practicing Theory in Second Language Writing

Part I. The Nature and Role of Theory in Second Language Writing

1 Between Theory with a Big T and Practice with a Small p: Why Theory Matters

Dwight Atkinson

> The English teacher can cooperate in her own mar-
> ginalization by seeing herself as a "language teacher"
> with no connection to . . . social and political issues.
> Or she can . . . accept her role as one who social-
> izes students into a world view that, given its power
> [in the U.S.] and abroad, must be viewed critically,
> comparatively, and with a constant sense of the possi-
> bilities for change. Like it or not, the English teacher
> stands at the very heart of the most crucial educa-
> tional, cultural, and political issues of our time. (Gee,
> 1990, pp. 67–68)

Written by James Gee, these words mark the terrain I would like to
cover in this chapter. My aim is to develop a way of thinking about
theory and practice that differs from dominant approaches but that
can still help clarify relationships between thinking and acting in L2
writing and education. Gee's words are especially important here because they indicate what is at stake in talking about these issues—not
engaging in ivory-tower debate but in understanding one's own place,
and the place of others, in local and world systems. In line with this
aim, let me offer a second quotation, this time from Michel Foucault:
"People know what they do. They frequently know why they do what
they do. What they don't know is what what they do does" (quoted
in Dreyfus & Rabinow, 1983, p. 187). It is in helping people "know
what what they do does" (or *may* do) that theory as I will define it can

5

contribute to our profession. But I am getting ahead of myself here, so let me begin closer to the beginning.

For the past 10 years, I have mainly taught two kinds of courses to graduate students in second language education and applied linguistics: "research methods" courses and "theory" courses. The latter, in my case, mostly introduce students to "thinking tools"—concepts regarding education, language learning, culture, and postmodernism which can inform, but not directly convert into, educational practice in the universities where most of my students are (or will be) employed. The question I often ask myself—and the question my students sometimes ask me as well—is what is the relationship of the "theory" I teach to the "practice" they perform, and which, in fact, they are largely interested in. In this paper, I try to construct an answer to that question—a better answer than those I commonly give. In doing so, I hope to suggest the importance of theory to L2 teaching generally and L2 writing specifically. In a sense, one could say that I am trying to theorize my own practice—to reflect on and better understand why I do what I do in the classroom, and perhaps what what I do does.

To preview, my argument will be that a simple theory-practice distinction is not a productive way to think in L2 writing and teaching. Instead, it is the speculative and thoughtful nature of theory *combined* with practice—and the lively and necessary dialogue between them—that gives them an invaluable place in helping teachers and researchers do what they do. But theory in this sense is not a panacea; it is more like a spark, or sometimes an irritant.

DEFINING "THEORY," DEFINING "PRACTICE"

Before jumping into the deep sea of theory and practice, however, it is necessary to define some terms. While dictionaries are not final authorities on anything, they seemed like a reasonable place to start in this case: I therefore examined three influential dictionaries—*Webster's New World Dictionary*, the *American Heritage Dictionary*, and the *Oxford English Dictionary* (or *OED*)—to get a sense of how the terms *theory* and *practice* have been commonly understood.

The most common meanings I found for *theory*—in no special order of importance—are three: (1) a system of principles, ideas, and concepts, used to explain, understand, or predict some phenomenon or phenomena; (2) a set of ideas or scheme which guides doing—a guide to practice; and (3) a speculative approach to something. This last seems closest to the original meaning of *theoria* in Greek and Late Latin, and according to the *OED* it is often pejorative, as in "That's just a theory."[1]

The most common meanings of "practice," on the other hand, are four: (1) customary or habitual action; (2) performance (i.e., "the act or process of doing something"—*American Heritage Dictionary*, p. 972); (3) repeated action for the sake of learning; and (4) the practice of a profession or business. The *OED* also mentioned two additional meanings that may be relevant to the present discussion: as *an application of* theory or *in contrast to* theory (i.e., theory vs. practice); and as a synonym for the Marxist term *praxis*—"social action which should result from or complement the theory of communism" (*OED*, vol. 7, pt. 2, p. 271). This, then, was my first attempt at understanding the significance of theory and practice to our field—I looked them up in the dictionary. Based partly on what I found there, let me now give a brief, initial account of my proposal.

THEORY WITH A BIG T VS. THEORY WITH A SMALL t; PRACTICE WITH A BIG P VS. PRACTICE WITH A SMALL p

I propose that we distinguish between different forms of theory and practice in L2 writing and education. My basic scheme for theory and practice has four categories: *Theory with a big T; theory with a small t; Practice with a big P, and practice with a small p.*[2] Each category relates to a different definition of theory or practice as found in my review of dictionary meanings. I will now briefly describe each category generally before trying, in the next section, to relate them specifically to second language writing and education.

Theory with a big T relates to the first meaning of theory in my dictionary search: "a system of principles, ideas, and concepts, used to explain, understand, or predict some phenomenon or phenomena." There are two kinds of Theory with a big T as I conceptualize it: The first—*scientific theory*—is the form of theory which is commonly thought to emerge from the natural sciences—exceptionless, objective, truthful, and empirically confirmed accounts of some part of the natural world. Atomic theory, relativity theory, evolutionary theory, and ecological theory are four examples that seem to fit this model.

The second form of Theory with a big T is what I will call *social macro-theory*. Social macro-theory represents grand attempts to explain how the human world—or some critical part of it—works. Examples include capitalism, Marxism, Christianity, rationalism, individualism, positivism, and social constructionism.

Theory with a small t is harder to define and exemplify, but it corresponds closely to meaning #3 in my dictionary search: "a speculative approach to something." It is perhaps most easily understood as the opposite of Theory with a big T, although I will complicate this understanding below. One source for my thinking about theory with a small t is the postmodernist idea of *petits récits*—theories that engage with particular, local situations because, postmodernistically conceived, that is largely or only what societies are composed of (e.g., Lyotard, 1984). As examples, I would give Foucault's partly theory-informed interventions regarding prisoners' rights in France (e.g., Eribon, 1991), or J. Robert Oppenheimer's work against the hydrogen bomb after his crucial role in developing the atomic bomb (Foucault, 1984a; Goodchild, 1981).

Let me turn now to practice: First, practice with a small p corresponds to meaning #1 in my dictionary review: "customary or habitual action." It is meant to capture what people, including teachers, do when they assume a "commonsense" view of reality (i.e., what is real is what I see in front of me, and how I respond to it). Examples of practice with a small p are the everyday tasks we accomplish without much reflection: listening to the radio, going to work, making small talk with acquaintances, cooking dinner. Much of the conduct of everyday life takes place at the level of practice with a small p—it has to: If every human action required sustained thought, we would never get out of the house in the morning or maybe even out of bed. Thus, everyday life is substantially unexamined, leading to what Frederick Erickson (1986) has called "the invisibility of everyday life."

Finally, Practice with a big P is practice which is outward-looking, reflective, and open to reformulation. It is also practice that has the potential to "speak truth to theory"—to dialogue with, inform, and even instigate or upset theory, especially in the small-t sense of the word. General examples of practice with a big P, like theory with a small t, are harder to find because they are usually local and contextual. But at least the idea is captured, more or less, in the above-mentioned Marxist concept of praxis: In this view, theory always directly informs practice, and practice, for its part, dialectically informs theory in turn.

T/THEORY IN SECOND LANGUAGE WRITING & EDUCATION

Let me now relate this general scheme specifically to work in L2 writing and education, beginning once again with theory. My first form of theory with a big T, scientific theory, can certainly be found in L2 education, and arguments, at least, for why we *need* such theory can certainly be found in L2 writing studies. In L2 education, the best-known example is Krashen's Monitor Model (1985). Less famous but more relevant these days is what I will call Focus on Form theory, whose foremost proponent is Michael Long (Long & Robinson, 1998), and which has its main theoretical basis in Richard Schmidt's Noticing Hypothesis (1990). The idea here—which many readers will already be familiar with—is that basically *all* language learning requires *some* level of conscious noticing or attention to form. Theories like Focus on Form and the Monitor Model are scientific in the sense that they basically claim to be exceptionless, objective (at least in their implicit epistemologies), truth-telling, and seek their confirmation in empirical research.

One of the strongest proponents of scientific theory in second language writing has been William Grabe. At the first Symposium on Second Language Writing in 1998, Grabe proposed that a scientific theory of L2 writing would benefit the field in many ways, especially concerning how academic writing is taught and evaluated. He argued that such a theory should be built on a knowledge foundation of "the writing processes and products of expert writers" (2001, p. 42). He further described two forms such theory might take—*descriptive* or *predictive*—with the descriptive version basically synthesizing what is known about L2 writing empirically, and the predictive version going much further to provide a hierarchical model of "processes, purposes, and outcomes" (p. 48) which would "predict relative difficulty of performance based on task, topic, and writer knowledge," as well as "general stages of writing development" (p. 48). Grabe himself clearly favored the predictive form of scientific theory, but he expressed caution as to whether such a theory was currently attainable.

Examples of my second type of Theory with a big T, social macro-theory, can be found in what I will call the neo-Marxist strand of L2 education and writing. This is work which supports a "critical pedagogy" approach to teaching and researching second or additional languages (e.g., Benesch, 2001; Crookes & Lehner, 1998; Kubota, 1999). In this work, a modernist narrative of oppressor vs. oppressed is clearly

represented—it is the "system" (represented by institutions, administrators, frequently teachers, and sometimes TESOL in general) against
the student, and the clear message is that to redress this imbalance
students must be given their own voices and power. The direct basis
of critical pedagogy is in Paulo Freire's work—a fairly straightforward
application of neo-Marxism to ameliorating the extreme disempower-
ment of Brazilian peasants through the teaching of critical literacy.
And the direct basis of Freire's attempt is in Marx's opposition of false
consciousness to true consciousness, where true or *critical* consciousness represents the Marxist theory of the means by which capitalism
(and, by extension, imperialism) oppresses (Marx, cited in Tucker,
1978, pp. 154–155; McLaren, 2000, p. 153). Unlike Marx, however,
who at least sometimes believed that worker revolution was inevitable,
neo-Marxists such as Lukács, Gramsci, Adorno, and Marcuse saw no
signs of its inevitability. As a result, intellectuals were assigned the role
of leading the way toward a classless society by actively opening the
eyes of the disempowered to their own oppression. This, in my understanding, is the core idea behind Freirian critical pedagogy (e.g.,
McLaren, 2000)—in the words of Lukács, quoted by Freire early in
his classic *Pedagogy of the Oppressed,* revolutionary intellectuals: "must
. . . *explain to the masses their own action* not only in order to insure the
continuity of the revolutionary experiences of the proletariat, but also
to *consciously activate the subsequent development* of those experiences"
(Lukács, 1965, quoted in Freire, 1970, p. 34; my translation & italics).
Or, as Herbert Marcuse, perhaps the best-known neo-Marxist, put it:

> [Society] must first enable its slaves to learn and see
> and think before they know what is going on and
> what they themselves can do to change it. And, to the
> degree to which the slaves have been preconditioned
> to exist as slaves and be content in their role, *their
> liberation necessarily appears to come from without and
> from above. They must be "forced to be free," to "see ob-
> jects as they are, and sometimes as they ought to appear."
> They must be shown the "good road" they are in search
> of.* (Marcuse, 1964, p. 40, including quotations from
> Rousseau; my italics)

Finally, in the words of Freire himself:

> For me the question is not for the teacher to have
> less and less authority. The issue is that the demo-
> cratic teacher never, never transforms authority into
> authoritarianism. He or she can never stop being an
> authority or having authority. *Without authority it is*
> *very difficult for the liberties of students to be shaped.*
> (Freire, in Shor & Freire, 1987, quoted in Johnston,
> 1999, p. 560; my italics)

In providing these quotes, I do not mean to dismiss critical pedagogy as simply an attempt to force one's truth on others. I do, however, want to set it in contrast to the form of theory I describe and exemplify next: theory with a small t.

Theory with a small t is a conscious response to both forms of Theory with a big T I have just described. It sees them, in postmodernist terms, as "metanarratives" (Lyotard, 1984). Metanarratives are all-encompassing, all-explanatory theories, based on what Donna Haraway (1988) has called "god's eye views." According to postmodernists like Lyotard and Foucault, the dominant thought styles of the Western world over the last three centuries have been founded on such grand narratives—offering some single, reductive, humanity-saving, and ultimately controlling truth. The view of humans as fundamentally rational, autonomous, and therefore perfectable; the idea that democracy *or* communism, once fully realized, would set humans free; the sense that capitalism together with technoscience could somehow permanently banish want and need—all have come in for withering critique from postmodernists. So what is left after the conceptual foundations of the last three centuries are disavowed? For postmodernists, the answer is *petits récits*—little narratives—which I would like to equate with (or at least relate to) theory with a small t.

Theory with a small t foregrounds the partial and speculative nature of theory. It suggests that, instead of totalizing narratives, there are only small, locally constructed, and locally relevant stories. It also suggests that those Theories with a big T—the totalizing metanarratives—can be modalized; that is, instead of filling the whole screen, they can be put to work in specific situations on specific problems, but as "thinking tools," with modesty and partiality built in, rather than asr "the one right story" by "the one who knows" (Lather, 2001, pp. 184 & 191). In other words, theory with a small t presents no already-made, all-knowing prescription for what is wrong with the world and how to fix it. Rather, it offers *small* tools that will help people build their *own* understandings (or not—there is no sense in which one *must* use these tools)[3] of social situations and power structures which will be relevant and useful in their own situations, including how to change them.

Let me now give two examples of theory with a small t as I am trying to conceptualize it, and as it relates to my own situated experience as a teacher and researcher of L2 writing and education. The first example comes from a six-year period in which I taught university EFL teachers in Japan. It is not about L2 writing per se; rather, it involves basically all aspects of English language teaching and learning in the Japanese context.

During the first semester we are together, and then later on from time to time, I would usually say to the doctoral students in my classes something like the following: "Doesn't it strike you as odd that here *I* am, a white, middle-class, middle-aged American male, standing in front of you and professing, in English, about how to think, research, and teach EFL *in Japan,* a place where I last taught EFL some 20 years ago, and never at the university level? Is this not, on the face of it, a strange situation? Is it not, furthermore, strange that the institution which brings us together is an *American* university, offering classes only in English? Is this just a strange occurrence, or might it not be related to other things, like the fact that half a century ago our two countries fought a terrible war, or that there are now more American military bases in Japan than in any similar-sized chunk of the U.S.— 38 in Okinawa alone and at least four ringing the capital city, Tokyo? What do you make of these facts? And what might they say to your practice as EFL teachers?"

I must admit that I do not know exactly what my students think when I say this, although I do know they listen, and occasionally nod or comment. My questions are rhetorical ones, except that I do not know the exact answers. What I do know is that, over my years in Japan, it seemed more and more obvious that Japan was in many ways umbilically attached to the U.S. and in a substantially unequal relationship. Certainly, there are Theories with a big T which give a basis on which to theorize the relationship—theories of neo-colonialism and imperialism (e.g., Young, 2001). Such theories offer all-encompassing explanations, and these have doubtless influenced my views. But I do not automatically take them on board when I ask my questions. Instead,

I am merely developing—and trying to provide—thinking tools that might complicate and enrich my students' and my own understanding of what we do in the classroom, and just possibly—in the words of Foucault quoted earlier—what what we do does.[4]

Let me now give my second example—one which relates directly to L2 writing. This example comes from my experience teaching and researching TESOL in U.S. universities. It occurred to me some time ago, again under the influence of theory with a big T but not purely as its consequence, that the concept of coherence in writing can be problematized (Atkinson, 2003, 2004). Again, let me put it as a series of questions: What is this thing we call clear writing? And why is it effectively deified in U.S. university writing programs (e.g., Bartholomae, 1998/1999)? Why, more specifically, do we teach thesis statements; top-down organizational structures; the careful building of arguments based on general statements supported by concrete examples; advance organizers and summary statements; the meticulous citing of sources; and hypercorrect form, format, and presentation?

The simple answer, of course, is so our students can write clearly, but to what larger end? Could this obsession with coherence relate to the widely-held claim that the American economy has shifted from one based on *material* production to one based on *information* management and production (e.g., Lyotard, 1984)? In what sense might the technology of clear writing be part of a larger, even global system for moving knowledge quickly and efficiently between different points in a complex network of production and consumption? And if clear writing *is* in some sense a technology for the progressive accumulation of capital, what does this mean for what we do as writing teachers, or, once again, for what what we do does (Atkinson, 2003)?

Practice in Second Language Writing & Education

Let me turn now to practice. Practice with a small p—that is, basically unreflective, commonsense practice—is no doubt a reality in our field. Possible reasons for this may include: (1) the deskilling of teachers, and the current dominant definition of teaching as an instrumental activity—that is, if writing is defined simply as efficient literate communication, then its teaching is likely to be conceived of as the *transmission of skills* of efficient literate communication;(2) the very real problem of class size, with numbers in U.S. tertiary-level writing classes, for example, ranging from 20–50 students; and (3) the power-

ful grip of tradition on teacher beliefs, practices, and experience, such
that, in Freeman and Johnson's words, "Much of what teachers know
about teaching comes from their memories as students, as language
learners, and as students of language teaching" (1998, p. 401).

But teachers are not simply technicians, and this is where practice
with a big P may come in. Teachers are also master mediators, mediating between institutional requirements and students, curriculum and
students, textbooks and students, specialist knowledge and students,
assignments and students, grading rubrics and students, even students
and students. This mediation is part and parcel of learning—it is di-
recting and redirecting the negative and positive forces impacting
learning in such a way, hopefully, that learning itself can take place. In
this sense, the many roles of the teacher—facilitator, counselor, evalu-
ator, cheerleader, and even expert knower and knowledge-giver—all
involve mediation, although we may not typically think of them this
way. To the extent that such mediation is conscious and reflective,
practice with a big P is part of what teachers do: Instead of being
against theory, as is commonly believed, teachers consciously mediate
what they know, including but not only what they have discovered for
themselves through the act of teaching, and rework, redirect, and re-
distribute it in ways that allow learning to go on.

And this is exactly where theory with a small t can play an important role. By developing and using thinking tools which are local
enough yet flexible enough to allow connections to be made between
the classroom and the world, teachers involve themselves in the dialectical fashioning of knowledge—of small narratives. It is this kind of
knowledge that I see as the goal of theory with a small t and practice
with a big P—the development, in Holliday's (1996, p. 235) words, of
"the ability to locate oneself and one's actions critically within a wider
community or world scenario."

Conclusion

Although I have discussed both theory and practice—and their all-
important interaction—in this chapter, my primary aim has been to
rethink theory in second language writing and education. My main
argument can be summarized as follows: Theory with a big T reveals
Truth with a big T—it tells the Truth about something, usually an important something, in the world. But that Truth often (if not always)
becomes an end in itself, an oppressive end—it becomes absolute or

"totalizing" (Foucault, 1984b, p. 375). According to the postmodernist critique, Western history has for the last three centuries been dominated by such theories. Theory with a small t, on the other hand, may also be a kind of truth—but it is a quite different kind: local, contingent, experimental, and diffident. It says: "Ok, let's take this idea and test it against our experience. Let's not get down on our knees and worship it, let's not let it tell us what to do or not to do or how to live a good life. No, let's see how it stacks up *in* our life, *in relation to* our experience—not as an all-encompassing interpretation and foundation, but as a thinking tool. Let's use it to see if we can do *more* thinking—and *different kinds* of thinking—than we've done before." It is with exactly such thinking that we perform the hard labor of building our *own* understandings of the world, and quite possibly our own political action. It is not by taking someone else's theory and throwing ourselves into it and becoming its servant that we can hope to change our world and ourselves. Rather, let us make our theories our own.

Coda

At the 6th Symposium on Second Language Writing, where this chapter was originally presented, I was struck by the "commonsense" way in which theory was approached and conceptualized. That is, the almost-universal background assumption seemed to be that there is something called practice—i.e., the teaching (and sometimes researching) of L2 writing—which our field is basically concerned with and which justifies its existence. And the role of theory—virtually always conceived of as (in my terms) scientific theory—is to help us to improve our practice.

Now I do not want to criticize those who think this way, in part because I often think this way myself. However, I would like to note a quite different role for theory, one which I have indirectly been trying to get at in my chapter. This difference basically recapitulates Horkheimer's (1972) distinction between "traditional theory" and "critical theory."

The argument goes as follows: Linking theory so closely to practice, and in fact making it subservient to practice, is a politically conservative move. That is, by grounding our thinking and actions mostly or solely in the view that we have a "real situation" on our hands which needs to be addressed—"real problems" which need to be solved—we commit ourselves to a quite limited domain of possibility: the "real" present. In other words, by assuming for practical purposes that our current reality is the *only possible* reality, for all intents and purposes we make it so. As an example, consider the fact that by approaching writing instruction in purely "process" terms —e.g., idea generation, revision, drafting, feedback, etc.—and by basing our research agenda (including developments in theory) on this conceptualization as well, we reduce our view of writing to a quite particular and limited set of possibilities of how writing can be taught and thought.

One alternative to this general approach—and the one I would like to foreground here—is (in a sense) to *delink* theory and practice. That is, if we think of theory as I have tried to do in this chapter, as "a speculative approach to something"—as a letting the mind roam free of practice, if you will—then we open up a whole new range of possibilities, many of them almost by definition "impractical," since the limitations of (current) practice are intentionally being avoided. This attempt to envision other worlds—including worlds in which practice would *follow from* theory rather than lead it, and thereby be considerably altered—is what Horkheimer meant by "critical theory." I am particularly interested in such theory for what it might help us do in terms of meeting the challenge set by James Gee in the quotation which opens the present chapter—in helping us as teachers of English envision our role and place in the wider world. But I do not see this as an issue that is separable from what we teach, or how we teach it.

NOTES

1. The *OED* was also the only dictionary to mention the "theory vs. practice" opposition—there it featured in two different definitions, one of which cast theory in a pejorative light.

2. Although I am aware that the expression "theory with a big T" (and quite possibly one or more of the other three category descriptors used here as well) has been used by others, I have been unable to find references to it in a search of the literature. At any rate, I believe the basic meanings I give these terms are rather different than the meanings given them by others.

3. In conversation with Foucault, Gilles Deleuze stated: "A theory is exactly like a box of tools. . . . It must be useful. It must function. If no one uses it, beginning with the theoretician himself (who then ceases to be a theoretician) then the theory is useless, or the moment inappropriate. . . . It is strange that it was Proust, an author thought to be a pure intellectual, who said it so clearly: treat my book as a pair of glasses directed to the outside; if they don't

suit you, find another pair; I leave it to you to find your own instrument, which is necessarily an instrument of combat" (Bouchard, 1977, p. 208).

4. Compare Foucault (quoted in Lather, 2004, p. 282): "I absolutely will not play the part of one who prescribes solutions. . . . My role is to address problems effectively, really: to pose them with the greatest possible rigor, with the maximum complexity and difficulty so that a solution does not arise all at once because of the thought of some reformer or even the brain of a political party. . . . It takes years, decades of work carried out at the grassroots level with the people directly involved. . . . Then perhaps a state of things may be renewed."

References

Atkinson, D. (2003). Writing and culture in the post-process era. *Journal of Second Language Writing, 12,* 49–63.

Atkinson, D. (2004). Contrasting rhetorics/contrasting cultures: Why contrastive rhetoric needs a better conceptualization of culture. *Journal of English for Academic Purposes, 3,* 277–289.

Bartholomae, D. (1998/1999). "Stop being so coherent": An interview with David Bartholomae by John Boe & Eric Schroeder. *Writing on the Edge, 10,* 9–28.

Benesch, S. (2001). *Critical English for academic purposes: Theory, politics, & practice.* Mahwah, NJ: Erlbaum.

Bouchard, D. F. (Ed.) (1977) *Language, counter-memory, practice: Selected essays and interviews by Michel Foucault.* Ithaca, NY: Cornell University Press.

Crookes, G., & Lehner, A. (1998). Aspects of process in an ESL critical pedagogy teacher education course. *TESOL Quarterly, 32,* 319–328.

Dreyfus, H., & Rabinow, P. (1983). *Michel Foucault: Beyond structuralism and hermeneutics,* 2nd ed. Chicago: University of Chicago Press.

Eribon, D. (1991). *Michel Foucault.* Cambridge, MA: Harvard University Press.

Erickson, F. (1986). Qualitative methods in research on teaching. In M. C. Wittrock (Ed.), *Handbook of research on teaching,* 3rd. ed. (pp. 119–161). New York: Macmillan.

Foucault, M. (1984a). Truth and power. In P. Rabinow (Ed.), *The Foucault reader* (pp. 51–75). New York: Pantheon.

Foucault, M. (1984b). Politics and ethics: An interview. In P. Rabinow (Ed.), *The Foucault reader* (pp. 373–380). New York: Pantheon.

Freeman, D., & Johnson, K. E. (1998). Reconceptualizing the knowledge-base of language teacher education. *TESOL Quarterly, 32,* 397–418.

Freire, P. (1970). *Pedagogy of the oppressed.* (M. B. Ramos, Trans.). New York, NY: Continuum

Gee, J. P. (1990). *Social linguistics and literacies: Ideology in discourses.* London, England: Falmer.

Goodchild, P. (1981). *J. Robert Oppenheimer: Shatterer of worlds.* Boston, MA: Houghton-Mifflin.

Grabe, W. (2001). Notes toward a theory of second language writing. In T. Silva & P. K. Matsuda (Eds.), *On second language writing* (pp. 39–58). Mahwah, NJ: Erlbaum.

Haraway, D. (1988). Situated knowledges: The science question in feminism and the privilege of partial perspective. *Feminist Studies, 14,* 575–599.

Holliday, A. (1996). Developing a sociological imagination: Expanding ethnography in international English language education. *Applied Linguistics, 17,* 234–255.

Horkheimer, M. (1972). Traditional theory and critical theory. In *Critical theory: Selected essays* (pp. 188–243). New York: Herder & Herder.

Johnston, B. (1999). Putting critical pedagogy in its place: A personal account. *TESOL Quarterly, 33,* 557–565.

Krashen, S. (1985). *The input hypothesis: Issues & implications.* Harlow, England: Longman.

Kubota, R. (1999). Japanese culture constructed by discourses: Implications for applied linguistics research and ELT. *TESOL Quarterly, 33,* 9–35.

Lather, P. (2001). Ten years later, yet again: Critical pedagogy and its complicities. In K. Weiler (Ed.), *Feminist engagements: Reading, resisting, and revisioning male theorists in education & cultural studies* (pp. 183–195). New York: Routledge.

Lather, P. (2004) Foucauldian 'indiscipline' as a sort of policy application. In B. Baker & K. Hayning (Eds.), *Dangerous coagulations? The uses of Foucault in the study of education* (pp. 279–303). New York: Peter Lang.

Long, M. H., & Robinson, P. (1998). Focus on form: Theory, research, & practice. In C. Doughty & J. Williams (Eds.), *Focus on form in classroom second language acquisition* (pp. 15–41). Cambridge, England: Cambridge University Press.

Lyotard, J-F. (1984). *The postmodern condition: A report on knowledge.* Minneapolis, MN: University of Minnesota Press.

Marcuse, H. (1964). *One-dimensional man.* Boston, MA: Beacon.

McLaren, P. (2000). *Che Guevara, Paulo Freire, and the pedagogy of revolution.* Lanham, MD: Rowman & Littlefield.

Schmidt, R. W. (1990). The role of consciousness in second language learning. *Applied Linguistics, 11,* 129–157.

Tucker, R. C. (Ed.) (1978). *The Marx-Engels reader,* 2nd ed. New York: Norton.

Young, R. J. C. (2001). *Postcolonialism: An historical introduction.* London, England: Blackwell.

2 Theories, Frameworks, and Heuristics: Some Reflections on Inquiry and Second Language Writing

Alister Cumming

In thinking about the nature of theories in studies of second language writing, I realized that I could approach these matters most knowledgably in respect to my own experiences: How have theories featured in my research on second language writing? To answer this question, I have reflected on my personal thinking—trying to ascertain some key elements in my intellectual interests and efforts at principled reasoning—from early memories of childhood through to university studies and then teaching and research about L2 writing.[1] I have done so to be concrete—to avoid the abstractions that inevitably arise in discussing theory—as well as to consolidate some of my personal practical knowledge (Casanave, 2005; Connelly & Clandinin, 1988). Empirical inquiry and the organization of knowledge have always interested me. Making sense of them entails some form of theory, if only to describe things coherently. Descriptive frameworks account for relevant phenomena. Also important are heuristics that mobilize people's actions—such as writing, reading, learning, or teaching, as well as the interrelations among them—and organize them in practical and sometimes innovative ways.

No single theory might ever explain such complex phenomena as second language writing, which necessarily involves the full range of psychological, cultural, linguistic, political, and educational variables in which humans engage. Nancy Hornberger (2003) has demonstrated this in her "continua of biliteracy," outlining the many different factors that influence literacy in a second language. Her continua are also an elegant example of what I mean by a "descriptive framework."[2] I will argue in this chapter, delving unabashedly into my own experiences, that a coherent descriptive framework and practical heuristics are not only useful to guide empirical research but also to inform pedagogy and policies in such areas as second language writing. Theories help to conceptualize and extend these purposes.

CHIPPING SLATE AND SIFTING THROUGH A MIDDEN

I used to spend my childhood summers at my grandparents' beach-front cottage on Saltspring Island on the west coast of Canada. It was a marvelous location in every sense, full of relatively untouched natural wonders. At that time, the area was scarcely populated by the dozens of vacation cottages that now line the same beachfront that I, my sister, and a few young friends used to wander freely about. There were two things that I did during those idle summer hours that constitute the earliest inklings I can recall of the role of theory in empirical inquiry.

One activity was a rather odd interest I had in chipping away at a wall of slate stone that formed a small cliff against the beachfront that extended up to the property of our nearest neighbor to the south. I would find a hard rock on the beach, and use that to carve a progressively deeper niche out of the soft, brittle shale on this cliffside. The shale would, if I picked industriously at it, fall away in larger or smaller sheets out of the cliff and down to the beach. I spent long afternoon hours doing this, taking delight in my dexterity with the intricate network of stone and watching the slate pieces fall away, exposing unique nooks in spaces between the networks of stone. Sometimes cobwebs or other evidence of insects that had lodged themselves among the stone would emerge. My sister would sometimes join in, but she did not share much of my peculiar fascination in chipping away at stones. So she usually busied herself with some more animate activity nearby on the shoreline, such as overturning large stones to watch dozens of small crabs scurry away from their usual abodes.

I have no idea what motivated me to chip away at this cliff of slate, other than just to do it for the sake of occupying myself in the activity. This became painfully obvious one day when the fellow who owned the property above the cliff confronted me, and then later my parents, in outrage over the fact that I was progressively destroying the extent of his land above the cliff, close to which his chicken coop was located.

I had, over the summer, chipped away several feet of his property. I had no explanation, for him or my anxious parents, for my activity other than my pleasure in watching the sheets of slate tumble down as I ingeniously dislocated them. This incident was one of the first in which I understood that there could be unforeseen social consequences to my personal activities.

Contrast this activity with another at a different cliff at the other end of my grandparents' beachfront. On this other cliffside at the north end of the beach was a compressed conglomeration of ancient, broken shells of clams, oysters, and mussels, mixed with layers of moist black earth. The shells had been discarded, presumably after feasting, by some First Nations population in centuries past, then slowly buried over—but then half exposed again, vertically, as a low cliff, when a small roadway had, a decade or two previously, been bulldozed along the shoreline. This was, in archeological terminology, a midden, or as the *Oxford English Dictionary* states, "a refuse heap" or ancient garbage dump. One might pass by the site thinking the mound of compressed shells was a natural geological formation. But not my grandfather. He was an amateur anthropologist of the Indian peoples of the Pacific Northwest, a population with whom he regularly worked in his law practice, and among whom he had grown up in the interior of British Columbia, gaining a familiarity with their languages and cultures rare among the European-background settlers of western Canada. On a few occasions he took me to this midden, along with a small shovel and bucket, and we spent the day carefully digging into, then sifting through, the layers of broken sea shells and earth in search of artifacts. Every so often we would find an arrowhead or other small tool or item. Such discoveries were a great delight and curiosity, making for the topic of lengthy conversations afterwards about their significance. But most of the time this activity was just tedious, careful sorting through a mound of black earth mixed with sharp chunks of old broken seashells.

The contrast I want to make in these two cliffside sites and the respective digging activities is this: The latter had theoretical significance, which we approached with a particular heuristic method: There was a social history in the midden, more of which could be revealed by searching carefully through its contents to expose artifacts such as arrowheads. These we then interpreted in reference to my grandfather's knowledge of the history of local civilizations as well as the theories of anthropologists such as Franz Boas. Chipping away at slate, in contrast, was just an idle pastime without any intellectual or social significance other, perhaps, than inadvertently to bring down the mass of property above the cliff more rapidly than would otherwise have happened, and than our neighbor would have liked. It might be an exaggeration to say that my digging away at both sites was a child's form of empirical inquiry, but I would like to think of them that way. My point is that the activity of digging in the midden was principled and purposeful inquiry, guided by a descriptive framework and heuristics for discovering and making sense of what was there. I presume all that was more evident then to my aging grandfather than it was to my young mind.

BIOLOGY AND LITERATURE

In high school and university my intellectual interests pulled in various directions. From among them I ultimately had to make a choice, in declaring a university major, between biology or English literature. I enjoyed nature. I also enjoyed reading books. For my bachelor's degree, I was so hesitant to choose between the two fields that I fulfilled the course requirements for both, and I subsequently worked at jobs in both areas. Studies in biology led me to summer jobs as an assistant for an ecologist and as a laborer in a provincial park. Studies of English led me to teaching and graduate studies in literature and then ESL, composition, and education. As I reflect on those years of intellectual and professional apprenticeship, I am intrigued by the integral but differing roles of theory in biology and in literary studies. One field was the study of nature, the other the study of art. Both were informed by their respective theories, descriptive frameworks, and practical heuristics.

Biology: A Science of Nature

Studies in biology were organized as the accumulation of detailed knowledge in reference to three major theoretical schemes: One scheme was a *descriptive framework*—the Linnaean system of classification for the plant and animal kingdoms then all their detailed subsystems and species. The second was a full-scale *theory:* the theory of evolution (and all the more recent variants on and revisions to this theory) that aspired to explain the existence, development, and varieties of living things. The third scheme was a set of *heuristics,* established ways of making sense of particular phenomena or elements that spanned the natural world, constituting domains of inquiry within biology. One domain was embryology, which investigated the stages of growth from conception into mature beings, typically through examining cross-sections of embryos at specific stages of development under a microscope (e.g., Saunders, 1970, and I see in recent years studies of embryology have linked productively with the domain of genetics to produce major insights into the process of evolution, Rosenfield & Ziff, 2006). Another domain was functional morphology, which described the forms and operations of bodily structures across species, typically through examination and dissection of sample specimens (e.g., Waterman, 1971). Another was ecology, which described the interrelations among living systems and their habitats, typically in reference to the conditions of climate, geology, vegetation, and animal life within or across specific environments. Each of these (and other such) domains had their own principles, objects, and heuristic methods of inquiry Studying biology mainly involved observing, memorizing, and/or dissecting in great detail and precision particular specimens (or aspects of them) in regards to their defining characteristics, interrelationships, and processes of development, structure, or variation.

Mid-way through the program of biology courses I remember marveling at how magnificently all the empirical details fit within the theory and frameworks. My memorizing Latin and common names for and distinguishing features of every species of fish, amphibian, bird, or mammal in the local area was, on the one hand, the accumulation of immense quantities of factual knowledge. On the other hand, this knowledge all neatly linked to, and indeed was explicable within, the framework of Linnaean classification, evolutionary theory, and heuristics of inquiry in domains such as embryology, morphology, or ecology. In my later work as an ecologist's assistant, this organization of knowledge guided, and made purposeful, what was otherwise tedious labor. That job involved assisting a post-doctoral researcher to hike into remote sites in northern Canada to collect samples of plants and soils and indications of local animal life and climate. Later, back in the university laboratory, we evaluated these samples for their properties (e.g., in machines that sorted and measured the composition of soils) and charted their characteristics (e.g., on colored, carefully typed and labeled graphs). This work had the goal of defining the uniqueness of an ecosystem in a particular location, all in respect to the comprehensive descriptive framework devised by the professor who headed the laboratory as well as the heuristics we employed systematically to collect empirical evidence then analyze, synthesize, and present it to others (e.g., Krajina, 1965). The practical purpose for this inquiry was to designate several unique sites in northwestern Canada as "ecological reserves." By virtue of their unique ecology, substantiated by the evidence we had gathered and analyzed, these sites would be declared legally off limits for future mining, logging, or other industries or human development. To make a case for the designation of an ecological reserve, we worked as a team to present systematically and comprehensively a range of empirical evidence following an accepted set of theories, an explicit descriptive framework, and a practical set of heuristic procedures. Apart from that image of science, human effort, empirical evidence, and social purpose combining, I don't know that this knowledge has many direct applications to studies of second language writing. But I am intrigued that various scholars have recently argued for ecological orientations to issues in applied linguistics: Canagarajah (2005), Hornberger (2003), Lee and Schumann (2003), and van Lier (2004).

Literary Studies: Interpreting Written Art

Literary studies also had their theories and frameworks. But these were fragmented into different areas of scholarship. Many were even encapsulated within specific courses or the interests of particular professors. At the time that I undertook my master's studies (in the 1970s) the role of "theory" was just exploding into what would later be either lamented or rejoiced as the post-modern dilemma. There was the established canon of English literature, of course, extending from Anglo-Saxon poems through Shakespeare's plays to modern novels, poems, and drama, and then postcolonial and current literatures. This canon shaped the program of studies and its core and optional courses. At the graduate level, the canon underpinned what needed to be known—in terms of historical periods, great works, genres, and analytic methods—to pass a comprehensive exam. But within each course were unique and even conflicting theories or descriptive frameworks. One professor of Shakespeare might, for example, approach the plays in reference to genre conventions arising from mythic rites (e.g., Northrop Frye's [1957] *Anatomy of Criticism,* Fraser's [1922] *Golden Bough*), whereas another professor would pursue themes such as the metaphor of madness (e.g., in Lear, Hamlet, or Macbeth) in respect to Michel Foucault's theories of social and ideological control (1965). There were psychoanalytic theories that explained readers' responses to incidents in novels in respect to Freudian episodes in childhood (e.g., Holland, 1968) or Jungian archetypes (e.g., Campbell's [1949] *Hero with a Thousand Faces*). There were the theories of aesthetics contemporary to the Metaphysical, Romantic, Victorian, Symbolist, or Black Mountain poets—each with differing insights and values, around which courses on these topics were framed. There were even theories about theories in literary studies (e.g., Derrida, 1976; Eagleton, 1976). The courses in linguistics I took were based entirely on Noam Chomsky's (1965) theories of transformational-generative grammar. We learned to chart intricate tree diagrams of syntactic structures in English, though oddly, never any other languages nor with much consideration of any competing theories of linguistics. Coincidentally, Chomsky's entirely different set of theories had informed a course that I had taken in political philosophy (Chomsky, 1968). Of course, theories also featured in other fields of study that I ventured into, such as Gombrich's theory of representation in art history (1972) or Marx (1954) and Engel's theories of dialectical materialism in studies of history, and so on.

In short, most areas of inquiry in literature and the humanities had unique or competing sets of alternative theories. Within these, relevant details of knowledge, study, and discussion were founded, interpreted, and explained. These frameworks made the topics coherent. Indeed, a coherent framework or theory seemed virtually a prerequisite for the designation of a topic as the proper subject of intellectual knowledge. Looking back on this abundance of theories, and their compartmentalization into separate domains or interests, reminds me now of the skit from *Monty Python*'s television program, popular at the time: A pseudo-intellectual, invited guest on the TV talk show reiterated how her "theory of the brontosaurus" was "my theory," "mine," and "my theory"—without ever explaining exactly what the theory, or even a brontosaurus, was. Everyone and everything had a theory. Indeed, just claiming that seemed to be a goal of academic inquiry, as that parody of intellectual discourse jokingly proclaimed. As a fellow graduate student mused over coffee about two ten-cent pieces he had put on the table: "What's this? Yet another set of paradigms (pair of dimes)."

I personally did not, and still do not, have much ambivalence about holding multiple theoretical frameworks in mind nor applying them uniquely or differently to particular areas of inquiry. The nature, purposes, and organization of human activity are too complex and multifaceted to expect a single over-arching theory to encompass everything in a meaningful or useful way. (And I might add, for this reason, religious fundamentalism seems to be a misguided distortion of the personal value of spiritual faith.) Indeed, this seems to be the operating assumption in most conceptualizations of applied linguistics and of education. For instance, literacy education necessarily involves multiple sets of knowledge because of the sheer complexity of and extensive variability in the processes, forms, and organization of literacy and of education (Bascia, Cumming, Datnow, Leithwood, & Livingstone, 2005). Even Chomsky, in putting forward what he called his "grand theory" of linguistics and human cognition, cautioned that he was making an abstract theoretical formulation rather than proposing principles that had much heuristic value for practical activities such as language teaching (Chomsky, 1988, p. 180):

> People who are involved in some practical activity such as teaching languages, translation, or building bridges should probably keep an eye on what's happening in the sciences. But they probably shouldn't take it too seriously because the capacity to carry out practical activities without much conscious awareness of what you're doing is usually far more advanced than scientific knowledge.

What then was the practical value of literary studies? Apart from the joy of reading extensively and my accumulating knowledge about literature, language, human experience, and social history, I learned two sets of practical heuristics that I have productively applied many times since to various research and pedagogical situations. One was the idea of "practical criticism" put forward by I.A. Richards (1966) and advocated by most of the professors of English literature with whom I studied. This was a heuristic for making sense of a piece of literature in a way that was useful for teaching (which my professors recognized would eventually be the vocation of most of their masters' students). The heuristic was simple: Identify the speaker(s) and contextual situation in a piece of literature and relate these to the forms of language expressed. Who was speaking, to whom, in what manner, and why? Applied to, for example, a lyric poem, this simple heuristic provided a straightforward method for solving the problem of what the poem "meant" and why it was expressed in the manner that it was. With the basic contextual situation in mind, one's task as reader (and writer/analyst) was to make sense of the relations between the ideas, situation, and language forms. With any well crafted piece of literature there was always a fantastically rich set of issues to explore and explicate. Doing so was both an intellectual puzzle of the highest order as well as a paradigm for understanding human experience and expression (cf. Widdowson, 1975). As I learned how to practice this method of inquiry (developing some of the strategies that, e.g., Warren, 2006 describes as heuristics for literary interpretations), I marveled at how it helped me puzzle over and eventually to reveal the craft and significance of any piece of literature. This recognition was akin to the feeling that I had experienced when appreciating how the practices, descriptive frameworks, and theories of biology fit together into a complete schematic whole. The challenge that emerged, of course, to this analytic approach was that interpretations of literature vary by socio-historical context, a point made emphatically by Stanley Fish's (1980) provocative question, *Is there a text in this class?* and all the other socio-historical orientations to literary studies that subsequently followed.

A related but more idiosyncratic heuristic was what Ezra Pound (1934, pp. 17–18) called, in his didactic writings about literary history, the "biological method." This involved the studious comparison of related texts, as a biologist does in comparing the forms of plants or animals, to identify their similarities, differences, and unique characteristics: "The proper METHOD for studying poetry and good letters is the method of contemporary biologists, that is careful first-hand examination of the matter, and continual COMPARISON of one 'slide' or specimen with another" (Pound, 1934, p. 17; capitals in the original). Given what I have said already about my interests in biology and social history, you can appreciate why this principle for literary inquiry appealed to me. This orientation subsequently inspired my approach to most of my course papers during my master's studies in English literature.

This heuristic (or principles akin to it) has also guided much of my own empirical inquiry into second language writing—in research evaluating significant points of contrast in essential aspects of second language writing. For example, I have designed research that attempted to establish differences between the following groups: composing processes in first versus second languages and among skilled versus unskilled writers (Cumming, 1989, 1995); the decisions that novice versus expert raters make while evaluating students' compositions (Cumming, 1990a; Cumming, Kantor & Powers, 2002); writing curricula and assessment practices in second versus foreign language contexts (Cumming, 2001a, 2003); or discourse features of texts that students write for personal expression versus those written to integrate ideas from reading or listening passages (Cumming, et al., 2005). Given the complexity of factors that bear on second language writing, establishing significant points of contrast in human behaviors is, I continue to believe, one of the few feasible and illuminating ways of discerning elements integral to this form of human activity. Moreover, many of the research designs and statistical methods common to psychological and educational inquiry were developed to assess whether significant relations or differences exist between contrasting phenomena through, for instance, factorial designs and control-group experiments or analyses of variance and correlational analyses. But research, and the resulting knowledge it produces, needs to go beyond just describing or evaluating contrasting behaviors. Doing so may constitute little more than the kind of chipping away at things as I did at the cliff of slate during my childhood. There need to be, as in the contrasting Indian midden of my childhood, relevant descriptive frameworks and theories to interpret, explain, and extend accounts of these phenomena.

LANGUAGE AND COMPOSITION TEACHING

Entering the field of language teaching in the mid-1970s, I saw that it was dominated by practical heuristics, but people had varying commitments to their theoretical substantiation. How to teach was *the* crucial issue, particularly for a novice instructor (like me). The field was then establishing itself, both as a subset of the discipline of applied linguistics and as the object of professional qualifications for Teaching English as a Second Language (TESL). Books and articles invariably featured or led up to "implications for teaching." They defined their primary purpose as heuristics for pedagogy rather than as the development of knowledge in a theoretical or comprehensively descriptive sense. In the courses I took for a TESL certificate, the practical heuristics advocated for teaching were grounded in certain descriptive frameworks. For example, the all-important formulae for lesson plans had—we were instructed—to be framed in respect to behavioral objectives, typically derived from a combination of Bloom's (1956) taxonomy, linguistic descriptions from Quirk and Greenbaum (1973), and the textbook that dominated local curricula for adult ESL teaching (Martin, 1963). Other foundations for organizing relevant pedagogical activities derived from, for instance, principles of contrastive analysis (Lado, 1964), the sophisticated scheme of the International Phonetic Alphabet (Albright, 1958), transformational-generative grammar (Chomsky, 1965), and an odd smattering of so-called humanistic concerns (e.g., Stevick, 1976).

These few frameworks were, I quickly found when starting to teach, hardly sufficient to address all that people needed to learn to acquire English while orienting themselves to living or studying in a new society. Nor were they sufficient to inform all that I had to organize and do to teach classes of 20 to 30 immigrants or visitors to Canada, from highly divergent backgrounds, for four to six hours per day. Some of these frameworks presented relevant information, but none guided me in how to teach. Their value quickly shifted to the background as I prepared to organize for hours of activities for classrooms full of adults enthusiastic to improve their English and their life situations. What leapt into the foreground were questions such as: What might I organize these people to do that will usefully improve their abilities in English while engaging and interesting them? From this perspective, the most vital and productive heuristics that I learned for language and composition teaching came from pedagogical experience and reflective analysis—either in my working collaboratively with colleagues or from my analyzing the relative successes or failures of certain classroom activities or individual students (as I have described in Cumming, 2002). This is how analysts such as Johnson (1999) suggest language teacher development usually proceeds.

In the terms I used above, there was a disjuncture between the descriptive frameworks and theories that informed applied linguistics and the practical heuristics for classroom pedagogy. Teaching ESL and/or composition had to be more than just an activity, such as chipping away at a cliff of slate. Descriptive frameworks and relevant theories were necessary to make sense and purpose of pedagogical phenomena—to know what to do and why I was doing it—as in digging through the Indian midden with my grandfather. But there was no comprehensive organization of knowledge, explanation of phenomena, or principles for action such as featured in biology nor much in the way of the canons, theories, or heuristics that guided the work of literary critics.

Many people have argued that our field has matured since those days. Theoretical foundations tend now to be multidisciplinary, research involves complementary methods of data collection and analyses, basic concepts have been reconceptualized, and orientations toward education are more profound (Cumming, 1994, 1998a, 1998b). Nonetheless, trends in pedagogical methods continue to vacillate, leading recently, for example, to communicative then task-based teaching, from method-based to post-method pedagogies, or to critical, ethical principles (e.g., Kumaravadivelu, 2006; Stern, 1983). I won't bother to recount my personal involvement with these. But I do want to emphasize that each such change in, development of, or challenge to pedagogical principles has introduced new and different theoretical frameworks to describe phenomena relevant to the contexts and foci of language or composition teaching and learning. The rationale is usually that the new perspective better reconciles the dilemma between frameworks to describe phenomena and heuristics to act on them. Sometimes a theory may inform the descriptive framework or guide the pedagogical heuristics, but nobody has proposed anything as grand as the theory of evolution or Linnean system of classification to unify them irrevocably. Krashen (1982) was perhaps the last researcher to try to make such a claim—in a flourish of exclamation marks and simple, formulaic principles—and that, after some faddish popularity, rightly led to a decade or so of "Krashen-bashing" publications by theorists and researchers.

Theories, Frameworks, and Heuristics in Research on Second Language Writing

After I gained enough pedagogical experience to feel confident that I knew my way around the practical matters of teaching ESL and composition, I found myself coordinating programs, instructing others to become teachers or better informed educators, developing curricula or assessment instruments, or evaluating programs. In each of these activities, though, I found my own, and the available published, knowledge lacking. So I opted to pursue doctoral studies to learn how to do research and, I hoped, to contribute purposefully to enhancing knowledge about second language writing as well as such related matters as student assessment, curriculum evaluation, and educational policies. In pursuing these interests over the past twenty years, the role of theory has appeared at every juncture, either prominently as an issue needing to be addressed or implicitly as an assumption made. As I have stated above, two elements usually figured in my experiences. One is the need to adopt or develop a framework that describes relevant phenomena credibly and coherently. The other is to identify, derive, or apply some form of heuristic to guide my actions effectively or to interpret those of others meaningfully.

Descriptive frameworks are where theories are most conspicuously located and vigorously debated. Zuengler and Miller (2006) have recently portrayed the current frameworks about second language acquisition as dichotomized between cognitive-rationalist and sociocultural-relativist viewpoints—or to put personal faces on things, a long-standing debate between Jim Lantolf (e.g., 1996) and Michael Long (e.g., Long & Doughty, 2003). In some respects, this observation holds for studies of second language writing as well. Moreover, the debate parallels my accounts above of differences in theories between the scientifically oriented field of biology and the interpretively oriented field of literary studies. But that distinction is too simple a formulation to be of much explanatory value, as Widdowson (1983) has argued all the simple dichotomies that have featured in applied linguistics usually prove to be.

A more penetrating, and I think useful, question was posed by Bill Grabe (2001) at a previous symposium at Purdue University when he asked, what do we want a theory for? His functional perspective recognizes the heuristic dimensions of theories as applied to pedagogical actions while also appreciating, with due humility, that most of our work—be it teaching, researching, or writing—is limited to certain situations and interests, not the totality of relevant phenomena. Grabe (2001) speculated that a theory of second language writing might, for example, lead to better understanding of teaching and learning, improved educational applications, and explanations of otherwise puzzling phenomena. At the same time, Grabe recognized the futility of supposing that there might ever be a single unified theory about second language writing—because of the different, competing interests and functions that any single theory would necessarily have to encompass. Instead, he concluded, as I have above, that the best, unified perspective for which we might hope is of the order of Spolsky's (1989) general framework of the conditions that influence the learning of languages (or, I would also suggest, Hornberger's [2003] framework of the conditions that influence biliteracy or Stern's [1983] bases of knowledge that influence the teaching of languages). These broad descriptive frameworks have the heuristic value of helping us to make sure that we have, in any one endeavor, accounted for a full range of relevant variables and not unduly emphasized some while neglecting others.[3]

To return to the question with which I opened this chapter, I can now address it from Grabe's (2001) functional perspective: How have theories featured in my research on second language writing? My inclinations in research have usually been to investigate a worthwhile, manageable problem, and see what it reveals, somewhat as I described doing above at the two cliffsides of my childhood. That is, I have usually designed research to address one or two intriguing issues in a specific context, using a certain heuristic to produce data that I then interpret within a descriptive framework to account for the phenomena investigated. I have not personally aspired to create a theory, though I have often speculated on which theories apply to specific circumstances. Most of the research I have done has been in the context of funded grants or contracts, the results of which are subsequently submitted as reports to funding agencies and/or published as articles in scholarly or professional journals or books. Such inquiry virtually necessitates specifying one's theoretical orientation. Typically, from the start, a theoretical orientation needs to appear in the context of a proposal that is reviewed and evaluated by others, who in turn are looking to see that, in addition to a relevant research question and feasible research plan, there is a theoretical foundation to guide the investigation and the interpretation of its results. In these ways, certain technologies, interested communities, and conventions have determined some of the scope and dimensions of my inquiry as well as the content and form of my reporting it. But these endeavors have also been shaped by my personal interests, knowledge, curiosity, and sense of what is worth investing efforts into.

Theoretical Orientations in Controlled but Emergent Research Designs

My first serious attempts at research were cognitively oriented studies of composing processes. Research done by colleagues with whom I was working in the early 1980s at Carleton University—such as Aviva Freedman, Ian Pringle, and Stan Jones—on writing development in

English inspired me to pursue doctoral studies in applied linguistics. So I moved to the Ontario Institute for Studies in Education, where I studied and also worked as a research assistant with Carl Bereiter and Marlene Scardamalia and took courses with, among others, David Olson, Jim Cummins, David Stern, Merrill Swain, Patrick Allen, and Gordon Wells. Research and emerging theories about first-language composing processes intrigued me. I wanted to know what these phenomena were like for the adult students to whom I had taught ESL composition in previous years. Might they differ for students who had highly developed writing abilities in their mother tongue compared to students who did not? Or for students who had high levels of proficiency in the second language, compared to those who did not? Answers to those questions, I thought, would advance knowledge beyond the then widely cited studies by Raimes (1987) or Zamel (1983), which had investigated only a few students and analyzed little of the variation associated with second language writing. Research for my doctoral thesis on this topic resulted in several articles (Cumming, 1989, 1990b, 1995).

There was a distinct heuristic to elicit data for such research: think-aloud verbal reports. Moreover, Ericsson and Simon (1984) had produced a compelling descriptive framework to guide such inquiry, demonstrating how concurrent verbal reports could reveal the thinking processes that people attended to while solving complex cognitive tasks. Their framework was a key element in a burgeoning set of theories called Cognitive Science, of which research into composing processes and linguistic knowledge were prominent, productive examples (Bereiter & Scardamalia, 1987; Chomsky, 1988; Flower & Hayes, 1981). Smagorinsky's (1994) collection of reflective essays by researchers about various types of verbal report data provided some useful cautions about this method of data collection while also demonstrating the multiple theoretical orientations to which verbal data could lend itself. Later, I also applied these heuristics and descriptive frameworks to investigate the decision making involved in evaluating ESL compositions for assessment purposes (Cumming, 1990a; Cumming, Kantor & Powers, 2002). Although a few first-language researchers had conducted such inquiry (e.g., Huot, 1990), I realized nobody had yet described systematically the decisions people made while evaluating second language writing, leaving unexamined an integral aspect of the validity of the common practice of holistic scoring of second language writing.

Like most others using verbal report data, I designed these studies to document and discover qualities of phenomena rather than to test hypotheses or confirm any particular theory. The designs of these studies were emergent but controlled. I followed certain theoretical orientations, considering writing or evaluating compositions as a constrained, specialized activity of mental problem solving (as suggested by Bereiter & Scardamalia, 1987; Ericsson & Simon, 1984). Moreover, I selected the participants in these studies carefully to form contrasting groups (e.g., of expert or novices with specific, comparable backgrounds). In this way, my analyses could evaluate whether people's behaviors during tasks differed according to these characteristics. I also designed (or adopted) these tasks to be comparable for each person and realistic, even though the conditions of administering them were more like experiments rather than genuinely natural experiences. Because the designs were emergent—in the sense of my not knowing exactly what people would do in these conditions—my uses of theories typically came while interpreting the results of the analyses.

A case in point was Cumming (1990a). In that study, I initially had no idea what to make of my findings for novice raters of ESL compositions (i.e., student-teachers). They tended to do one of three very different things: to read sample compositions either (a) just for their ideas, (b) by editing the grammar and spelling (while knowing that the students who had written the compositions would never see their editing), or (c) by speculating on who the authors of the compositions might have been. In contrast, the skilled raters in my research sample tended to do all of these things in conjunction (except for editing the texts) along with dozens of other intricate reading and evaluation strategies. In trying to make sense of the unusual and disparate behavior of the student-teachers in my research, I looked to Kintsch's (1988) construction-integration model of reading comprehension. Kintsch's theory proposes that skilled reading involves interactively processing verbatim, propositional, and situational representations of a text. The skilled composition raters whom I had studied had practiced evaluating ESL compositions for years, so they had developed complex mental models and procedural strategies for evaluating them, using all three levels of Kintsch's text representation in an integrated and effective manner. In contrast, the student-teachers mostly were evaluating students' compositions for the first time, and I had not given them any guidelines or criteria to help them do so. As a consequence, the student-teachers had only partial representations of what evaluating ESL compositions involved. So they tended to operate at only one of the three levels of text representation. That is, they performed the evaluation tasks by either, in Kintsch's terms, acting on the verbatim representations (e.g., by correcting the grammar and spelling), attending to propositional representations (e.g., by just reading to interpret the main ideas), or trying to develop situational representations (e.g., by trying to envision the authors of the compositions and their motivations and circumstances for writing). Kintsch's theory provided a comprehensive, satisfying explanation for what otherwise seemed puzzling or even erratic behaviors. It also provided some basis to indicate the varied aspects of evaluating students' compositions these novice instructors might need to develop.

In my classroom observation studies, theories became especially fruitful to interpret the data I had gathered. I did two studies in the early 1990s where I sat in the classrooms of experienced ESL instructors throughout the duration of their courses, attempting to document everything that I saw happen. I had intentionally begun these studies without any theoretical orientations, so as to try to come to fresh, unbiased viewpoints on what I realized few other researchers had done: just describe ESL composition teaching as it naturally occurs. Inevitably, though, I found myself appealing to theoretical constructs to make sense of what I had documented. In Cumming (1992) I observed three teachers skillfully repeating common sets of verbal routines as ways of organizing and engaging their students. Probing into the literature on education, I found that others had documented similar pedagogical behaviors in various classroom contexts. These researchers proposed that skilled teachers structure the discourse of classroom interaction so that it continuously involves students in routines, on the one hand, to engage them comfortably, but on the other hand, to serve as a foundation on which to construct new learning (e.g., Burns & Anderson, 1987; Leinhardt, Weidman & Hammond, 1987). In Cumming (1999), I documented how a different instructor literally "orchestrated" her ESL classes around a set of routines that involved complex musical metaphors. I appealed to theories of metaphor (e.g., Lakoff & Johnson, 1981) and educational rituals (McLaren, 1986) to interpret these findings.

I made radically different uses of theories in an action research project that provided a program of culturally-relevant instruction for women from the Punjab who were settling in Vancouver and lacked both English and literacy (Cumming & Gill, 1991). Inspired by similar projects by Auerbach (1992) for Haitian adults in Boston and by Moll (1989) for young Hispanic learners of English in the Southwest U.S., Jas Gill and I devised a unique ESL literacy curriculum to address a problem that was then evident throughout the Vancouver area: Local ESL programs were not serving large numbers of women immigrants from India because of cultural barriers to their participating in such programs. We developed a program of ESL literacy instruction specifically for this population, using both English and Punjabi as the media of instruction (taught by an experienced and successful female Indo-Canadian instructor), focusing on situations important in the women's lives (e.g., interactions with their children's schools, shopping, reading mail, telephone conversations), and providing logistical supports that enabled these women to attend such classes (e.g., situating classes and field trips in their neighborhood, child-minding services).

The design of this project was, again, controlled but emergent. Our guiding heuristic was to set up classroom conditions to address all barriers to participation that we could identify. Then our research documented the pedagogy and interactions that ensued. We also systematically interviewed and assessed, over half a year, the women's progressively increasing uses of literacy in English and Punjabi in their homes and communities. We initiated the project from the theoretical (Vygotskian and Freirian) premise that the perceived problem of this population not participating in ESL or literacy programs arose from cultural barriers to their accessing such programs, barriers that were inherent in the organization of the programs, not the characteristics of Indo-Canadian women. If an ESL literacy program were created to cater particularly to their cultural interests and circumstances, then Indo-Canadian women could participate in and benefit from such programs as well as improve their language and literacy abilities to interact meaningfully in their local communities. Our research findings documented and demonstrated this. The value of theory here was to envision and demonstrate new forms of pedagogy and curriculum organization that were culturally-relevant for this population which was otherwise disadvantaged and excluded from conventional formats for both ESL and literacy education.

Theoretically Motivated Inquiry

I became increasingly interested in the question of how instruction influences learning to write in a second language. In a project in the 1990s, I tried to approach these matters from a purely descriptive perspective in natural contexts of classroom ESL teaching or tutoring. The empirical results were not satisfying. There was such enormous variability and complexity in the factors that influenced learning to write among ESL students that it proved difficult to relate these processes effectively to students' achievements (Cumming & Riazi, 2000). Moreover, the experienced instructors participating in our study differed greatly in their stated beliefs about writing and about their teaching but nonetheless tended to teach in similar ways (Shi & Cumming, 1995; Riazi, Lessard-Clouston & Cumming, 1996). We also found that the expectations dominating teacher-student verbal interactions about students' written drafts were so highly conventionalized that they tended to defy innovations aimed at improving them (Cumming, 1993; Cumming & So, 1996).

If these concertedly empirical investigations yielded conclusions, they concerned the utter complexity of teaching, learning, writing, languages, and cultural diversity. So I decided to design some studies that were based explicitly on theories that addressed these matters. These studies do, I believe, help to understand things better than my straightforward descriptive research did, though their findings remain encapsulated within the terms of the theoretical frameworks. One example was Nassaji and Cumming (2000). Hossein Nassaji came into my office one day with a box of booklets, saying that he had collected two years' of dialogue journals written between his son (an ESL learner from Iran, then in grades 1 and 2 of initial schooling in Toronto) and his experienced teacher. Could we discuss what he might do with them? Hossein proposed analyzing the long-term development of his son's morphosyntax in English using established techniques and linguistic categories (e.g., reviewed in Goldschneder & DeKeyser, 2005). When I read through the data, I was struck by the interactive qualities of the teacher's and student's responses to each others' texts as well as the long-term development of these ongoing written "conversations." Rather than just documentation of the student's progressive uses of English morphosyntax, here were long-term, dynamic interactions between a teacher and her ESL student. I realized these were unique data to investigate how instruction and second language writing interrelate

and develop. We adopted a coding scheme from Shuy (1993) to categorize the functions of the student's and teacher's discourse, and we
appealed to Vygotskian theories to interpret the progressions of these
discourse functions as instances of pedagogy in the student's zone of
proximal development (Lantolf, 2000; Vygotsky, 1978; Wells, 1999).
Shuy's scheme provided a heuristic to make sense of the enormous
amount of data. Sociocultural theory provided a conceptual framework to explain the student's and teacher's communications as ongoing support for the student's English writing development. Like many
such case studies, however, the theory also raised more questions than
it resolved, particularly in respect to the sufficiency of our data, evidence, and interpretations.

In recent years, I have increasingly used theories to design research
on second language writing development and instruction. My reason
is implicit in my shift (if you noticed) a few sentences above from the
terms "descriptive framework" to "conceptual framework." Theories
provide a conceptualization that is more profound and fully substantiated than the descriptions that might simply arise from empirical
inquiry, no matter how deeply grounded or verified those descriptions
may be in the actual data (cf. Strauss & Corbin, 1990). Theories conceptualize descriptions. Two particular theories that I have been uti-
lizing are activity theory and goal theory. These theories are related:
Both consider goals to be central to human actions and motivation.
Indeed, I see them as related theoretical conceptualizations rather than
as a single, unified theory (and so I write them in lower case rather
than capital letters). Activity theory is oriented toward socio-cultural
systems and interactions among people (Engeström, Miettinin & Punamaki, 1999; Leont'ev, 1972). Goal theory is oriented toward cognitive psychology and self-regulated learning (Austin & Vancouver,
1996; Pintrich, 2000).

I along with my graduate students, have been investigating students' goals for improving their writing during intensive ESL courses and university programs (Cumming, 2006; Cumming, Busch &
Zhou, 2002). We have also documented the goals of the instructors
for these courses (in ESL and various university courses), relating them
to the goals the students have for their writing and learning. The concept of goals serves a heuristic function. Students and teachers can
talk readily about them to explain their own actions and activities. In
analyzing their discourse, we have produced an empirically verified

and theoretically informed framework to describe these goals for ESL writing improvement (Cumming, 2006). Activity and goal theories have also given us a relatively comprehensive perspective on the complex phenomena of learning and teaching ESL writing. Using goals as a focus for our research, we have been able to document and relate ESL students' composing processes, written texts, and perceptions of their learning, and their instructors' perceptions of this writing and their aims for students' literacy development as well as changes in these elements or processes over several years and across ESL and university courses. This interrelated perspective contrasts with the main body of research on second language writing which has tended to compartmentalize, and thus fragment, current knowledge through separate investigations of either writing processes, written texts, teaching, or of specific types of social contexts or learner groups, rather than considering how these are integrated and interdependent (Cumming, 1998b, 2001b; Leki, Cumming & Silva, 2006).

A CONCLUSION

My conclusion from these admittedly self-indulgent reflections is simple: Purposeful empirical research is necessarily informed by theories, which serve to conceptualize thinking about phenomena, though to varying degrees of explicitness, design, or benefit. Heuristics provide useful tools for research and pedagogy to relate the practical actions of writing, learning, language, and teaching to theoretical conceptualizations. I have found my own research increasingly oriented toward theories because they help to conceptualize and interrelate complex phenomena. Studies of second language writing will probably never develop into the scientific status of, for example, biology (cf. Hacking, 1983). Nor do I imagine anyone really expects or wants that to happen. But studies of second language writing do need to overcome the compartmentalization of knowledge that characterizes the current state of the field, as it does in literary studies. One could try to move forward on this problem through elaboration of and consensus on specific theories and descriptive frameworks. But to hope for a single explanatory theory of second language writing seems futile, given the complexity and diversity of issues and situations involved.

The current, localized scope of inquiry into separate strands of research and program policies for different learner groups, ages of students, second or foreign languages, aspects of written literacy, social contexts, and types of educational programs (as shown in Leki, Cumming & Silva, 2006) compartmentalizes knowledge into separate interests. This makes it difficult to determine what exactly is integral to second language writing and what is not. To illustrate this problem, let me recount one final anecdote from my work in the 1990s. I joined a group of researchers to plan an international comparative study that aimed to survey second and foreign language education in 25 countries (which later resulted in Dickson & Cumming, 1996) under the auspices of the IEA (International Association for the Evaluation of Educational Achievement). At one of our initial meetings, the Director of IEA, Tjeerd Plomp—who had previously coordinated many of the major international studies of math, science, and computer education—recommended that a first step in planning such a project was to determine if there was a theoretical framework that could inform the overall design of the research. He sent us back to our respective countries to try to identify such a framework relevant to second language education, recommending that we meet again in a few months to consider the frameworks proposed. Most of us wrote arguments to explain why a single theory does not exist in second language education such as could describe, let alone even explain, all of the curricular, pedagogical, learner, linguistic, literacy, developmental, and societal variables that one would want to investigate in a comprehensive international survey. The purpose of a comparative study should, I argued, be to describe and analyze such situational variability, not to incorporate it within a single theory. A few participants in the project proposed we adopt theories by Krashen (1992) about second language acquisition or by Gardner (1985) about motivations and language learning. These theories were quickly dismissed because people felt they focused on limited aspects of educational phenomena. Moreover, their status was questionable, even among the small group of us. A few people derided them as Anglo-centric, biased toward North American educational systems, and uninformed about situations in other parts of the world or research literatures that were not published in English.

The point I take from this experience is not so much that comprehensive theories are lacking in the field of language education, though they obviously are. The point I want to make is that to describe second language writing, research and theories need: (a) to determine what is essential to this domain, distinguishing it from what is peripheral or interdependent on other phenomena; (b) to address the basic phenomena that commonly feature in education; and (c) to relate integrally to a range of situations both locally and around the world. I believe these are the major challenges for theories and research about second language writing in the coming years. Without addressing these issues in a comprehensive way, research into specific aspects of second language writing risk being activities like my chipping away at slate, as a child, without a guiding purpose or benefit. Moreover, researchers risk adopting or proposing partial theories, like those in literary studies, that provide insights or benefits only for certain situations, issues, peoples, or topics, but not others.

Notes

1. I thank Razika Sanaoui and Lourdes Ortega for useful comments on an initial draft of this chapter. Lourdes as well as Dwight Atkinson usefully reminded me that the conceptualizing value of theories extends to envisioning possibilities for transforming existing educational or societal circumstances (as in Cumming & Gill, 1991).

2. Other notable examples of descriptive frameworks are Spolsky's (1989) account of the various "conditions" that influence a person's learning a second or foreign language and Stern's (1983) analysis of the foundations of knowledge that inform the teaching of languages.

3. Nonetheless, we need to be cautious. Particular applications of concepts inevitably involve particular interpretations. Theories about genres are a case in point. The concept of genres is well described and widely accepted in writing research and pedagogy, providing a useful, comprehensive means to relate writing practices, textual characteristics, and social situations. But as Hyon (1996) and Johns (2003) have observed, three different and potentially conflicting theories about the concept of genres have been elaborated and put into practice. These emphasize, to varying degrees, the textual organization of discourse (Swales, 1990), the semiotics of linguistic systems (Halliday & Hasan, 1985), or cultural-psychological dimensions of power within specialized communities (Berkenkotter & Huckin, 1995).

References

Albright, R.W. (1958). *The international phonetic alphabet: Its background and development*. Monograph of the *International Journal of American Linguistics*, 24.
Auerbach, E. (1992). *Making meaning, making change : Participatory curriculum development for adult ESL literacy*. Washington, DC: Center for Applied Linguistics and Delta Systems.

Austin, J. T., & Vancouver, J. (1996). Goal constructs in psychology: Structure, process, and content. *Psychological Bulletin, 120,* 338–375.

Bascia, N., Cumming, A., Datnow, A., Leithwood, K., & Livingstone, D. (2005). Introduction. In N. Bascia, A. Cumming, K. Leithwood, & D. Livingstone (Eds.). *International handbook of educational policy,* Vol. 1 (pp. xi-xxxvi). Dordrecht, The Netherlands: Springer.

Bereiter, C., & Scardamalia, (1987). *The psychology of written composition.* Hillsdale, NJ: Erlbaum.

Berkenkotter, C., & Huckin, T. (1995). Genre knowledge in disciplinary communication: Cognition/culture/power. Hillsdale, NJ: Erlbaum.

Bloom, B. (Ed.) (1956). *Taxonomy of educational objectives: The classification of educational goals.* New York: McKay.

Burns, R., & Anderson, L. (1987). The activity structure of lesson segments. *Curriculum Inquiry, 17,* 31–53.

Campbell, J. (1949). *The hero with a thousand faces.* Princeton, NJ: Princeton University Press.

Canagarajah, S. (2005). Conclusion. In S. Makoni (Ed.), Toward a more inclusive applied linguistics and English language teaching: A symposium. *TESOL Quarterly, 39,* 745–753.

Casanave, C. (2005). Uses of narrative in L2 writing research. In P. Matsuda & T. Silva (Eds.), *Second language writing research: Perspectives on the process of knowledge construction* (pp. 17–32). Mahwah, NJ: Erlbaum.

Chomsky, N. (1969). *American power and the new mandarins.* New York: Vintage.

Chomsky, N. (1965). *Aspects of the theory of syntax.* The Hague: Mouton.

Chomsky, N. (1988). *Language and problems of knowledge: The Managua lectures.* Cambridge, MA: MIT Press.

Connelly, M., & Clandinin, J. (1988). *Teachers as curriculum planners: Narratives of experience.* New York: Teachers College Press.

Cumming, A. (1989). Writing expertise and second-language proficiency. *Language Learning, 39,* 81–141.

Cumming, A. (1990a). Expertise in evaluating second language compositions. *Language Testing, 7,* 31–51.

Cumming, A. (1990b). Metalinguistic and ideational thinking in second language composing. *Written Communication, 7,* 482–511.

Cumming, A. (1992). Instructional routines in ESL composition teaching. *Journal of Second Language Writing, 1,* 17–35.

Cumming, A. (1993). Teachers' curriculum planning and accommodation of innovation: Three case studies of adult ESL instruction. *TESL Canada Journal, 11,* 30–52.

Cumming, A. (Ed.) (1994). Alternatives in TESOL research: Descriptive, interpretive, and ideological orientations. *TESOL Quarterly, 28,* 673–703.

Cumming, A. (1995). Fostering writing expertise in ESL composition instruction: Modeling and evaluation. In D. Belcher & G. Braine (Eds.), *Academic writing in a second language: Essays on research and pedagogy* (pp. 375–397). Norwood, NJ: Ablex.

Cumming, A. (1998a). Issues and prospects: Introduction to the 50th jubilee special issue. *Language Learning, 48,* 453–463.

Cumming, A. (1998b). Theoretical perspectives on writing. *Annual Review of Applied Linguistics, 18,* 61–78.

Cumming, A. (1999). The orchestration of ESL performance. In D. Albrechtson, B. Henrikson, I. Mees, & E. Poulson (Eds.) *Perspectives on foreign and second language pedagogy* (pp. 41–52). Odense, Denmark: Odense University Press.

Cumming, A. (2001a). ESL/EFL writing instructors' practices for assessment: General or specific purposes? *Language Testing, 18,* 2, 207–224.

Cumming, A. (2001b). Learning to write in a second language: Two decades of research. In R. Manchon (Ed.), *Writing in the L2 classroom: Issues in research and pedagogy,* special issue of *International Journal of English Studies, 1,* 2, 1–23.

Cumming, A. (2002). If I'd known twelve things . . . In L. Blanton & B. Kroll (Eds.), *ESL composition tales: Reflections on teaching* (pp. 123–134). Ann Arbor, MI: University of Michigan Press.

Cumming, A. (2003). Experienced ESL/EFL writing instructors' conceptualizations of their teaching: Curriculum options and implications. In B. Kroll (Ed.) *Exploring the dynamics of second language writing* (pp. 71–92). New York: Cambridge University Press.

Cumming, A. (Ed.) (2006). *Goals for academic writing: ESL students and their instructors.* Amsterdam: John Benjamins.

Cumming, A., Busch, M., & Zhou, A. (2002). Investigating learners' goals in the context of adult second-language writing. In S. Ransdell & M. Barbier (Eds.) *New directions for research in L2 writing* (pp. 189–208). Dordrecht, Netherlands: Kluwer.

Cumming, A., & Gill, J. (1991). Learning ESL literacy among Indo-Canadian women. *Language, Culture and Curriculum, 4,* 181–200.

Cumming, A., Kantor, R., Baba, K., Erdosy, U., Eouanzoui, K., & James, M. (2005). Differences in written discourse in independent and integrated prototype tasks for Next Generation TOEFL. *Assessing Writing, 10,* 5–43.

Cumming, A., Kantor, R., & Powers, D. (2002). Decision making while rating ESL/EFL writing tasks: A descriptive framework. *Modern Language Journal, 86,* 67–96.

Cumming, A., & Riazi, A. (2000). Building models of adult second-language writing instruction and achievement. *Learning and Instruction, 10,* 55–71.

Cumming, A., & So, S. (1996). Tutoring second language text revision: Does the approach to instruction or the language of communication make a difference? *Journal of Second Language Writing, 5,* 197–226.

Derrida, J. (1976). *Of grammatology.* Washington, DC: Johns Hopkins University Press.

Dickson, P., & Cumming, A. (Eds.). *Profiles of language education in 25 countries.* Slough, UK: National Foundation for Educational Research.

Eagleton, T. (1976). Criticism and ideology: A study in Marxist literary theory. London: Humanities Press.

Engeström, Y., Miettinen, R., & Punamaki, R. (Eds.). (1999). *Perspectives on activity theory.* Cambridge, UK: Cambridge University Press.

Ericsson, K., & Simon, E. (1984). *Protocol analysis: Verbal reports as data.* Cambridge, MA: MIT Press.

Fish, S. (1980). Is there a text in this class? The authority of interpretive communities. Cambridge, MA: Harvard University Press.

Flower, L., & Hayes, J.R. (1981). A cognitive process theory of writing. *College Composition and Communication, 32,* 365–387.

Foucault, M. (1965). *Madness and civilization: A history of insanity in the age of reason.* (R. Howard, Trans.). New York: Vintage Books. (Original work published 1961)

Fraser, J.G. (1922). The golden bough: A study in magic and religion. London: Macmillan.

Frye, N. (1957). *Anatomy of criticism: Four essays.* Princeton, NJ: Princeton University Press.

Gardner, R.C. (1985). *Social psychology and second language learning: The role of attitudes and motivation.* London: Arnold.

Goldschneider, J., & DeKeyser, R. (2005). Explaining the "natural order of L2 morpheme acquisition" in English: A meta-analysis of multiple determinants. In R. DeKeyser (Ed.), *Grammatical development in language learning* (pp. 27–71). Malden, MA: Blackwell.

Gombrich, E.H. (1972). *The story of art.* London: Phaidon Press.

Grabe, W. (2001). Notes toward a theory of second language writing. In T. Silva & P. Matsuda (Eds.), *On second language writing* (pp. 39–57). Mahwah, NJ: Erlbaum.

Hacking, I. (1983). Representing and intervening: Introductory topics in the philosophy of natural science. Cambridge, UK: Cambridge University Press.

Halliday, M. A. K., & Hasan, R. (1985). *Language, context, and text: Aspects of language in a social-semiotic perspective.* Geelong, Australia: Deakin University Press.

Holland, N. (1968). *The dynamics of literary response.* New York: Oxford University Press.

Hornberger, N. (Ed.) (2003). *Continua of biliteracy: An ecolological framework for educational policy, research, and practice in multilingual settings.* Clevedon, UK: Multilingual Matters.

Hyon, S. (1996). Genre in three traditions: Implications for ESL. *TESOL Quarterly, 30,* 693–722.

Huot, B. (1990). The literature of direct writing assessment: Major concerns and prevailing trends. *Review of Educational Research, 60,* 237–263.

Johns, A. (2003). Genre and ESL/EFL composition instruction. In B. Kroll (Ed.). *Exploring the dynamics of second language writing* (pp. 195–217). New York: Cambridge University Press.

Johnson, K. (1999). *Understanding language teaching: Reasoning in action.* Boston: Heinle & Heinle.

Kintsch, W. (1988). The role of knowledge in discourse comprehension: A construction-integration model. *Psychological Review, 92,* 163–182.

Krajina, V. (1965). *Ecology of the Pacific Northwest and of the western Canadian Arctic and Subarctic.* Vancouver, B.C.: Department of Botany, University of British Columbia.

Krashen, S. (1982). *Principles and practice in second language acquisition.* Oxford: Pergamon.

Kumaravedivelu, B. (2006). TESOL methods: Changing tracks, challenging trends. *TESOL Quarterly, 40,* 59–81.

Lakoff, B., & Johnson, M. (1981). The metaphorical structure of the human conceptual system. In D. A. Norman (Ed.), *Perspectives on cognitive science* (pp. 193–206). Norwood, NJ: Ablex.

Lado, R. (1964). *Language teaching: A scientific approach.* New York: McGraw-Hill.

Lantolf, J. (1996). SLA theory building: "Letting all the flowers bloom." *Language Learning, 46,* 713–749.

Lantolf, J. (2000). Second language learning as a mediated process. *Language Teaching, 33,* 79–96.

Lee, N., & Schumann, J. (2003, March). The evolution of language and the symbolosphere as complex adaptive systems. Paper presented at the Annual Meeting of the American Association for Applied Linguistics, Arlington, VA.

Leinhardt, G., Weidman, C., & Hammond, K. (1987). Introduction and integration of classroom routines by expert teachers. *Curriculum Inquiry, 17,* 135–176.

Leki, I., Cumming, A., & Silva, T. (2006). Second-language composition teaching and learning. In P. Smagorinsky (Ed.), *Research on composition: Multiple perspectives on two decades of change* (pp. 141–169). New York: Teachers College Press, Columbia University.

Leont'ev, A. (1972, trans. 1979). The problem of activity in psychology. In
    J. Wertsch (Ed.), *The concept of activity in Soviet psychology* (pp. 37–71).
    Armonk, NY: Sharpe.

Long, M., & Doughty, C. (Eds.) (2003). *The handbook of second language
    acquisition*. Malden, MA: Blackwell.

Martin, C. (1963). *An introduction to Canadian English*. Toronto: New Ca-
    nadian Publishers.

Marx, K. (1954). *Capital: A critique of political economy* (Vols. 1-3). New
    York: Progress Publishers.

McLaren, P. (1986). *Schooling as a ritual performance*. London: Routledge
    and Kegan Paul.

Moll, L. (1989). Teaching second language students: A Vygotskian perspec-
    tive. In D. Johnson & S. Roen (Eds.), *Richness in writing* (pp. 55–69).
    New York: Longman.

Nassaji, H., & Cumming, A. (2000). What's in a ZPD? A case study of a
    young ESL student and teacher interacting through dialogue journals.
    Language Teaching Research, 4, 95–121.

Pintrich, P.R. (2000). The role of goal orientation in self-regulated learning.
    In M. Boekaerts, P. R. Pintrich & M. Zeidner (Eds.), *Handbook of self-
    regulation* (pp. 451–502). San Diego, CA: Academic Press.

Pound, E. (1934). *ABC of reading*. New York: New Directions.

Quirk, R., & Greenbaum, S. (1973). *A university grammar of English*. Lon-
    don: Longman.

Raimes, A. (1987). Language proficiency, writing ability, and composing
    strategies: A study of ESL college student writers. *Language Learning, 37,*
    357–385.

Riazi, A., Lessard-Clouston, M., & Cumming, A. (1996). Observing ESL
    writing instruction: A case study of four teachers. *Journal of Intensive Eng-
    lish Studies, 10,* 19–30.

Richards, I.A. (1966). *Practical criticism, a study of literary judgement*. Lon-
    don: Routledge and Kegan Paul. (Original work published 1929)

Rosenfield, I., & Ziff, E. (2006, May 11). Evolving evolution. *New York Re-
    view of Books, 53,* 8, 12–17.

Saunders, J. W. (1970). *Patterns and principles of animal development*. New
    York: Macmillan.

Shi, L., & Cumming, A. (1995). Teachers' conceptions of second-language
    writing instruction: Five case studies. *Journal of Second Language Writing,
    4,* 87–111.

Shuy, R. (1993). Using language functions to discover a teacher's implicit
    theory of communicating with students. In J. Peyton & L. Staton (Eds.),
    Dialogue journals in the multilingual classroom (pp. 127–154). Norwood,
    NJ: Ablex.

Smagorinsky, P. (Ed.) (1994). *Speaking about writing: Reflections on research methodology*. Thousand Oaks, CA: Sage.

Spolsky, B. (1989). *Conditions for second language learning*. Oxford: Oxford University Press.

Stern, H.H. (1983). *Fundamental concepts of language teaching*. Oxford: Oxford University Press.

Stevick, E. (1976). *Memory, meaning, and method*. Rowley, MA: Newbury House.

Strauss, A., & Corbin, J. (1990). *Basics of qualitative research: Grounded theory procedures and techniques*. Newbury Park, CA: Sage.

Swales, J. (1990). *Genre analysis: English in academic and research settings*. Cambridge: Cambridge University Press.

van Lier, L. (2004). *The ecology and semiotics of language teaching: A sociocultural perspective*. Nordrecht, The Netherlands: Kluwer.

Vygotsky, L. (1978). *Mind in society: The development of higher psychological processes*. Cambridge, MA: Harvard University Press.

Warren, J. (2006). Literary scholars processing poetry and constructing arguments. *Written Communication, 23*, 202–226.

Waterman, A. (1971). *Chordate structure and function*. New York: Macmillan.

Wells, G. (1999). *Dialogic inquiry: Towards a sociocultural practice and theory of education*. Cambridge: Cambridge University Press.

Widdowson, H. (1975). *Stylistics and the teaching of literature*. London: Longman.

Widdowson, H. (1983). *Learning purpose and language use*. Oxford: Oxford University Press.

Zamel, V. (1983). The composing processes of advanced ESL students: Six case studies. *TESOL Quarterly, 17*, 165–187.

Zuengler, J., & Miller, E. (2006). Cognitive and sociocultural perspectives: Two parallel SLA worlds? *TESOL Quarterly, 40*, 35–58.

3 Multicompetence, Social Context, and L2 Writing Research Praxis

Lourdes Ortega and Joan Carson

Theory building is nourished by empirical data, but the data generated by empirical investigations can be only as good as the theories that guide research practices. Empirical research is a cyclical process that begins and ends with theories and theory-driven interpretations (Norris & Ortega, 2003). If we accept this position, then the congruence between theoretical insights and research praxis is a prerequisite for generating useful disciplinary knowledge. It is important, then, for members of any research community to reflect on how well they "practice" their theories in the research programs they pursue. This is our point of departure in this chapter. We ask ourselves: To what extent are prevalent research practices in work at the interface between second language (L2) writing and second language acquisition (SLA) reflective of and congruent with cutting-edge theoretical understandings currently available to the research community? Our answer is that there is a misalignment between theory and actual research practice in this line of work. We then identify and discuss four areas for expansion that have the potential to improve the alignment of cutting-edge theoretical insights and empirical efforts at the interface between L2 writing and SLA.

A Brief Map of L2 Writing-SLA Interfaces

The kind of work we address in this chapter pursues a better understanding of linguistic and cognitive dimensions of L2 writing. Because of its emphasis on text, cognition, and skills, we conceptualize it as SLA-oriented L2 writing research, or research conducted at the interface between L2 writing and SLA. Perhaps the following are among the best researched areas in this domain:

- text-based studies where L2 writers are profiled into developmental levels through textual linguistic features (e.g., Ortega, 2003; Reynolds, 2005; see review in Polio, 2001)
- correlational studies that attempt to elucidate the moderating influence of L2 proficiency on L2 writing development (e.g., Cumming, 1989; Sasaki & Hirose, 1996; Schoonen et al., 2003)
- observational-introspective studies that address the posited distinct nature of L2 writing (Silva, 1993) by investigating cognitive processes and particularly the L2-constrained nature of formulation (e.g., Manchón & Roca de Larios, 2007)
- quasi-experimental studies that investigate the effectiveness of providing error correction on writing (see contrasting reviews in Ferris, 2004, and Truscott, 2007)

One can think of other areas of research where SLA and L2 writing insights and interests converge. At the broadest level, however, L2 writing-SLA interfaces revolve around the fundamental question of how linguistic expertise in the L2 may constrain the development of L2 composing abilities and, conversely, the less frequently explored question of how L2 writing may foster overall second language development. In terms of research praxis, work exploring L2 writing-SLA interfaces is empirical and post-positivist, and it typically emphasizes textual (including linguistic and rhetorical) dimensions and cognitive dimensions of L2 writing at the expense of the wider social context. While we believe the focus on textual and cognitive dimensions of writing is a legitimate one for researchers who are so inclined to direct their efforts, we will argue that research praxis must nevertheless go beyond text and individual writer and be attuned to contemporary theoretical insights. These insights call for a redefinition of linguistic competence and an expansion of the scope of inquiry.

MULTICOMPETENCE, SOCIAL CONTEXT, AND THEORY-RESEARCH PRAXIS MISALIGNMENTS

In recent years, a concerted critique has emerged that problematizes and deconstructs the status of the native speaker as a benchmark for building theories, conducting research, or designing pedagogies. More and more scholars have articulated the same critique against the subtle but dangerous monolingual bias behind the native speaker myth (Seidlhofer, 2001). The consequences have been far-reaching, in that this theoretical appraisal has also cast doubts on the appropriacy of typical culture-language associations in pedagogy and materials (McKay, 2003) and has raised fundamental questions as to who has the right to own a language, define it, promote it or resist it, and shape the ways in which it is used, taught, learned, and researched (Canagarajah, 1999; Sridhar, 1994). Perhaps the most transformative consequence for our present purposes is what hasn't been called yet (but we would like to call here) an imminent bilingual turn in applied linguistics.

The bilingual turn began with the realization that, just as applied linguistic research can no longer stand on the native speaker as model and norm, so is it no longer tenable to hold monolingualism as the starting point of inquiry. Vivian Cook, one of the earliest SLA voices to raise these concerns (e.g., Cook, 2002, 2008), argues that the best psycholinguistic evidence tells us L2 competence is fundamentally different from the linguistic competence of a monolingual (see also Grosjean, 1989). "L2 users" are not two monolinguals in one. Instead, they possess a psycholinguistically distinct form of "multi-competence." And as Cook (2002) puts it, "multi-competence is not just the imperfect cloning of mono-competence, but a different state" (pp. 7–8). Thus, multicompetence is a worthwhile proposal that the research community has available for making theoretical progress in the study of linguistic dimensions of L2 learning.

A second, long-ranging theoretical development has been what many have recognized as a social turn in applied linguistics. Over the last fifteen years or so, it has become apparent that many traditional theories in SLA are ill-equipped to deal with the social context of language learning and language use in theoretically rigorous ways. Newer theories have thrived that provide strategies and practices for studying human phenomena as embedded in experience and situated in context (Matsuda et al., 2003). They offer social respecifications of a number of areas that are central for a full understanding of L2 learning, including cognition (Lantolf & Thorne, 2006), grammar (Schleppegrell, 2004), interaction (Markee & Kasper, 2004), sense of self (Kanno & Norton, 2003; Pavlenko & Blackledge, 2004), and learning (Duff, 2007). Explanatory constructs that cut across these theories are agency, power, and identity; they are theoretical signposts pointing at the realization that the social must be researched, not as externally documented experience or fixed environmental encounters, but as experience that is lived, made sense of, negotiated, contested, and claimed by learners in their physical, inter-personal, social, cultural, and historical contexts.

Despite these compelling theoretical developments, work generated at the interface between L2 writing and SLA does not appear to be concerned with the need to respond to questions raised by the critiques of multicompetence and social context. For example, much L2 writing research to date, particularly L2 writing research at the interface with SLA, has treated the process of composing in a language other than the mother tongue as a monocultural and monolingual act of a special (secondary) nature, as Valdés (1992, 2000) has repeatedly denounced. Moreover, to our knowledge, concerns about how to incorporate the social context into the research produced have not been voiced by researchers at the interface between L2 writing and SLA. This is despite the fact that historically social and constructivist epistemologies have in general been prevalent in the field of L2 writing (Silva & Leki, 2004).

If we use Ivanič's (2004) multilayered view of writing, then work at the interface between L2 writing and SLA falls within the first two layers, text and cognition, and neglects the other two layers, the micro-context in which the writing event is embedded and the macro-context comprising the historical, social, cultural, material, and relational worlds in which writers participate. Ivanič also identifies an associated system of prevalent discourses that characterize theory, research, and pedagogy of L2 writing. Each of these discourses, she argues, reflects and creates the beliefs and values underlying the range of theories and practices one can encounter in the field of L2 writing. Work at the interface between L2 writing and SLA participates in the dominant discourse of writing as skill, with some inclusion of two other discourses, genre and process. The remaining three discourses of writing identified by Ivanič (creativity, social practices, and sociopolitical discourse) are practically absent from research generated in this line of work. Thus, a misalignment between research praxis and theoretical understandings is apparent when L2 writing researchers investigate linguistic and cognitive dimensions without concern for these intellectual developments.

Towards the Attunement of SLA-Oriented L2 Writing Research Praxis and Theory

How can theoretical insights about the multicompetent and social nature of writing better inform and guide research practices in SLA-oriented investigations of L2 writing? The challenge, at least in part, involves crafting new investigative prisms that might allow researchers to more fully investigate L2 composing as a multicompetent (i.e., biliterate and bilingual) act that is situated and understood in its social context. Motivated by this goal, we identify a constellation of practices that are congruent with recent theoretical understandings of multicompetence and social context in applied linguistics. In the remainder of the chapter, we discuss the following research strategies in turn:

- Investigating the same writers as they compose across languages;
- developing analytical systems to be applied to a writer's two or more languages;
- Employing raters who themselves are multilingual and multicompetent; and
- Engaging in empirical research programs across systematically diverse contexts and populations, with an emphasis on understanding the contextual bounds of disciplinary findings and theoretical interpretations.

If adopted, or at least explored, these strategies have the potential to transform the research praxis embraced by researchers at the interface between SLA and L2 writing, by challenging them to fine-tune theories of L2 writing from a multicompetent lens and by advancing the research community's ability to incorporate social context in its empirically driven theory building efforts. This move may make it possible to achieve a better balance between linguistic, cognitive, and social dimensions in future theory building efforts.

Studying Multicompetence via Within-Writer Designs

In his seminal comparative review of L1 and L2 writing, Silva (1993) synthesized 72 studies that fit two broad study designs. The majority of studies (n = 41 or 57 percent) featured a comparison of the writing produced by an L2 group to that of a baseline L1 group, whereas a smaller group (n = 27 or 38 percent) offered a comparison of the L1 and L2 writing by the same bilingual writers. A few years later, Kubota (1998) advocated strongly for what she called a within-subject approach to L2 writing, that is, for the second type of design. Kubota argued that this option is desirable because it allows comparisons not only across languages but within writers.

Once the native speaker (or the L1 writer) is no longer thought to be a viable norm and point of departure for research, the direct comparison of L1 to L2 groups becomes problematic as the sole or dominant empirical basis for theory building—in L2 writing as much as in SLA. Native-nonnative speaker comparisons may be legitimate for some research purposes but they are severely limited and fraught with dangers. As Cook (2008) has recently noted:

> There is no reason why one thing cannot be compared to another; it may be useful to discover the similarities and differences between apples and pears. SLA research can use comparison with the native speaker as a tool, partly because so much is already known about monolingual speakers. The danger is regarding it as failure not to meet the standards of natives: apples do not make very good pears. Comparing L2 users with monolingual native speakers can yield a useful list of similarities and differences, but never establish the unique aspects of second language knowledge that are not present in the monolingual . . . (p. 19)

Thus, we concur with Kubota (1998) and believe that much can be gained by investigating L2 writing as a within-writer phenomenon, by means of designs that treat writers as multicompetent individuals and thus require elicitation and analysis of writing by the same people in their two (or more) languages.

Within-writer designs are not rare in L2 writing research, although they still constitute a minority, some fifteen years since Silva's influential review. Recent studies of formulation in L2 writing (e.g., Chenoweth & Hayes, 2001; Roca de Larios et al., 2001) have featured this kind of design with particularly fruitful outcomes. Thus, for instance, the direct comparison of temporal formulation patterns by the same writers across their two languages, English and Spanish, recently allowed Roca de Larios et al. (2006) to make an unexpected finding. As predicted, the twenty-one writers they investigated spent more of their time engaged in problem solving behavior when they wrote an essay in their L2 than when they did a similar L1 essay task a week later. More specifically, problem solving consumed about a fourth of total composition time in their L2 (twice as much as in their L1), and this was true regardless of proficiency level. The unexpected finding, however, was that a key L1-L2 difference regarding the quality of problem solving during formulation was experienced by writers at intermediate but not at lower or higher proficiency levels. Specifically, the seven writers in the intermediate proficiency group devoted over twice as much time in the L2 than in the L1 to what the researchers call "upgrading" behavior (i.e., attempts to embellish and elaborate, as opposed to compensating for an L2 knowledge gap). By contrast, the seven least and seven most proficient writers were able to allocate similar relative percentages of upgrading time during L2 and L1 writing. Roca de Larios et al. link this finding to previous ones and suggest the possibility of "a more consistent correspondence between L1 and L2 performance at some proficiency levels (lower and advanced) than at others (intermediate)" (p. 109). This interpretation needs to remain tentative, because (as the researchers recognize) a confounding effect between proficiency and general composing expertise cannot be discarded, given the decision to compare across high school students, undergraduates, and graduates. However, the possibility is tantalizing and certainly consistent with the well attested nonlinear nature of language and skill development.

The within-writer design has also proven particularly fruitful for challenging traditional contrastive rhetoric claims that may be essentializing. Thus, both Kubota (1998) and Hirose (2003) were able to convincingly show with their same-writer findings that some writers do transfer the rhetorical preferences of their L1 into their L2 writing, whereas others do not (for a recent discussion of this issue, see Kubota & Lehner, 2004, and ensuing responses).

An additional possibility for L2 writing researchers interested in understanding multicompetent writers across their languages is to adopt within-writer designs in combination with monolingual writing baselines for all the languages under investigation. This option, which amounts to combining in single studies the two designs identified above, has remained an exception in the field. For example, only four such studies (or 5 percent of 72) were found in Silva (1993), all dealing with textual analyses. Neff et al. (2004) offer a good illustration of the advantages of such design, particularly for the study of research questions where L2 writing and SLA intersect. As their main focus, these researchers elicited L1 and L2 essays on the same topic from 60 EFL students in Spain at two different levels, first- and fourth-year in college EFL classes. In addition, they included three L1 baselines intended to represent differing degrees of writing expertise with full linguistic competence remaining constant. Specifically, two sets of argumentative writing samples of English and Spanish published newspaper articles were chosen as representative of expert native writing in each language; and one set of argumentative essays written by English L1 college-level students in the United States were considered to represent native writers who were novice relative to the journalist writers and closer in general writing expertise to the EFL college students. To the researchers' surprise, the EFL students employed as much subordination in their L2 English essays as the English newspaper writers did, and even slightly more subordination than the L1 English college writers. However, a comparison of the two L1 expert writer baselines revealed that the seemingly "advanced-like" use of subordination in the L2 college samples was best interpreted as a case of L1 transfer of a strong preference for subordination. Namely, English journalists prioritized elaboration at the clausal level through the use of dense nominalization and clause reduction (see Halliday, 1998), whereas Spanish journalists preferred elaboration by heavy subordination (they used on average one subordinate clause per main clause). In essence, Neff et al. were able to interpret more fully the interacting developmental and cross-rhetorical influences at play, precisely because the within-writer design was supplemented with (novice and expert) L1 baselines for the two languages involved.

Enough L2 writing research has accumulated by now to suggest that multicompetent writers are likely to use both (or all) their languages to aid themselves during the writing process (Wang & Wen, 2002; Woodall, 2002) and to negotiate multiple cultural and educational influences on their development of composing abilities (Kubota, 1998, 1999). Moreover, multicompetent writers recruit capacities across their languages in order to eventually learn how to navigate the demands of writing for very different communities depending on the language of choice, and they do so with varying degrees of confidence and mastery in their several languages, including their mother tongue, depending on their professional and life circumstances (e.g., Canaga-rajah, 2001, 2006; Chiang & Schmida, 1999; Curry & Lillis, 2004; Kellman, 2002; Yi, 2007). The logical corollary of so much evidence is that a full understanding of L2 writing must be based on the systematic study of the same writers as they engage in writing across all their languages, not only the L2, if we hope to capture the complexity of multicompetent writing as a process and an achievement in constant flux, and one that always recruits fluid and reciprocal capacities across the writer's languages.

DEVELOPING ANALYTICAL SYSTEMS TO STUDY OTHER LANGUAGES VIS-À-VIS ENGLISH

The endorsement of within-writer designs as a regular staple of L2 writing research praxis, while beneficial and feasible at first glance, would have a number of complex consequences. For one, the field would need to devise new strategies for making analyses across languages reasonably comparable. This poses no small challenge.

For example, when McCarthey et al. (2005) decided to investigate the two-year L1 and L2 writing trajectories of five elementary-age children schooled in English, they were faced with the challenge to create comparable analytical systems to apply to their L1 Mandarin and L2 English texts. This study was ambitious in scope because it involved the development of rubrics not only for formal linguistic aspects of the writing, but also for voice and rhetorical style across the two languages. While most of the rubrics and categories were parallel, a few ended up being language-specific. The composite scores on the various rubrics were then combined to yield judgments about writers' ability (advanced, competent, average, below average, and poor). Although the researchers were able to demonstrate rich developmental patterns in both languages through this analytical effort, they also commented that the need for comparability had probably the undesirable effect of making certain analyses more superficial or mechanical than they would have liked them to be (p. 98).

Comparisons involving cognitive, linguistic, and rhetorical dimensions of writing across languages always demand great care. When the contested construct of "writing quality" is at the center of research programs, we wade into even murkier waters. Indeed, among the most thorny analytical challenges in within-writer research would be the development of appropriate non-English writing scoring systems that can be used to judge writing quality across a writer's two (or more) languages. Two individual studies and a larger-scale research program have tackled this challenge in the past.

Carson et al. (1990) had their native-speaking Chinese and Japanese raters follow a pile-sorting technique and divide essays into six groups. They then asked the same raters to collaboratively develop scoring rubrics that described essential qualities in each pile. This led to six-point scoring rubrics in Chinese and Japanese that paralleled the scales and scoring system used for the L2 English essays while at the same time capturing the L1-specific content of perceptions of quality in writing. The second individual study, Sasaki and Hirose (1999), appeared almost a decade later and was designed much more elaborately. Sasaki and Hirose first derived 24 rubric descriptors by involving informants in two stages: first two Japanese L1 writing experts, and subsequently 102 Japanese teachers. At a third stage, another 106 teachers used the descriptors to evaluate two essays. This led to the establishment of six sub-scales derived from regression analysis of the teachers' scores. Finally, two L1 Japanese raters scored 69 new essays twice, first using the Japanese rubrics and, six months later, using a Japanese translation of Jacobs et al. (1981), the scoring rubrics most often employed in L2 writing studies to rate English essays. Both scales yielded similar, satisfactory inter-rater reliabilities and the scores obtained with the two scales correlated strongly ($r = 0.76$). Thus, the psychometric soundness of the developed scoring rubrics seems warranted for use in the context of EFL and Japanese writing in Japan.

Interestingly, Sasaki and Hirose commented positively on the Japaneseness of the resulting rubrics, noting that certain descriptors "reflect[ed] a particularity of the Japanese L1 composition teachers' judging criteria" (p. 170). Thus, the content validity of the rubrics was enhanced because of a greater attunement to the rhetorical and linguistic context of L1 Japanese academic writing. On the other hand, in another publication (Sasaki & Hirose, 1996), the researchers suggest that the use of L1-specific rating scales may actually result in a weaker relationship between L1 and L2 essay scores than the relationship typically obtained when parallel translated rubrics are used (e.g., as they had done in Hirose & Sasaki, 1994). They even raise the possibility that L1 writing ability "may not be so powerful in explaining L2 writing ability when the two languages have different rhetorical conventions" (Sasaki & Hirose, 1996, p. 156). Clearly, creating language specific, non-English scoring rubrics of writing quality is a delicate balancing act.

Similar difficulties are also underscored in the large-scale, comparative research program led by Alan Purves (Purves, 1992a). This well known project was undertaken in the context of an international study of educational achievement in writing, conducted under the auspices of the International Association for the Evaluation of Educational Achievement (IEA). One of the steps in the research process was to develop a scoring rubric that would capture international dimensions of writing across cultures and languages (Gorman, Purves, & Degenhart, 1988). While acknowledging that "good writing" was likely to vary from culture to culture, the international team's assumption was that texts have both language-specific and language-transcendent features. What emerged from the extensive development process was a scoring guide that featured four categories—content, organization, style, and tone—each of which could be defined to allow for appropriate variation in conventions across cultures. Ultimately, the researchers were unable to make direct comparisons across educational systems. The lack of uniformity in the organization of scoring sessions meant that the variability found in student competence was confounded by the variability in the application of the scale. Even so, researchers concluded that the existence of other types of variation (e.g., in teacher ideology, instructional practices) requires that writing be seen in a cultural context and not considered a general cognitive capacity. Purves (1992b) argues that a common core identifying "good writing" is illusory:

> Across the systems of education, the terms relating
> to written composition and its judgment are easily
> shared; the nuances and values given those terms are
> a part of the national culture that makes such sharing
> superficial at best. . . . We suspect that writing is not
> as unitary a construct as many national assessments
> and writing researchers would have it. (p. 200)

In sum, it would be naïve to imagine that an inclusion of target languages other than English in our studies would be simply that, just a linguistic addition to our research praxis. Rather, the change would also entail a concomitant expansion of the educational contexts, the sociocultural milieus, and the rhetorical and intellectual traditions that we will be compelled to accommodate within single studies. Recent advances in contrastive rhetoric (Connor, 2002; Kubota & Lehner, 2004; Matsuda, 1997) and comparative studies of literacy experiences across education systems (Carson, 1992; Kobayashi & Rinnert, 2002; Foster & Russell, 2002) should help inform this research program. In addition, qualitative studies of expert bilingual composing competence (Belcher & Connor, 2001; Casanave & Vandrick, 2003; Curry & Lillis, 2004; Kellman, 2002; Yi, 2007) and ethnographic studies of specific cultural understandings of what students, teachers, and raters mean by "good writing" (Li, 1996) are under-utilized in current SLA-oriented L2 writing research, and they would prove invaluable in putting empirical efforts regarding the development of non-English analytical systems into full theoretical perspective. Given recent discussions on the politics of difference in the study of L2 writing (e.g., Kubota & Lehner, 2004), such an area of inquiry is likely to be complex, contested, and challenging, yet theoretically profitable.

JUDGING THE QUALITY OF MULTICOMPETENT WRITING THROUGH A BILINGUAL LENS

It is no exaggeration to say that the ideal rater of L2 writing has usually been assumed to be a native speaking teacher or writing expert. This has been so even in studies of English L2 writing conducted in EFL and outer circle English contexts, where in non-research circumstances students are at least as likely to be evaluated by bilingual non-native English speaking teachers as by native English speaking ones. It should be noted that the same preference for native speaking raters is found when judging writing in other languages besides English. For example, McCarthey et al. (2005) recruited elementary teachers from Taiwan in order to assess the Chinese writing of their U.S.-based participants. Likewise, Carson et al. (1990) and Sasaki and Hirose (1999) involved native speakers in the development of Japanese and Chinese writing rubrics, respectively. Thus, what is known about the essay rating process (e.g., Connor & Carell, 1993; Hamp-Lyons, 1991; Weigle, 1994) and about the features that raters seem to pay attention to when evaluating writing quality on time-compressed essay tasks (e.g., Chiang, 1999; Watanabe, 2001), derives mostly from investigations of raters who may or may not have been aware of and familiar with the linguistic and rhetorical backgrounds of the writers whose L2 products they evaluated. When one considers the many ways in which the crisis of the native speaker has challenged applied linguists and TESOL educators to question deeply ingrained practices (e.g., Kamhi-Stein, 2004), it is indeed surprising that native-speaking raters are still held as the ideal norm in many L2 writing studies. The issue simply does not appear to ignite the imagination of L2 writing researchers.

Yet, an early call for studies that compare monolingual and bilingual ratings of quality was made by Pennington and So (1993). These researchers noted that it is important to understand the impact of employing "ratings obtained by using groups of monolingual speakers to make assessments in different languages, as opposed to having bilingual raters evaluate quality across languages" (p. 57). Looking back at the research conducted since then, studies addressing this call have been scarce. In fact, to the best of our knowledge, no study has directly investigated the L1 and L2 ratings produced by the same bilingual writing experts, as Pennington and So proposed. A small body of research, however, has looked comparatively at how native and nonnative speaking raters compare in their judgments of writing quality (Connor-Linton, 1995; Kobayashi, 1992; Kobayashi & Rinnert, 1996; and Shi, 2001, who also reviews other studies).

Perhaps the best known of these studies is Kobayashi and Rinnert (1996). These researchers set out to compare the rhetorical preferences of two groups of teachers, native and nonnative English speaking, both serving EFL student populations in Japan. They did so by asking all teachers to rate an L2 essay that—unbeknownst to them—followed a more prototypical American English rhetorical pattern and another that followed a more prototypical Japanese rhetorical pattern. They found that the Japanese EFL teachers (all of whom were by implicit definition multicompetent users of English) did not rate one version higher or lower than the other. By contrast, the native English speaking teachers of EFL rated the essay containing the more prototypical American English rhetorical organization higher. They preferred the more American English style despite the fact that more than half of them had resided in Japan for 6 or more years and had taught English composition for a minimum of eight years. The difference in rhetorical preferences between the native and nonnative English speaking raters is even more striking when one considers that with regard to other aspects of the writing (e.g., sentence-level errors) both groups of teachers responded very similarly to the two essays. Thus, Kobayashi and Rinnert's findings throw the following question into sharp relief:

In what ways could the customary practice of using native-speaking raters be influencing the results of existing studies? Much more research will be needed before the research community can truly appraise the extent to which observations reported across studies reflect particular biases when applying monolingual and monocultural values to L2 writing (Kobayashi & Rinnert, 1996; Kubota, 1998; see also discussion in Basham & Kwachka, 1991; Land & Whitley, 1989; McKay, 1993; Rubin et al., 1990; Valdés, 1992, 2000).

In fact, we would argue that the term *native speaking* raters in many L2 writing studies is almost coterminous with "monolingual" and "monocultural," and we cannot but make the inference that what is sought under the native-speaking attribute of raters in such studies is some kind of warrant of linguistic and cultural purity. Yet, a challenging question needs to be asked: Assuming other things (e.g., writing expertise, teaching experience) are equal, could bilingual, bicultural experts be more qualified than monolingual experts to evaluate the L2 (and L1) texts that are generated by emerging multicompetent writers? In the long run, it is an empirical matter to determine whether expert and fully developed L2 writers might be ideal raters to employ in future L2 writing studies, and particularly in studies that adopt within-writer designs. For that reason, we would welcome future research that not only compares the ratings of groups of native and nonnative speakers, but that more purposefully illuminates the judgments of L1 and L2 quality made by language teaching and writing experts who are themselves multicompetent speakers of all the languages in a given study.

We would also like to raise a cautionary note to consider in future research efforts in this direction. It is rather uninformative to study raters and their judgments as if they stemmed exclusively from a context-free, fixed, and dichotomous status as native or nonnative speakers of the target language. Instead, it will be crucial in the future to go even further and explore raters' judgments of L2 writing quality against the ecological context of particular raters' and teachers' professional and institutional cultures. This is important for two reasons, at least. First, views about what is to be valued in student writing are shaped by membership in particular institutions and by participation in specific professional cultures (e.g., Atkinson & Ramanathan, 1995). Second, L2 writing experts capable of rating and evaluating multicompetent writing may resist being dichotomized into native and nonna-

tive speakers (e.g., Liu, 1999).Therefore, it might be more productive
to consider multicompetent raters' perceptions and skills as differing
along complex dimensions of language expertise, inheritance, and af-
filitation (the triadic perspective proposed by Rampton, 1990; see also
Leung et al., 1997). Both linguistic and cultural allegiances and actual
degree of multicompetencies developed by bilingual writers and raters
are no doubt important in understanding value judgments about L2
writing quality. This future area of research seems to us of crucial importance when investigating L2 writing-SLA interfaces.

GROUNDING THEORETICAL MODELS IN A
VARIETY OF SOCIAL CONTEXTS

The fourth area which we argue is in need of expansion pertains to a
much broader issue regarding the social context and populations currently investigated. L2 writing theories would be strengthened considerably if the research community could expand the focus of inquiry to
include underrepresented populations of second, foreign, and heritage
writers with differing degrees of literacy in L1 and L2, varying ages,
and diverse needs for writing and using the L2. We view it as a theoretical imperative to investigate multicompetent writing across a fuller
spectrum of contexts where biliteracy is a needed cultural capital.

A first important step is to acknowledge that some contexts are
typically excluded from scholarly discussions at the interface between
SLA and L2 writing. A telling fact is that of 154 empirical studies
published in the *Journal of Second Language Writing* between 1992
and 2007, we tallied a mere 26 that did not involve writers or writing issues that are specific to college-level populations in ESL or EFL
contexts. Extrapolating from this number, L2 writing theories may
be informed by empirical findings with less than a fifth of grounding
in any contexts but those involving English L2 writers functioning in
colleges and universities in second and foreign language settings. The
exclusion of diverse social contexts has serious ethical consequences,
because it silences the existence of large and diverse populations of L2
writers, and it leaves their educational needs ill-served (Ortega, 2005).
It should be recognized, furthermore, that it also has devastating consequences for theory building.

For example, the relationship between linguistic expertise and
composing ability has been theorized in the field of L2 writing thus
far on the premise that linguistic and literate competencies are well

developed in the L1 in the first place. This is no surprise given that, of course, college-level writers represent highly literate populations, having been schooled in both their L1 and their L2. On the other hand, this means that current L2 writing theories do not account for writing development in populations that are non-literate or semi-literate in their L1 (e.g., Acton & Dalphinis, 2000). Yet, such populations comprise truly large numbers of (child and adult) immigrant and refugee populations as well as many bilingual indigenous populations in the United States, and even larger numbers in other parts of the world.

Research concerning various populations where literate competencies are less than fully developed in the L1, or where L1 literacy cannot be assumed to exist at all, is still largely to be done (at least within the field of L2 writing; see Tarone & Bigelow, 2005, for a review of relevant literature in other fields). Thus, we can only speculate about several theoretical possibilities. One proposal is that of a "reversed" positive transfer from L2 composing into L1 composing ability, probably constrained by critical levels of L1 maintenance. This has been suggested for contexts where instruction in L2 literacy antedates reading and writing instruction in the L1. For example, Verhoeven (1994) found evidence for such a reversed influence among Turkish children enrolled in submersion school curricula in the Netherlands.

A second, perhaps more difficult step in beginning to address the social context in our research praxis is to break free from another assumption that will not be tenable for much longer, namely, that linguistic and literate competencies are static and fixed in the L1, and only dynamic and in flux in the L2. We need future research that helps us understand how the development of L2 composing competence interacts with, destabilizes, and most likely transforms the nature of L1 composing competence, and how the experiences afforded by different social contexts shape these processes. Perhaps the most salient observation to date in this area is that erosion and even loss of L1 composing capacities may be expected in certain contexts. The study by McCarthey et al. (2005) is relevant here. These researchers witnessed an overall loss of L1 writing competencies in their five Chinese-English elementary school participants over two years. Interestingly, the amount of loss was inversely proportional to the already acquired level of literacy in their L1 at the time of arrival in the United States, a constraint also suggested in the work by Verhoeven (1994). The differences across individuals, however, were also large. Of the five children,

Chung Min experienced the least loss, going down from advanced to competent L1 Chinese skills. Hui-Tzu showed neither progress nor loss and remained 'average' in her L1 writing over the two years. Yi Lin's written Chinese vocabulary slowly shrank while her English writing quickly grew in voice and sophistication. Both Paul and Suzie steeply deteriorated in their L1 Chinese writing competencies while their L2 English writing showed signs of incipient dominance. Perhaps not coincidentally, these last two children came from working-class parents with plans to reside in the United States permanently. Finally, McCarthey et al. noted that voice developed dramatically in both Chinese and English for all five children, hinting at the hybridization of expression of voice across the two languages. Apparently, the children were inspired by the English instruction they received in school to use first person and to personalize the topic for the reader, regardless of the language in which they wrote (p. 97). In sum, McCarthey et al.'s rich findings suggest anything but static or fixed L1 capacities in multicompetent writers.

We do not know what new theoretical models will need to be advanced, or how the present ones will need to be modified, once L2 writing researchers begin to investigate L2 plus L1 writing development in populations which are currently seriously understudied. Research into L2 writing that is grounded in contexts across a range of settings and that aims at expanding our theoretical understanding of multicompetence in writing would prove invaluable for making progress in theory building.

We hasten to acknowledge here that the appropriate characterization of contexts for language learning posits in itself an elusive theoretical challenge (see varying attempts in Block, 2003, chapter 3; Rampton, 1999; Siegel, 2003; Valdés, Brookes, & Chávez, 2003). Moreover, the pitfall of essentializing groups is very real when research programs embark on developing theories of human learning and cultural cognition by unwittingly defining populations monolithically according to cultural, linguistic, ethnic, or racial membership. Harklau (in her contribution in Matsuda et al., 2003) warned us against this danger with regard to the use of the label "1.5 generation," and a special issue of *Educational Researcher* (Lee, 2003) is entirely devoted to exploring such problems when studying education for ethnic and racial minority populations. (This issue also offers some useful strategies to counter essentializing assumptions in educational research practices.) There will be a great need to address these challenges in the kind of future research program we are envisioning for studying L2 writing-SLA interfaces.

Closing Thoughts

In this chapter we have explored the need for researchers who work at the interface between L2 writing and SLA to be more attuned in their research praxis to cutting-edge theoretical insights about L2 development and L2 writing available to the research community. We identified and discussed what we believe are some desirable expansions in the research practices that are prevalent at the interface between SLA L2 and writing. The attunement is needed in response to the broad realization that, in order to be useful to the communities it serves, L2 writing research of any kind, and particularly linguistically and cognitively oriented L2 writing research, needs to vigorously engage with the notions of multicompetence and social context. The field can hope best to understand multicompetent writing in its full social complexity if writing events are studied across a writer's languages and in context. We have argued that this would entail the investigation, within single research projects, of the same writers as they compose across languages, making space for writing in other languages alongside English writing, and employing raters and rubrics that are truly multicompetent. In addition, it would demand investigating diverse populations of L2 writers with their own range of uses, stakes, and developmental concerns for the attainment of competence in bilingual composing in particular, and bilingual literacy in general. The ongoing challenge will be to formulate new methodologies and investigative prisms that allow researchers to study linguistic and cognitive dimensions of writing through models of inquiry that are congruent with and support these theoretical insights.

A reorientation of research praxis in the directions we envision would have two beneficial side consequences. First, it would enable L2 writing researchers to better capture what multicompetent writers can do, as opposed to only understanding what they cannot or wish not to do in their L2, English. Additionally, we suspect the changes we have discussed would by necessity lead to a healthy increase of dialogue and collaboration among L2 writing researchers (where the term "L2 writing" is often associated with English writing exclusively) and researchers working on L2 writing within the perspectives of foreign and heritage language education (see Reichelt, 1999, 2001; and Colombi,

2002). We look forward to future research at the interface between L2
writing and SLA that strives for depth and breadth and is grounded in
the social context of learning and guided by a multicompetent view of
language and literacy development.

ACKNOWLEDGMENT

We are grateful to Alister Cumming, Bill Grabe, and Tony Silva for
their comments on earlier versions of this draft.

REFERENCES

Acton, T., & Dalphinis, M. (Eds.). (2000). *Language, blacks and gypsies: Languages without a written tradition and their role in education.* London: Whiting & Birch.

Atkinson, D., & Ramanthan, V. (1995). Cultures of writing: An ethnographic comparison of L1 and L2 university writing/language programs. *TESOL Quarterly, 29,* 539–568.

Basham, C. S., & Kwachka, P. E. (1991). Reading the world differently: A cross-cultural approach to writing assessment. In H. Hamp-Lyons (Ed.), *Assessing second language writing in academic contexts* (pp. 37–49). Norwood, NJ: Ablex.

Belcher, D., & Connor, U. (Eds.). (2001). *Reflections on multiliterate lives.* Clevedon, UK: Multilingual Matters.

Block, D. (2003). *The social turn in SLA.* Washington, DC: Georgetown University Press.

Canagarajah, S. (1999). Interrogating the "native speaker fallacy": Non-linguistic roots, non-pedagogical results. In G. Braine (Ed.), *Non-native educators in English language teaching* (pp. 77–92). Mahwah, NJ: Erlbaum.

Canagarajah, S. (2001). The fortunate traveler: Shuttling between communities and literacies by economy class. In D. Belcher & U. Connor (Eds.), *Reflections on multiliterate lives* (pp. 23–37). Buffalo, NY: Multilingual Matters.

Canagarajah, A. S. (2006). Toward a writing pedagogy of shuttling between languages: Learning from multilingual writers. *College English, 68*(6), 589–604.

Carson, J. G. (1992). Becoming biliterate: First language influences. *Journal of Second Language Writing, 1,* 37–60.

Carson, J. E., Carrell, P. L., Silberstein, S., Kroll, B., & Kuehn, P. A. (1990). Reading-writing relationships in first and second language. *TESOL Quarterly, 24,* 245–266.

Casanave, C. P., & Vandrick, S. (Eds.). (2003). *Writing for scholarly publication: Behind the scenes in language education.* Mahwah, NJ: Erlbaum.

Chenoweth, N. A., & Hayes, J. R. (2001). Fluency in writing: Generating text in L1 and L2. *Written Communication, 18,* 80–98.

Chiang, S. Y. (1999). Assessing grammatical and textual features in L2 writing samples: The case of French as a foreign language. *Modern Language Journal, 83,* 219–232.

Chiang, Y.-S. D., & Schmida, M. (1999). Language identity and language ownership: Linguistic conflicts of first-year university writing students. In L. Harklau, K. M. Losey & M. Siegal (Eds.), *Generation 1.5 meets college composition: Issues in the teaching of writing to U.S.-educated learners of English as a second language* (pp. 81–96). Mahwah, NJ: Erlbaum.

Colombi, M. C. (2002). Academic language development in Latino students' writing in Spanish. In M. J. Schleppegrell & M. C. Colombi (Eds.), *Developing advanced literacy in first and second languages* (pp. 67–86). Mahwah, NJ: Erlbaum.

Connor, U. (2002). New directions in contrastive rhetoric. *TESOL Quarterly, 36,* 493–510.

Connor, U., & Carrell, P. L. (1993). The interpretation of tasks by writers and readers in holistically rated direct assessment of writing. In J. Carson & I. Leki (Eds.), *Reading in the composition classroom: Second language perspectives* (pp. 141–160). Boston: Heinle & Heinle.

Connor-Linton, J. (1995). Crosscultural comparison of writing standards: American ESL and Japanese EFL. *World Englishes, 14,* 99–115.

Cook, V. (2002). Background to the L2 user. In V. Cook (Ed.), *Portraits of the L2 user* (pp. 1–28). Buffalo, NY: Multilingual Matters.

Cook, V. (2008). Multi-competence: Black hole or wormhole for second language acquisition research? In Z. Han (Ed.), *Understanding second language process* (pp. 16–26). Clevedon, UK: Multilingual Matters.

Cumming, A. (1989). Writing expertise and second language proficiency. *Language Learning, 39,* 81–141.

Curry, M. J., & Lillis, T. (2004). Multilingual scholars and the imperative to publish in English: Negotiating interests, demands, and rewards. *TESOL Quarterly, 38,* 663–688.

Duff, P. (2007). Second language socialization as sociocultural theory: Insights and issues. *Language Teaching, 40,* 309–319.

Ferris, D. R. (2004). The "grammar correction" debate in L2 writing: Where are we, and what do we go from here? (and what do we do in the meantime?). *Journal of Second Language Writing, 13,* 49–62.

Foster, D., & Russell, D. R. (Eds.). (2002). *Writing and learning in cross-national perspective: Transitions from secondary to higher education.* Mahwah, NJ: Erlbaum.

Gorman, T.P., Purves, A.C., & Degenhart, R.E. (Eds.). (1988). *The IEA study of written composition I: The international writing tasks and scoring scales.* Oxford: Pergamon Press.

Grosjean, F. (1989). Neurolinguists, beware! The bilingual is not two monolinguals in one person. *Brain and Language, 36,* 3–15.

Halliday, M. A. K. (1998). Things and relations: Regrammaticising experience as technical knowledge. In J. R. Martin & R. Vell (Eds.), *Reading science: Critical and functional perspectives on discourse of science* (pp. 185–235). New York: Routledge.

Hamp-Lyons, L. (1991). Reconstructing "academic writing proficiency." In L. Hamp-Lyons (Ed.), *Assessing second language writing in academic contexts* (pp. 127–153). Norwood, NJ: Ablex.

Hirose, K. (2003). Comparing L1 and L2 organizational patterns in the argumentative writing of Japanese EFL students. *Journal of Second Language Writing, 12,* 181–209.

Hirose, K., & Sasaki, M. (1994). Explanatory variables for Japanese students' expository writing in English: An exploratory study. *Journal of Second Language Writing, 3,* 203–229.

Ivanič, R. (2004). Discourses of writing and learning to write. *Language and Education, 18,* 220–245.

Jacobs, H., Zinkgraf, S., Wormuth, D., Hartfiel, V., & Hughey, J. (1981). *Testing ESL composition: A practical approach.* Rowley, MA: Newbury House.

Kamhi-Stein, L. D. (Ed.). (2004). *Learning and teaching from experience: Perspectives on nonnative English-speaking professional.* Ann Arbor, MI: University of Michigan Press.

Kanno, Y., & Norton, B. (2003). Imagined communities and educational possibilities: Introduction. *Language of Language, Identity, and Education, 2*(4), 241–249.

Kellman, S. G. (Ed.). (2002). *Switching languages: Translingual writers reflect on their craft:* University of Nebraska Press.

Kobayashi, H. (1992). Native and nonnative reactions to ESL compositions. *TESOL Quarterly, 26,* 81–112.

Kobayashi, H., & Rinnert, C. (1996). Factors affecting composition evaluation in an EFL context: Cultural rhetorical pattern and readers' background. *Language Learning, 46,* 397–437.

Kobayashi, H., & Rinnert, C. (2002). High school student perceptions of first language literacy instruction: Implications for second language writing. *Journal of Second Language Writing, 11,* 91–116.

Kubota, R. (1998). An investigation of L1-L2 transfer in writing among Japanese university students: Implications for contrastive rhetoric. *Journal of Second Language Writing, 7,* 69–100.

Kubota, R. (1999). Japanese culture deconstructed by discourses: Implications for applied linguistics research and ELT. *TESOL Quarterly, 33,* 9–35.

Kubota, R., & Lehner, A. (2004). Toward critical contrastive rhetoric. *Journal of Second Language Writing, 13,* 7–27.

Land, R. E., & Whitley, C. (1989). Evaluating second language essays in regular composition classes: Toward a pluralistic U.S. rhetoric. In D. M. Johnson & D. H. Roen (Eds.), *Richness in writing: Empowering ESL students* (pp. 284–293). New York: Longman.

Lantolf, J. P., & Thorne, S. L. (2006). *Sociocultural theory and the genesis of second language development.* New York: Oxford University Press.

Lee, C. D. (Ed.) (2003). Theme Issue: Reconceptualizing race and ethnicity in *educational research. Educational Researcher, 36*(5), 3–37.

Leung, C., Harris, R., & Rampton, B. (1997). The idealised native speaker, reified ethnicities, and classroom realities. *TESOL Quarterly, 31*, 543–560.

Li, X.-M. (1996). *"Good writing" in cross-cultural context.* Albany, NY: State University of New York Press.

Liu, J. (1999). Nonnative-English-speaking professional in TESOL. *TESOL Quarterly, 33*, 85–102.

Markee, N., & Kasper, G. (2004). Classroom talks: An introduction. *Modern Language Journal, 88*, 491–500.

Manchón, R. M., & Roca de Larios, J. (2007). On the temporal nature of planning in L1 and L2 composing: A study of foreign language writers. *Language Learning, 57*, 549–593.

Matsuda, P. K. (1997). Contrastive rhetoric in context: A dynamic model of L2 writing. *Journal of Second Language Writing, 6*, 45–60.

Matsuda, P. K., Canagarajah, A. S., Harklau, L., Hyland, K., & Warschauer, M. (2003). Changing currents in second language writing research: A colloquium. *Journal of Second Language Writing, 12*, 151–179.

McCarthey, S. J., Guo, Y.-H., & Cummins, S. (2005). Understanding changes in elementary mandarin students' L1 and L2 writing. *Journal of Second Language Writing, 14*, 71–104.

McKay, S. L. (1993). Examining L2 composition ideology: A look at literacy education. *Journal of Second Language Writing, 2*, 65–81.

McKay, S. L. (2003). Toward an appropriate EIL pedagogy: Re-examining common ELT assumptions. *International Journal of Applied Linguistics, 13*, 1–22.

Neff, J., Dafouz, E., Díez, M., Prieto, R., & Chaudron, C. (2004). Contrastive discourse analysis: Argumentative text in English and Spanish. In C. L. Moder & A. Martinovic-Zic (Eds.), *Discourse across languages and cultures* (pp. 267–283). Philadelphia, PA: John Benjamins.

Norris, J. M., & Ortega, L. (2003). Defining and measuring SLA. In C. Doughty & M. H. Long (Eds.), *Handbook of second language acquisition* (pp. 717–761). Malden, MA: Blackwell.

Ortega, L. (2003). Syntactic complexity measures and their relationship to L2 proficiency: A research synthesis of college-level L2 writing. *Applied Linguistics, 24*, 492–518.

Ortega, L. (2005). For what and for whom is our research? The ethical as transformative lens in instructed SLA. *Modern Language Journal, 89,* 427–443.

Pavlenko, A., & Blackledge, A. (Eds.). (2004). *Negotiation of identities in multilingual contexts.* Philadelphia, PA: Multilingual Matters.

Pennington, M. C., & So, S. (1993). Comparing writing process and product across two languages: A study of 6 Singaporean university student writers. *Journal of Second Language Writing, 2,* 41–63.

Polio, C. (2001). Research methodology in second language writing research: The case of text-based studies. In T. Silva & P. K. Matsuda (Eds.), *On second language writing* (pp. 91–115). Mahwah, NJ: Erlbaum.

Purves, A.C. (Ed.). (1992a). *The IEA study of written composition II: Education and performance in fourteen countries.* Oxford: Pergamon Press.

Purves, A.C. (1992b). Conclusion. In A. C. Purves (Ed.), *The IEA study of written composition II: Education and performance in fourteen countries* (pp. 199–202). Oxford: Pergamon Press.

Rampton, B. (1990). Displacing the "native speaker": Expertise, affiliation, and inheritance. *ELT Journal, 44,* 97–101.

Rampton, B. (1999). Dichotomies, difference, and ritual in second language learning and teaching. *Applied Linguistics, 20,* 316–340.

Reichelt, M. (1999). Toward a more comprehensive view of L2 writing: Foreign language writing in the US. *Journal of Second Language Writing, 8*(2), 181–204.

Reichelt, M. (2001). A critical review of foreign language writing research on pedagogical approaches. *The Modern Language Journal, 85,* 578–598.

Reynolds, D. W. (2005). Linguistic correlates of second language literacy development: Evidence from middle-grade learner essays. *Journal of Second Language Writing, 14,* 19–45.

Roca de Larios, J., Manchón, R. M., & Murphy, L. (2006). Generating text in native and foreign language writing: A temporal analysis of problem-solving formulation processes. *Modern Language Journal, 90,* 100–114.

Rubin, D., Goodrum, R., & Hall, B. (1990). Orality, oral-based culture, and the academic writing of ESL learners. *Issues in Applied Linguistics, 1,* 56–76.

Sasaki, M., & Hirose, K. (1996). Explanatory variables for EFL students' expository writing. *Language Learning, 46,* 137–174.

Sasaki, M., & Hirose, K. (1999). Development of an analytical rating scale for Japanese L1 writing. *Language Testing, 16,* 457–478.

Schleppegrell, M. J. (2004). *The language of schooling: A functional linguistics perspective.* Mahwah, NJ: Erlbaum.

Schoonen, R., van Gelderen, A., de Glopper, K., Husltijn, J., Simis, A., Snellings, P., et al. (2003). First language and second language writing: The role of linguistic knowledge, speed of processing, and metacognitive knowledge. *Language Learning, 53,* 165–202.

Seidlhofer, B. (2001). Closing a conceptual gap: The case for a description of English as a lingua franca. *International Journal of Applied Linguistics, 11,* 133–158.

Shi, L. (2001). Native and nonnative-speaking EFL teachers' evaluation of Chinese students' English writing. *Language Testing, 18,* 303–325.

Siegel, J. (2003). Social context. In C. Doughty & M. H. Long (Eds.), *Handbook of second language acquisition* (pp. 178–223). Malden, MA: Blackwell.

Silva, T. (1993). Toward an understanding of the distinct nature of L2 writing: The ESL research and its implications. *TESOL Quarterly, 27,* 657–677.

Silva, T., & Leki, I. (2004). Family matters: The influence of applied linguistics and composition studies on second language writing studies—Past, present, and future. *Modern Language Journal, 88,* 1–13.

Sridhar, S. N. (1994). A reality check for SLA theories. *TESOL Quarterly, 28,* 800–805.

Tarone, E., & Bigelow, M. (2005). Impact of literacy on oral language processing: Implications for second language acquisition research. *Annual Review of Applied Linguistics, 25,* 77–97.

Truscott, J. (2007). The effect of error correction on learners' ability to write accurately. *Journal of Second Language Writing, 16,* 255–272.

Valdés, G. (1992). Bilingual minorities and language issues in writing. *Written Communication, 9,* 85–136.

Valdés, G. (2000). Nonnative English speakers: Language bigotry in English mainstream classrooms. *ADE Bulletin, 124,* 12–17.

Valdés, G., Brookes, H., & Chávez, C. (2003). Bilinguals and bilingualism. In G. Valdés, *Expanding definitions of giftedness: The case of young interpreters from immigrant communities* (pp. 25–61). Mahwah, NJ: Erlbaum.

Verhoeven, L. T. (1994). Transfer in bilingual development: The linguistic interdependence hypothesis revisited. *Language Learning, 44,* 381–415.

Wang, W., & Wen, Q. (2002). L1 use in the L2 composing process: An exploratory study of 16 Chinese EFL writers. *Journal of Second Language Writing, 11,* 225–246.

Watanabe, Y. (2001). *Read-to-write tasks for the assessment of second language academic writing skills: Investigating text features and rater reactions.* Unpublished doctoral dissertation, University of Hawai'i at Mānoa.

Weigle, S. C. (1994). Effects of training on raters of ESL compositions. *Language Testing, 11,* 197–223.

Woodall, B. R. (2002). Language-switching: Using the first language while writing in a second language. *Journal of Second Language Writing, 11,* 7–28.

Yi, Y. (2007). Engaging literacy: A biliterate student's composing practices beyond school. *Journal of Second Language Writing, 16,* 23–39.

4 Finding "Theory" in the Particular: An "Autobiography" of What I Learned and How about Teacher Feedback

Lynn M. Goldstein

When asked to participate in the 2006 Purdue Symposium on Second Language Writing by "addressing the topic of the nature and role of theory in second language writing studies," I had to take a step back because I have never thought of myself as a theoretician. I thought for while about the request and what I could contribute and then wrote back that "when I think of my own research in teacher feedback, I am hard pressed to define what I would call theory. I have always been leery of wide all-encompassing theories, have never been satisfied by any I have encountered, and feel that theory is best arrived at in the local or in the particulars. Would I say that my research starts from theory?—well, perhaps a "hunch" that something is going on, but even more so from a question I wanted to answer about practice. I have actually never hypothesized/theorized at the start of any of my research studies but instead have let the data "speak" for itself. Thus, it's by asking these questions and then collecting data to analyze that I have arrived at an understanding (theory) about what happens when teachers and students interact through the process of feedback and revision. So my cycle has been practice leads to questions (broadly conceived ones) leads to research leads to theory—my notion is that building theory is aggregating what happens at the "local." My chapter thus searches through the key defining moments in my own practices as a second language writing teacher, researcher, and teacher educator to see how my understandings, a word I prefer to use instead of theory, have developed about the processes of teacher feedback and students' revision using teacher feedback. In doing so, I hope to illuminate both my current understanding of teacher feedback and student revision and of the processes of arriving at these understandings.

FINDING UNDERSTANDINGS IN THE PARTICULARS

If the truth be told, I have never had any formal education to be a second language writing teacher. In 1977, in the first semester of my doctoral program, with two years of ESL teaching under my belt, none of which was focused on writing, a friend asked me if I needed any work and recommended that I apply to teach writing at a local community college where she also worked. She hushed me when I told her I had never taught writing and told me to apply anyway, I did and was hired. My understanding of feedback and revision from that time is shown in Figure 1.

Teacher Reads Paper → Teacher Gives Feedback → Student Revises using this feedback

Figure 1. 1977 Conceptualization of the Feedback and Revision Process

In contrast, here is my current understanding of this process (something that I will return to at the end of my chapter), but it is evident that the simple, linear figure has morphed into a complex, non-linear model as shown in Figure 2.

When comparing my 1977 representation to my 2005 representation, the question that arises is how I moved from the figure of 1977 to the model of 2005. The general answer is that I started with the particular, that is, practice and data which consisted of actual feedback and revisions, and derived from them both how to do research and how to develop my understandings of the processes of feedback and revision. More specifically, in examining this process chronologically—"my research autobiography," if you will—I have uncovered six principles that have helped me make sense of my practices and my data and have helped me arrive at my present understandings and my current model. The following discussions look at the particulars, that is, the data, the six principles, as well as the understandings about the feedback and revision process that these particulars and principles allowed.

The first principle is derived from what I call my "bingo" moment, both because it came from a student named Bingo and because it was a

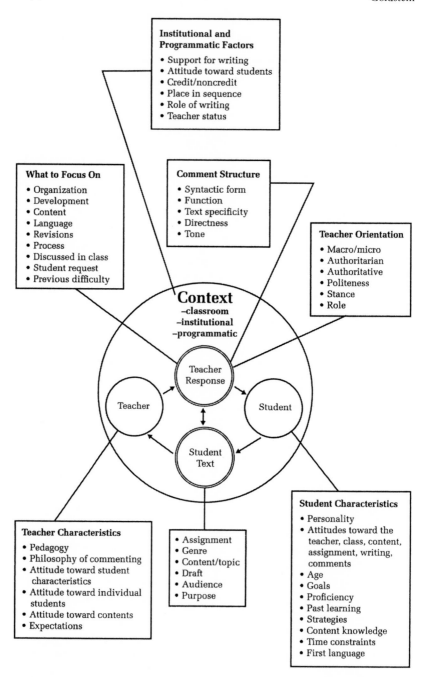

Figure 2. 2005 Conceptualization of the Feedback and Revision Process (Goldstein, 2005; reprinted with permission)

moment of enlightenment. Bingo, a student in a writing class I taught in 1985 at a large public California university, attached the following letter to an essay he gave me to read:

Questions about the 3rd essay

> In the introduction, I say 7th line that "he earn his living out of this 'remote' profession." Do you know what I mean?
>
> You say that in the introduction I don't need evidence to support my idea. But if Patrick tell lie and I sum up the ideas of what his "lie" is, them I may make the wrong introduction. For example, Patrick told me divorce happen one out of 2 marriage and the figure doesn't match this.
>
> In the bottom part of P. 3, I say that violating law is painful and violating custom is disastrous. Is it more effective if I give some example of how painful and disastrous it is?
>
> In the bottom part of p.4 the effect of discrimination is disrespect by friend, disrespect by family and so on. But I think I didn't make the point of how disastrous it was comparing the violating the law. What do you think?
>
> In page 7. I said that the child had to obey their parent & so on to make the effect of hierarchy. But I found that all society more or less also obey parent, abide to custom. In this case, I think I didn't effectively make the comparison of hierarchy and democratic society. What do you think?
>
> In page 3. I use 'rule' rather than 'custom,' but in a sense rule is a written law and custom is just commonly acceptable knowledge about some behavior or activity. So there is a difference between 'rule' and 'custom.' Then can I use 'rule'? If not, which words can I use if I don't want to repeat 'custom' again and again?
>
> In top of page 3, I said that the answer lie in its cultural tradition. Do I need to specific and give some detail? I think that cultural tradition that such a broad meaning that it may not be appropriate to use. If not, which words do I need to use?" (Goldstein, 2005)

I had not requested he do so, nor had I requested that any of my students attach any cover notes with their essays. In the process of answering Bingo's note and questions, I realized that I could understand what he wanted to do in his essay and what he was concerned about. I suddenly realized what had been missing from my practice and from my understanding of what makes for effective processes of giving feedback: A way to understand students' rhetorical contexts and their concerns and the need to respond within these contexts and to these concerns. I started asking students to attach cover notes that let me know their rhetorical context and let me know what their concerns were.

In doing so, I saw that I read their papers differently, that is, no longer in a "vacuum," and my feedback changed and was responsive to the students' rhetorical contexts. I stopped appropriating. What I also learned from this experience is my first principle: Understandings do not just come from formal research, but also come from the classroom, learning from our students and from our practices. In following this principle, I learned that effective feedback doesn't start with the text, and isn't just about responding to texts; it starts with the student, responding to the student, what the student wants to accomplish, what the students needs, and ultimately about teachers and students communicating with each other. Listening to and learning from students can inform our understandings of the feedback/revision process.

My second principle, one that I have followed in all of my research on feedback and revision the past twenty years, developed from the research that I, along with my co-researcher Susan Conrad, carried out on conference feedback (Goldstein & Conrad, 1990). In doing this research, we did not start with any hypotheses but started instead with curiosity about the relationship between conference feedback and revision. At that time, many people seemed to be suggesting that conferences were more effective than written feedback because students could be active participants, but no one was actually looking at the actual conference discourse and its relationship to what students were doing with the feedback when they revised their papers. This led us to wonder about what students actually did in the conference and with the conference feedback. What we discovered in our three case studies is that when we looked at how active students were in conferences, they ranged from inactive to active; conferences did not automatically guarantee active student participation (see Tables 1 and 2). Next, as we looked at the conference transcripts, we noticed that sometimes the students negotiated for meaning with the teacher when discussing potential revisions, and sometimes they did not. We became curious as to whether there was a relationship between negotiation or lack of negotiation and the effectiveness of the students' revisions and we discovered that in fact there was (see Table 3): Students almost always revised successfully when they had negotiated that revision, and almost always either did not attempt any revision or revised unsuccessfully when they had not negotiated that revision.

The principle we were following was "let the data speak for itself"; rather than starting with hypotheses, we started with just a broad question of what the relationship might be, and in the process we noticed negotiations, leading us to ask what role they might play. Following this principle led to our understanding that first, students differed greatly in terms of how actively they participated in conferences, and second, that discourse where teacher and student negotiate meaning while discussing potential revisions leads to effective revision.

Table 1. Comparison of Student Input Discourse Features. Goldstein & Conrad, 1990; reprinted with permission.

Discourse features per conference	Student[a]		
	M	Z	T
Nominations made by student (%)	19.5	47.3	50
Of student nominations, % invited	42.88	41	20
Turns per episode (M)[b]	2.33	3.68	5.94
Questions asked by student (M)[b]	1.43	2.33	4.5
Questions asked by teacher (M)[b]	14	6	6.75
Negotiations made by student (%)	33.2	55.75	60.78
Negotiations made by student (M)[b]	1.66	6.3	7.75

[a] M = Marigrace, Z = Zohre, T = Tranh

[b] M = mean number

Table 2. Comparison of Student Input: Discourse Structure (%). Goldstein
& Conrad, 1990; reprinted with permission.

	Student[a]		
Episodes per conference	M	Z	T
Conversational work done primarily by teacher			
T questions/S answers	27.27	13.89	3.57
T talks/S backchannels	33.33	36.11	10.71
Total[b]	60.6	50	14.28
Student/teacher sharing work			
T talks/S talks	21.21	36.11	53.57
Total[b]	21.21	36.11	53.57
Conversational work done primarily by student			
S questions/T answers	0	8.33	10.71
S talks/T backchannels	0	0	3.57
Total[b]	0	8.33	14.28

Note. Percentages do not total to 100 because the remainder consisted of mixed episodes.

[a] M = Marigrace, Z = Zohre, T = Tranh

[b] T = Teacher, S = Student

The next principle that guided what data I collected and how arose when I began research where I was no longer both the researcher and teacher (Goldstein & Kohls, 2002). In this research, Robert Kohls, my co-researcher, and I realized that we needed to know why the teacher did the things she did when she responded, so I interviewed her, asked her to keep a journal and asked her to annotate her comments on her students papers in terms of why she commented the way she did. In addition, in previous work, I had conference transcripts where students detailed what was affecting their revisions, but here, because this class was online, we did not have these data. Instead, I interviewed the students and also asked them to go over each essay with me and explain how and why they used the teacher's feedback for their revisions. As in previous studies, we coded revisions in terms of whether or not the students revised in response to the teacher's feedback, and if

Table 3. Negotiations of revision (%). Goldstein & Conrad, 1990; reprinted with permission.

		Student[a]		
		M	**Z**	**T**
Negotiated Revisions (n = 3)		(n = 6)	(n = 12)	
	Successful	100	100	91.66
	Unsuccessful	0	0	0
	No revision			
		Student[a]		
Nonnegotiated Revisions (n = 6)		(n = 5)	(n = 10)	
	Successful	33.33	0	20
	Unsuccessful	66.77	40	60
	No revision	0	60	20

[a] M = Marigrace, Z = Zohre, T = Tranh

so, the degree of revision success. In doing so, we discovered that one student, in response to her teacher's feedback, was frequently either not revising and leaving her text as is or removing text that needed revision (see Table 4). We also discovered that for this student, unlike for the other students, the teacher was repeating the same comments she had given this student on the previous draft, and we wondered why (see Table 5). The different data sources we collected allowed us to answer our questions:

(1) The interview data allowed us to understand that because the student's time was devoted to the demands of a full load of graduate courses and because she didn't receive grades on her drafts, the student made a strategic decision where she frequently did not revise until her final draft. As she said when I interviewed her: "First I will finish my IPS (International Policy Studies) things. If it's the final draft, I'll focus on the ES (English Studies) course. Otherwise I'll do my best, but next to the main course"

(2) The interview data also allowed us to see that this student did not ask for help in areas where she needed help and did not revise when either she did not understand the comments or know how to revise in response to the comments. For example, when

discussing citations with me and the possibility of asking her teacher for help, she stated that she did not understand "about the citation comments" and continued that "I couldn't find enough information about the citation online. But, yeah—unfortunately, I couldn't ask her how to find the information . . . I didn't have time to ask her"

Table 4. Percent of Comments on the Draft in Response to which No Revision Attempted or Text Removed on the Subsequent Draft. Goldstein & Kohls, 2002; Goldstein, 2006; reprinted with permission.

Draft	ABa NATe	TRf	RPb NATe	TRf	ILRc NATe	TRf	LRd NATe	TRf
1	14.8% (7/47)	12.8% (6/47)	0.0%	0.0%	0.0%	47.2% (17/36)	77.1% (27/35)	0.0%
2	100.0% (27/27)	0.0%	8.3% (1/12)	0.0%	6.2% (1/16)	0.0%	30.0% (9/30)	0.0%
3	40.6% (13/32)	0.0%						
4	75.0% (12/16)	0.0%						

(3) The teacher's journal, interview data, and annotations of her comments provided insight into her commenting behaviors, particularly her repeating of comments from a previous draft on the subsequent draft when responding to this student. We discovered that many of the teacher's repeated comments resulted from (1) the teacher's assumption that the student understood her comments and understood how to revise in response to these comments and (2) given this assumption, the teacher's conclusion that the student had just decided not to take the time to revise in response to her comments. She did not consider a lack of revision to indicate that the student didn't understand the comment or didn't know how to revise. In our interviews, she stated that "Hiroko didn't hardly incorporate any of my feedback, um, and it's not that I think she misunderstood it. I think that my feedback to her was task-specific, related to providing

citations to some of her—full citations—and that would have meant that she would have had to go back and actually find the source and include the citation, and I think that was a lot of work for her." In her annotations of her comments, she wrote: "Most of my comments were related to citations or lack of. She was aware that citations were an integral part of the assignment. I think she just lacked time to complete this."

Table 5. Number of Comments Teacher Repeated From Previous Draft. Goldstein & Kohls, 2002; Goldstein, 2006; reprinted with permission.

	Number of repeated comments despite revision already successfully done	Number of repeated comments despite revision attempted and partially successful	Number of repeated comments when revision attempted but unsuccessfully done	Number of repeated comments when revision not attempted
# Repeated comments/Total number of comments				
Annotated Bibliography				
Repeated from draft 1 on draft 2 (n = 34/52)	7	6	10	11
Repeated from draft 2 on draft 3 (n = 4/33)	0	0	0	4
Introduction to Literature Review				
Repeated from draft 2 on draft 3 (n = 35/36)	17	0	13	2
Literature Review				
Repeated from draft 2 on draft 3 (n = 6/30)	0	0	0	6

The principle we followed, employing multiple data sources that allowed the teacher and students to speak for themselves, allowed us to arrive at the understanding that teachers and students mutually influence each other and may misinterpret each other's behaviors and that feedback and revision need to be understood within this process of co-construction.

Table 6. Relationship between Type of Revision Problem and Revision Success Across Category Types (excluding unattempted revisions). Data from Conrad & Goldstein, 1999; used with permission.

	Explanation/analysis/ explicitness		Other problems	
	total number (n = 12)	# success-fully revised (n = 1.5)	total number (n = 20)	# success-fully revised (n = 18.5)
Syntactic Category				
declarative (n = 22)	6.5	1.5	15.5	14
question (n = 10)	5.5	0	4.5	4.5
Semantic/Pragmatic Content				
declaratives				
state opinion (n = 1)	1	0	0	—
need to (n = 12)	2	1.5	10	8.5
characterize text (n = 5)	3	0	2	2
suggestion (n = 4)	0.5	0	3.5	3.5
questions				
yes/no (n = 4)	0.5	0	3.5	3.5
WH (n = 5)	5	0	0	—
either/or (n = 1)	0	—	1	1
Directness				
direct (n = 20)	3	1.5	17	15.5
indirect (n = 12)	9	0	3	3
Revision Strategy				
included (n= 17)	0	0	17	15.5
not included (n = 15)	12	1.5	3	3

Principle number two focused on letting the data speak for itself. What I have also discovered is that even when we let the data speak for itself, sometimes what we "hear" the first time in looking at the data may not be correct. In another study that Susan Conrad and I carried out (Conrad & Goldstein, 1999), we examined the relationship between written comments and student revision. We arrived at a point where we had already analyzed our data and were "done." We thought that there was a relationship between comment type and revision success: Comments phrased as Questions seemed to result in less successful revision than did declaratives, with yes/no questions resulting more often in successful revision than did WH questions; revisions in response to declaratives seemed to be more successful when phrased as 'you need to . . . ' or as suggestions, such as 'you should . . . ' , than when phased as a description of what a student had done ("here you have a paragraph with two main ideas"). This made perfect sense.

However, in looking at the data one last time to verify the above findings, the data began to "speak" anew, and I began to sense that what we had found as described above might not be the whole picture and that we should take a look at the type of "problem" being commented on and revised for. In doing so, we discovered that regardless of the form or semantics of the comments students were almost always unsuccessful revising in response to teacher feedback about explanations or analyses (see Table 6). Thus, using the principle of being open to alternative analyses and interpretations of the data led us to better understand that the problem area needing revision can affect how feedback is used/success of revision, regardless of the comment type.

We also need to be open to reinterpretations happening "accidentally" and long after the original results are reported. In writing a chapter to bring together all of my work and look at different types of feedback (Goldstein, 2006), it was not my intention as I took a second look at data from previous studies to discover that I had misunderstood any of that data. However, in taking these second looks, I learned that by not listening carefully enough to Tranh, my feedback to Tranh characterizing his argument about postponing having children as overgeneralization missed his point; for Tranh, it was an issue of cultural differences as can be seen in this transcript, particularly in the italicized lines where Tranh is trying to explain that his sees these issues differently, given his cultural views.

Conference between Lynn and Tranh:

> L: Okay so here you are telling me is that now that I'm thirty-two and still hadn't have postponed having children, that wasn't a good idea.
> T: Um I I I I don't know. I feel that people postpone and then they keep postponing and- and until one day it's too late or it's too hard for them that they be maybe so
> L: Um, I have a friend who's forty and she has a four year old and a six month old.

T: Oh. ((laughter)). You know to me I think that over thir-
   ty is too late, yeah.
            [
L: too old
L: Most of my friends who have had children had their
   children in their early thirties. And when I have my
   first child I'll be somewhere around thirty-three thirty-
   four
T: Okay. ((laughter))
L: and the reason
T: I'll think about that too and see.
T: I don't know. I I feel y'know that in the Chinese um
   Chinese culture is is is a big problem for people
L: uhmm
T: If a women gets old and have a baby, It is always good
   to have it when
L: Mhm
T: one is young. So um I would think about that.
T: *Yes, I read the— what* Newsweek *and I know that many
   some example say that women over thirty-five so maybe
   there is different culture and different people may have
   different ways, may have different ideal, but I write here
   and I feel that um you know I heard people say um in our
   country or in the community is I write down there.*
T: *I really don't want to bring out this big piece about medical
   research. I just um I think that there is something is my um
   feeling about that.*
L: There are there are negative effects, there definitely are
   and I agree with you, um but there aren't negative effects for everybody, it's only a small proportion of the
   people so people in a sense need to make informed decisions. (Goldstein, 2006)

This principle of stepping back and taking a second look after a period
of time was discovered accidentally, but has proven to be an important
one. It allowed me to arrive at the understanding that how a student
uses teacher feedback is affected by who the student is and what beliefs
the student brings to what the student is writing about, and this interacts with who the teacher is and what beliefs the teacher brings to un-

derstanding the student's content. Importantly, my new understanding is that the teacher's beliefs can "block" the teacher's/researcher's understanding of how the student used the teacher's comments and why the student made the revisions as in the above case where what the teacher first thought was a case of overgeneralization was a case of different cultural expectations. Given this, second "looks" are warranted and informative.

The final principle derives from what I learned in my initial feedback research: Aggregating data hides what is going on with the individual, and thus more generally hampers our understandings of feedback and revision processes. For example, in my conferencing study (Goldstein & Conrad, 1990), by looking at each individual student separate from the others, we were able to see how differently they used feedback and understand why. For example, we can see this by comparing Marigrace and Tranh:

(1) Marigrace followed my feedback to the letter and never questioned it, something she expresses quite clearly in the conference excerpt below where she says "Yeah. You told me to" :

Student/Teacher Conference between Mari Grace and Lynn:

T: [. . .] What differences do you see between where you
    are now and where you
    began?
M: Um there's more direction in my paper than in my last
    paper.
T: mmmhm
T: Okay. Do you know how you got to this point?
M: Yeah. You told me ((laughter)) to. (Conrad & Goldstein, 1999)

(2) Tranh removed text, rather than look for needed content. He attributed this to time issues and to what he called the "game" of writing the papers for our course—the papers were not "real" to him as can be see in the following excerpt:

Lynn's Teacher Comment:

"Finally, on page seven, you say ancient feuds can cause discrimination. Can you go into this in more depth?

You say discrimination results in war but you don't
show/discuss how ancient feuds result in discrimination."

Conference between Lynn and Tranh:

Tr: in uh describing how the ancient feud the ancient feud
( ) to influence on people to another
T: okay
Tr: um I think
T: Yeah
Tr: it's true I understand that it's true you know
T: Yeah
Tr: for for some people they read about the history an they
know their pa- their ancestor were mistreated by the
other people, so they feel bad, they don't like
T: Mm
Tr: the others. Um I think this really affects one's atti-
tudes. But I cannot put them
in the Middle East situation because I can't think of any
any any
T: yeah
Tr: uh any uh Arabs against Jews in the past. But I do
know they are against them right now.
[. . .]
Tr: I I I I that's why I want to talk to you, I want
T: yeah
Tr: to cut it off because
T: okay
Tr: because I can't think of any example between the Jews an
the Arabs in the past that they are against each other now
is uh recently they are against each other.[. . .] So I take it
out, I still have plenty of example. (Conrad & Goldstein,
1999)

Following the principle of looking at each student as an individual allowed us to arrive at the understanding that what students bring to the
process of using teacher feedback and revising their texts is affected by
a number of individual factors unrelated to the teacher's comments:
their individuality, their expectations about student and teacher roles,

their understandings of what the class requires, their knowledge of the content they are writing about, and their being affected by outside influences, such as course load and work hours.

CONCLUSION

Through using the above six principles to look at the particulars, that is the data, I have arrived at my current understandings, depicted in my model. I agree with Dwight Atkinson that my work is not atheoretical (personal communication, Symposium on Second Language Writing, June 9, 2006), but would simply argue that by adhereing to the principles I describe above, my work is not "preconceived," but instead allows for understandings to develop out of the particulars. These particulars are not "manufactured" or manipulated, but come from actual teaching and what students communicate and do in the classroom, as well as students' papers, their revisions, teachers comments, transcripts of conference discourse, and teachers' and students' annotations and explanations for their behaviors and choices. The understandings derive from "acting" on these particulars through listening to and learning from students as we teach them, by asking broad questions instead of testing hypotheses, by letting the data speak for itself, by letting teachers and students speak for themselves, by reexamining and reconsidering data and findings and being open to the possibility of revision of findings, and by looking at individuals rather than aggregating.

From having looked at the above particulars and through following these principles, I have been able to understand the many factors that affect how a teacher comments and how a student revises with this commentary. The 2005 model shown in Figure 2 shows that, contrary to the 1977 model shown in Figure 1, this process is not a linear one, but rather a recursive one taking place within and being affected by particular contexts. It shows that the process is one of communication flowing back and forth between teacher and student, that many texts (teacher's commentary and the students' drafts) are created, that each teacher and each student brings his/her own sets of characteristics, knowledge and attitudes that influence and shape their texts and communications, that these texts get produced and these communications take place within particular contexts that also serve to shape teacher commentary and students revision, and that teachers and students mutually influence each other in the process of commenting and drafting and revision.

In concluding, I would like to encourage others who are in the process of developing their own understandings to consider the principles I have described above, following them to work from the particular, that is the data, to more the more general, that is, understandings. I would also like to suggest that more understandings await us:

- We need an understanding of what happens over time; that is, (how) do the processes of teacher feedback and student revision result in students learning and being able to apply what they learn to subsequent writing over time? In what ways? What factors work towards and against this?
- The understandings/model I have arrived at needs to be examined within many different settings and with different students and different teachers as what I wrote to the Symposium organizers, Paul Kei Matsuda and Tony Silva when they first asked me to participate in the Symposium " . . . what I would say is missing is the theory back to practice—the need for others to "test" out what I have found in their practices, as well as replication studies (there are a few such studies, but very few)."
- We need to bring the understandings from the particulars back to the particular, that is, back to practice so we can learn about what works, in what settings, with what students, under what conditions as ultimately our goal is being able to practice feedback in the best possible way to help our students become effective writers.

As I closed my email to Tony and Paul: "[there is] the need for the field to 'test' out theory by returning to practice—by returning to the local.

REFERENCES

Conrad, S., & Goldstein, L. (1999). ESL student revision after teacher-written comments: Text, contexts, and individuals. *Journal of Second Language Writing, 8*(2), 147–179.

Goldstein, L. (2005). *Teacher written commentary in second language writing classes*. Ann Arbor, MI: University of Michigan Press.

Goldstein, L. (2006). In search of the individual: Feedback and revision in second language writing. In K. Hyland and F. Hyland (Eds.), *Feedback in second language writing: Contexts and issues* (pp. 185–205). Cambridge, UK: Cambridge University Press.

Goldstein, L., & Conrad, S. (1990). Input and the negotiation of meaning in ESL writing conferences. *TESOL Quarterly, 24*(3), 443–460.

Goldstein, L., & Kohls, R. (2002). Writing, commenting, and revising: The relationship between teacher feedback and student revision online. Paper presented at American Association for Applied Linguistics, Salt Lake City, Utah.

Part II. Reflections on Theoretical Practices

5 Practicing Theory in Qualitative Research on Second Language Writing

Linda Harklau and Gwendolyn Williams

In recent years considerable attention has focused on the theories, approaches, and methods used in qualitative research on first (Schultz, 2006) and second language writing (Grabe, 2001; Silva, 2005; Silva & Leki, 2004). The starting point for this particular exploration of the subject is Ramanathan and Atkinson's (1999) review of ethnographic work on second language writing. There they concluded that while researchers had adopted methods associated with qualitative inquiry, in most cases they had dealt only superficially with the theory and philosophical underpinnings of the approach. They further observed that many of the central debates in the parental disciplines of anthropology and sociology have had little influence on qualitative scholarship in second language writing.

We wondered if in the ensuing years second language writing scholarship had made any headway in elaborating upon its underlying epistemological and philosophical premises. In this chapter, we begin by defining our own terms and assumptions about qualitative research and its relationship to theory and arguing that theory is always central to research whether it is explicitly identified or not. Next, we review the uses of theory in second language writing research literature in the past five years. We find that many recent research reports do not explicitly articulate the theoretical and methodological origins and ancestry of the approaches used and suggest some possible reasons for these omissions. We then conclude with some implications for the role of theory in future scholarship in our field.

DEFINING OUR TERMS AND ASSUMPTIONS

We need to first acknowledge that the term *qualitative research* is rather broad and inexact. For some, it denotes an entire field of inquiry in its own right (Denzin & Lincoln, 2000), a field that is marked by wide variation, internal overlap and inconsistencies, and contentiousness (Kamberelis & Dimitriadis, 2005). The breadth of the field and the difficulty of discussing it as a totality is recognized, for example, by *TESOL Quarterly's* move to differentiate guidelines for qualitative approaches, including conversation analysis, critical ethnography, and qualitative case study work (Teachers of English to Speakers of Other Languages, 2006).

On the face of it, "qualitative" could simply mean any research method or methodology that does not make use of numbers. However, we need to differentiate here between research *method* and *methodology*. A research method—be it participant observation, interview, survey, elicitation task, or experiment—is a tool. It is a means of collecting data. A methodology, on the other hand, is a theory of inquiry that directs which research methods might be used, how and why they are used, and how resulting data are analyzed. The term *qualitative research* is typically used to denote not just any non-quantitative method but rather a group of research methodologies that share a focus on naturalistic, holistic observation of complex social settings, and on how people interpret and make sense of these settings (Denzin & Lincoln, 2000). Qualitative researchers systematically collect and record empirical data such as fieldnotes, diaries, interviews, written texts and documents, and recorded speech in order to describe and theorize "routine and problematic moments and meanings in individuals' lives" (Denzin & Lincoln, 2000, p. 3) "Qualitative research" is therefore a misnomer in the sense that qualitative research methodologies are not distinguished by the absence of numerical measures but rather by their theoretical and epistemological orientation. In fact, qualitative studies can make use of methods that are quantitative in nature. Likewise, studies that are experimental or hypodeductive in nature might nevertheless include qualitative methods and analysis.

Theory in qualitative research is likewise a vast and historically situated issue (Denzin & Lincoln, 2000). We must emphasize that we are not philosophers. Then again, in our view, theory is not the exclusive province of philosophers. Rather, theory is ubiquitous in human activity. It governs how individuals make sense of the world around them and how they act upon that understanding. In other words, we all operate on the basis of theories even if they are implicit and not recognized as such or go by other names such as frameworks (Hayes, 2006), paradigms, or models.

Any second language writing research endeavor works simultaneously with different types and levels of theory. For the sake of discussion, we will call one type of theory *content theory*—a theory regarding the nature of writing and literacy, of second language acquisition, and of the nature of teaching and learning. *Methodology,* on the other hand, is a theory of inquiry that is focused on the sorts of data collection and analysis that are deemed necessary and appropriate. Although a given content theory might not be directly tied to a specific methodology, by its nature and the assumptions it makes about the nature of language, literacy, and learning, it will tend to co-occur with a certain range of methodologies. For example, content theories about multiliteracies, by their focus on how context shapes the form and meaning of messages, will tend to co-occur with methodologies that emphasize the role of context, including interpretivist, critical, and postmodern variants of ethnography. Content theories about cognitive processes involved in composing, on the other hand, are more likely to draw from methodologies that highlight the role of individual cognition such as mixed methods.

Another level of theory is the local theory that is generated in a specific study from a specific data set. In this sense, theory is never static nor simply imposed top-down. Rather, content theories and methodologies are constantly reinterpreted and reshaped by individual researchers in local contexts as they generate new theory and perspectives. While qualitative approaches tend to emphasize the generation of theory at the local level and experimental approaches tend to emphasize confirmation of existing theory, in practice both use existing theories as a starting point and augment and change them as well as generating new theory in the research process.

Content theories and methodologies are further undergirded by a more basic theory, a set of assumptions about truth and knowledge, a particular "view of the human world and social life within that world" (Crotty, 1998, p. 7). These include assumptions about what knowledge is or *ontology,* how we know it or *epistemology,* and what values go into it or *axiology* (Creswell, 2003, p. 6). Qualitative research can be conducted from a wide array of theoretical paradigms (Crotty, 1998).

Early work in anthropology, for example, tended to be characterized by an objectivist or ***positivist*** epistemology, assuming that the researcher can gain access to a reality that exists apart from any human consciousness of it (Goldschmidt, 2001). Often traced to Auguste Comte (1778–1857) (Lather & St. Pierre, 2005, June), objectivist epistemology assumes that "a tree in the forest is a tree regardless of whether anyone is aware of its existence" (Crotty, 1998, p. 8) and that "when human beings recognize it as a tree, they are simply discovering a meaning that has been lying there in wait for them all along" (p. 8). More recent philosophy of science tends to work within a "post-positivist" stance that recognizes that science is not always concise and argues that scientific facts are simply commonly held beliefs that cannot be absolutely proven (Avis, 2003; Crotty, 1998). The post-positivist paradigm continues to be highly influential in linguistics and applied linguistics (Lazaraton, 1995; Rajagopalan, 2004), and in other areas of social and behavioral science inquiry (see, e.g., Bernard, 2000). It is also what the general public would most associate with the idea of "research" as well as the implicit paradigm in current U.S. government initiatives on scientifically-based research.

However, there are certainly other paradigms apparent in current qualitative research. Qualitative research has also been strongly influenced by a strand of German philosophical thought originating with Immanuel Kant (1724–1804) and suggesting that human beings and the social world are fundamentally different in nature and behavior than physical and inanimate objects because of the capacities for language and meaning making. In this *interpretivist* view, "all human 'knowledge' is developed, transmitted and maintained in social situations" (Berger & Luckmann, 1966). Therefore, the social world cannot be reduced to what can be observed but rather is created, perceived, and interpreted by people themselves. To gain knowledge of the social world, one must gain access to actors' own accounts of it (Brewer, 2000, p. 35).

Neo-Marxist, emancipatory, and critical paradigms emerged out of the Frankfurt School after World War I (Rajagopalan, 2004) and social justice movements of the 1960s and 1970s (Lather & St. Pierre, 2005, June). These are often seen as aligned epistemologically with interpretivist perspectives but as having a distinctive axiological perspective that emphasizes the moral dimension of advocacy and action to remedy social inequities.

In the 1980s, presaged by the work of Geertz ([1966]1973) and Evans-Pritchard (1962), qualitative research experienced the same dramatic *postmodern and poststructuralist* shift that swept through the humanities and social sciences. Post paradigms grew out of a school of French thought in the 1960s and 1970s that included scholars such as Michel Foucault, Jacques Derrida, and Gilles Deleuze (Lather & St. Pierre, 2005, June). Proponents such as Clifford (1986), Marcus and Fischer (1986), and Van Maanen (1988) drew on trends in literary criticism to reject the possibility of objectivity in qualitative research as well as scientific notions of validity, reliability, and generalization (Brewer, 2000). Qualitative inquiry faced a "crisis of representation" (Denzin & Lincoln, 2000), questioning researchers' claims to privileged status and knowledge, and demanding that researchers acknowledge and explore their own subjectivity and place in their research conduct and findings (Tedlock, 2000). Post paradigms are also distinguished by their view of knowledge as constantly shifting and fragmentary. In contrast to the "tree of knowledge" positivist view of knowledge as cumulative and building into a structure, post paradigm researchers are more likely to see knowledge as "rhizomatic," without a clear beginning, end, or structure, and growing up and spreading from diffuse sources (Deleuze & Guattari, 1987). The shift towards poststructural and postmodern perspectives was marked in first language composition studies (see, e.g., Faigley, 1994; Harkin & Schilb, 1991) but muted in second language writing research. We should add that the philosophers and researchers working in post paradigms find typologies such as this antithetical and would tend to reject them as well as their placement within them.

Of course, there is considerably more multiplicity and complexity in theoretical stances in second language writing research than this "stick figure" philosophical review can suggest. The point is that these epistemological perspectives—objectivist, interpretivist, and postmodern—continue to inform current research on second language writing. We believe it is important to be aware of the perspectives from which researchers are approaching qualitative research because such perspectives have profound effects on the methods used, on modes of data analysis, and on how findings are ultimately reported. A corollary is that even if researchers never explicitly enunciate their theoretical framework, they still nevertheless have one that guides inquiry.

REVIEW OF THEORIES IN RECENT L2 WRITING SCHOLARSHIP

Given that there is a vast array of theoretical approaches available to the qualitative researcher in second language writing, what sort of approaches are in evidence in contemporary work in the field? To answer that question, like several other authors in this volume (see Flahive, this volume; Reynolds, this volume; Ortega, this volume), we conducted a search of the literature to survey the status of theory in current work in our field. We examined sources in the past five years, from 2001 to the present. We focused on journal articles with the assumption that this work is most rigorously reviewed in terms of methods and thus most representative of current standards for qualitative research in the field. Journal articles are also the source most likely to contain complete accounts of studies' research methodology. The search resulted in a corpus of forty-two journal articles. Most appeared in *Journal of Second Language Writing, TESOL Quarterly, Assessing Writing, Language Testing,* and *The Modern Language Journal.* We believe this corpus is broadly representative of the state of the art in qualitative work on second language writing. Of the articles identified, ten were essays and thirty-two were what we would define as research studies—studies in which data were systematically collected and analyzed.

Theory in Essays

Some essays were addressed primarily to content theories in second language writing. Atkinson (2003), for example, critiques the way that the concept of culture has been used in L2 writing research and suggests alternatives. Many essays point out topics and research methods that are currently underrepresented in L2 writing research. These included the use of a critical and poststructuralist lens on study of L2 writing (Atkinson, 2003), the need for more research on learners' perspectives on genre-based writing instruction (Cheng, 2006), and the need to move away from individualist container metaphors of literacy and towards communities of practice metaphors (Kern & Schultz, 2005). Some essays specifically addressed theories of qualitative research on L2 writing. Casanave (2003), for example, argues for more sociopolitically-oriented qualitative case study research of writing process, written products, and writer identity. DePew and Miller (2005) suggest a need for a "post-critical framework" to study digital writing practices. While not addressing methods dichotomously as qualitative or quantitative, Connor (2002) notes the need to go be-yond the analysis of text features in contrastive rhetoric research and develop more complex notions of the social and cultural contexts into which writers are socialized. Some essays are concerned primarily on the pedagogical implications of theories about second language writing (see, e.g., Hyland, 2003).

Content Theories in Research Articles

Research articles included a wide array of content theories; no single content theory predominated. One theory that appeared multiple times was activity theory, also known as "sociocultural theory" or "sociohistoric" theory (Prior, 2006). Based on the work of Vygotsky (1896–1934), Leontiev (1981), Voloshinov, and Bakhtin, content theories in this vein begin from the premise that the human mind develops from appropriating aspects of the surrounding environment (Lantolf & Pavlenko, 2001) in interaction with other individuals, objects, and symbols. Accordingly, activity theory tended to appear in articles in our corpus when the purpose was to investigate how L2 writing develops within a larger sociocultural context such as showing how bilingual nurses incorporated the written discourse patterns of patient care plans into their professional ways of thinking (Parks, 2001), how young L2 writers constructed identity through journal writing (Maguire & Graves, 2001), how middle school students learned to write in a technology rich environment (Parks, Huot, Hamers, & Lemonnier, 2005), or how university level L2 writers assessed their own writing based on their interpretations of success from interacting with their teacher through email journals (Basturkmen & Lewis, 2002). One study (Cho, 2004) drew from a related learning theory known variously as situated peripheral participation, communities of practice, and situated knowledge.

To give another example, some of the content theories presented in our corpus share an intellectual heritage from British and continental functionalist theories of language. These are grounded in the work of the "London school" of linguistics most associated with J.R. Firth as well as influenced by the Prague School of functional linguistics (Butt, 2001). Systemic functional theory, for example, emerged in the 1960s primarily in the work of M.A.K. Halliday (1973; 1978) and is the intellectual ancestor of several of the content theories we found in our corpus. These include the so-called "Sydney school" of genre theory (Hyland, 2003; Hyon, 1996). It also includes multiliteracies and literacy as social practice perspectives derived from a group of scholars that includes Street, Gee, and Lankshear. For example, Leibowitz (2005) and Hyland (2002) both based their studies on Hallidayan-derived work on appraisal or evaluation theory. Because functionalist perspectives on language from their outset set out to describe language in its social context and to tie meaning to "context of situation," this approach set their work apart from the more cognitive and formal structuralist orientation of American linguists Bloomfield and later Chomsky (Butt, 2001) and thus seems to co-occur frequently with qualitative research which likewise tends to emphasize the social and contextual aspects of teaching and learning L2 writing.

The corpus also included a wide variety of other productive and useful content theories such as "positioning theory" (Arkoudis & O'Laughlin, 2004), theories about the beliefs of teachers (Basturkmen & Lewis, 2002; Zhu, 2004), theories of the role of teacher-student interactions in learning (Blanton, 2002), "stream of thought" analysis (Myers, 2001), theories of process and post-process writing instruction in composition studies (Matsuda, 2003), learning strategy theories and Bachman's framework for factors influencing language test performance (Nikolov, 2006), the implications of Grician maxims for cross-cultural communication and writing (White, 2001), theories about the use of corpus analysis in teaching L2 writing (Yoon & Hirvela, 2004), theories about cognitive aspects of the writing process (de Larios, Manchon, & Murphy, 2006; L. Wang, 2003; W. Wang & Wen, 2002), theories of phonetic transparency and learning how to spell in two languages (Blese & Thomson, 2004), theories of identity and L2 writing (Hyland, 2002), and the "proficiency theory" of adult learning (M.-f. Wang & Bakken, 2004). Some studies combined content theories in new and potentially generative ways. For example, Kobayashi and Rinnert (2002) combine Swales' (1990) genre theory with Connor's iteration of contrastive rhetoric theory, Parks (2001) integrates activity theory with New Rhetoric (Hyland, 2003) and Myers' (2001) genre theory, and Young and Miller (2004) weave together theories about the "interactional architecture" governing composition revision talk with legitimate peripheral participation.

Almost all of the articles examined identified and explained a content theory, suggesting that this sort of theorizing is widely considered to be essential in contemporary reports of qualitative research on L2 writing.

Methods and Methodologies in Research Articles

The most common research methods in articles described as qualitative were interviews and collection and analysis of documents. Some also included fieldnotes, journals and email dialogs with participants (de Larios, Manchon, & Murphy, 2006), concurrent (de Larios, Manchon, & Murphy, 2006; Nikolov, 2006) or retrospective (L. Wang, 2003) think aloud protocols, reader feedback on second language learner texts (Cho, 2004), discourse analysis (Lave & Wenger, 1991; Leibowitz, 2005), audio or video recordings of classroom events (Parks, Huot, Hamers, & Lemonnier, 2005), proficiency tests (de Larios, Manchon, & Murphy, 2006), background questionnaires (de Larios, Manchon, & Murphy, 2006), and writing elicitation tasks (Parks, 2001; L. Wang, 2003).

In terms of methodologies, researchers invoked a number of paradigms including Geertzian ethnography and "thick description (Blanton, 2002), conversation analysis and ethnomethodology (Young & Miller, 2004), "social constructivist" paradigms associated with Vygotskian and Bakhtinian content theories (Maguire & Graves, 2001), and critical discourse analysis (Gebhard, 2004). In some cases, qualitative analysis served as a means of complementing and elaborating upon previous or concurrent quantitative analyses (Blese & Thomson, 2004; de Larios, Manchon, & Murphy, 2006; Nikolov, 2006; L. Wang, 2003; W. Wang & Wen, 2002).

Although no methodology could be said to predominate, one that appeared multiple times was grounded theory. First developed by Glaser and Strauss (1967), grounded theory found its origins in the work of George Herbert Mead and the school of American pragmatism (Greckhamer & Koro-Ljungberg, 2005). While the original formulation was positivist in orientation, a number of variants have developed in the ensuing years, and some take a social constructionist or interpretivist perspective (Charmaz, 2000; Piantanida, Tananis, & Grubs, 2004). Some examples of grounded theory work in our corpus include Weigle and Nelson's (2004) study of the interaction between ESL students and their tutors, Wang and Bakken's (2004) investigation of the experiences of nonnative speakers of English with academic and professional publishing in medicine, and Katznelson, Pegigan, and Rubin's (2001) study of how learning to write in a second language produces varying changes in individual attitudes and beliefs.

Another methodology that appeared multiple times was narrative inquiry. Narrative inquiry is a family of methodologies that examine how writers or storytellers use language to represent themselves (Wortham, 2001). Wortham traces its origins to Goffman's (1959) work on self-representation and Labov and Waletzky's (1967) ground-breaking work on the organization of narratives in interviews. Narrative inquiry has been used to examine how stories are told and organized (Ochs & Capps, 2001) as well as how stories are received and incorporated into lived experience (Heath, 1983/1996). In our corpus, Steinman (2005) used narrative analysis to study second language writers' autobiographies in order to examine how these authors portray their second language acquisition through their second language writing. Tannenbaum (2003) analyzed the published writings of two "translingual writers" (writers using a language other than their mother tongue) to examine the political and psychological motives for their linguistic choices.

Because post paradigms have been highly influential in composition studies over the past 15 years, we expected to find a similar degree of influence on qualitative research on second language writing. Surprisingly enough, we found very limited use in this work; in fact, only one article explicitly incorporated a postmodern paradigm (Steinman, 2005). Perhaps this is because, as Silva and Leki (2004) have pointed out, second language composition is in a unique position, situated in and influenced both by composition and rhetoric studies, traditionally a humanities based field, and by applied linguistics, a largely empirical field. Steinman (2005) notes that researchers using such paradigms might be caught between applied linguists who either do not understand these perspectives or do not recognize them as valid, and composition studies where, as Silva and Leki point out, empirical research reports are not the predominant form of inquiry.

While virtually all of the research studies elaborated on their content theory, almost half did not identify a methodology—a theory of inquiry—used to guide data collection and analysis. Instead, this work used qualitative methodological terms in broad and under-defined ways such as "ethnography," "interview study," "narrative," "discourse analysis," "case study," or even simply "qualitative." While these studies tended to make use of inductive thematic content analyses of interviews or written text (Merriam, 1998) that are common in qualitative approaches, they did not reference a specific variant of qualitative work or accompanying epistemological stance.

We also discovered that in many cases researchers cite generic qualitative research textbooks. In many cases, these were venerable but dated. The "usual suspects" included Glesne and Peshkin (1992), Glaser and Strauss (1967), Miles and Huberman (1994), Geertz ({1966}1973), and Hammersley and Atkinson (1983). Articles frequently made use of specific methods or key phrases from these texts and others such as "constant comparative method" (Glaser & Strauss, 1967), "thick description" (Geertz, {1966}1973), or "analytic induction" (Znaniecki, 1934) without elaborating on their underlying import for understandings of the social world or research methodology.

Unfortunately, our review can only confirm earlier observations that the field of second language writing research has yet to fully reckon with the questions about methodologies as well as their underlying epistemologies. It seems to be widely acknowledged at this point that qualitative research on second language writing (see, e.g, Atkinson, 2005; Li, 2005; Ramanathan & Atkinson, 1999) and on applied linguistics more generally (Holliday, 2004) often lacks explicitness and transparency when it comes to methodologies. We must emphasize that in most cases this was not a sign of sloppy or insufficient scholarship; these were studies published in major journals and were often quite specific about what data were collected and analyzed—just not why it was done that way.

Instead of yet again wagging our fingers at qualitative researchers in our field, we wanted to offer some speculations about why many scholars apparently do not see the lack of discussion about methodologies as a serious omission. One, we suspect, is the lingering dominance of positivist and post-positivist perspectives. For second language writing researchers with this orientation, truth is non-epistemic (Avis, 2003); that is, the nature and scope of reality are not considered subject to explanation or discussion because they are simply considered to be there, to exist. On the other hand, for qualitative L2 writing researchers, the predominance of positivist and post-positivist perspectives makes it possible or even necessary to define their work relatively generically as "not-positivism" rather than defining it in relation to other qualitative methdologies with differing epistemological and theoretical stances. So in one sense, the lack of identification of researchers' theories in work in our field can be interpreted as a defensive posture or post-positivist hangover from applied linguistics, where that perspective was once normative and is still influential.

We believe the second reason has to do with communities of practice or what Ramanathan (2002) has described as scholarly "thought collectives." Perhaps second language writing researchers believe that we share enough common referents and understandings about qualitative inquiry that other researchers will be able to intuit that a term such as "thick description" denotes a Geertzian interpretivist anthropological perspective, or that "constant comparative method" indicates an adherence to Glazer and Strauss' articulation of grounded theory. If we all shared the same theories of inquiry and assumptions in our field, there would indeed be little reason to repeat them over and over again in every research report. However, ours is a field that is blessed or cursed with considerable epistemological and theoretical diversity and widely varying approaches to research. It therefore seems necessary for qualitative researchers to make the theoretical premises of their work more explicit.

CONCLUSION AND IMPLICATIONS

So what points do we hope that readers come away with from this chapter? First, we believe that it is not *methods* per se that define a study or hold it together, be they qualitative, quantitative, or mixed. Rather, it is the underlying theory of inquiry—the *methodology*—that makes a study coherent and governs what methods might be used and how they are deployed. In this sense, it is impossible to do research about second language writing without a theory, although that theory may be implicit. Given the significance of methodology for how research is conducted and the methodological diversity of our field, it seems important to encourage more articulation of and reflexivity about our underlying theoretical assumptions in qualitative research on second language writing.

Second, although handbooks and manuals on various qualitative research methodologies have proliferated in the past decade and become much more sophisticated and differentiated in approach, work in our field still tends to rely on older, generic, and less theorized sources on qualitative methodology. There is still a tendency, for example, for "qualitative research" to be equated implicitly with "ethnography." We believe it is time for the field to recognize the breadth of possible qualitative methodologies and to situate our work more carefully and more specifically in relation to research traditions.

Third, while we advocate increased awareness and articulation of theoretical frameworks, that does not mean we believe in slavish adherence to existing content theories or methodologies. These might themselves become "metanarratives" (Lyotard, 1984) that steer research into a limited variety of legitimated paradigms (Silva, 2005). One implication of this view is the need to both diversify and innovate new methodologies. Because virtually all extant qualitative research methodologies originated outside of our field, they tend to have shortcomings for the purposes of studying second language writing. In particular, it seems as though existing methodologies have predisposed researchers to study cognitive processes in writing in isolation from texts produced and both in isolation from the local interactional, sociocultural, and political contexts in which texts are produced. However, approaches that look exclusively at cognitive process often have an impoverished theory of social context and functions of writing (Hyland, 2003). Likewise, ethnographies and other observational, naturalistic approaches often lack methodological and analytical power to look carefully at cognitive processes or text features. We should exploit the holistic nature of qualitative research to develop methodologies that can examine the interactive nature of cognition during the writing, texts produced, and the local and broad sociocultural and political context. Some innovative hybridized research methodologies in recent work include Flowerdew's (2004) integration of corpus analysis and ethnography, Hyland's (2002) combination of corpus analysis with L2 writer interview data, and Swales's (1998) notion of "textography." These, however, need to be more fully elaborated as theories of inquiry. We should also exploit other well established qualitative research traditions in the social sciences that are thus far rare in second language writing research such as historiography (see, e.g., Matsuda, 2003, 2005). As a field on the cusp of the humanities, second language writing studies could also draw productively from humanities-influenced research paradigms such as arts-based inquiry (see, e.g., Bochner & Ellis, 2003) and literary text analysis (Steinman, 2005; Tannenbaum, 2003).

Finally, in answer to the question "Can we have a theory of second language writing?" (Grabe 2001; Silva and Matsuda, this volume), we would ask why we would only want one. As Lantolf (1996) once wrote, "Let all the flowers bloom." Different content theories and methodologies lead to different understandings and insights into the nature of second language writing. Just as important, they have different epistemological and methodological blind spots. The more theories that are available to us, the deeper and more multidimensional our understanding of the phenomenon is likely to become and the less likely we are to overlook important dimensions (Lather, 2006).

References

Arkoudis, S., & O'Laughlin, K. (2004). Tensions between validity and outcomes: Teacher assessment of written work of recently arrived immigrant students. *Language Testing, 21,* 284–304.

Atkinson, D. (2003). Writing and culture in the post-process era. *Journal of Second Language Writing, 12,* 49–63.

Atkinson, D. (2005). Situated qualitative research and second language writing. In P. K. Matsuda & T. Silva (Eds.), *Second language writing research: Perspectives on the process of knowledge construction* (pp. 49–64). Mahwah, NJ: Erlbaum.

Avis, M. (2003). Do we need methodological theory to do qualitative research? *Qualitative Health Research, 13,* 995–1004.

Basturkmen, H., & Lewis, M. (2002). Learner perspective of success in EAP writing. *Assessing Writing, 8,* 31–46.

Berger, P. L., & Luckmann, T. (1966). *The social construction of reality; a treatise in the sociology of knowledge* (1st ed.). Garden City, NY: Doubleday.

Bernard, H. R. (2000). *Social research methods: Qualitative and quantitative approaches.* Thousand Oaks, CA: Sage.

Blanton, L. L. (2002). Seeing the invisible: Situating L2 literacy acquisition in child-teacher interaction. *Journal of Second Language Writing, 11,* 295–310.

Blese, D., & Thomson, P. (2004). The acquisition of spoken forms and written words. *Written Language and Literacy, 7,* 79–99.

Bochner, A. P., & Ellis, C. (2003). An introduction to the arts and narrative research: Art as inquiry. *Qualitative Inquiry, 9,* 506–514.

Brewer, J. D. (2000). *Ethnography.* Buckingham, England: Open University Press.

Butt, D. G. (2001). Firth, Halliday and the development of systemic functional theory. In S. Auroux (Ed.), *History of the language sciences. Volume 2. An international handbook on the evolution of the study of language from the beginnings to the present* (Vol. 2, pp. 1806–1838). Berlin: de Gruyter.

Casanave, C. P. (2003). Looking ahead to more sociopolitically-oriented case study research in L2 writing scholarship. (But should it be called "post-process"?") *Journal of Second Language Writing, 12,* 85–102.

Charmaz, K. (2000). Grounded theory: Objectivist and constructivist methods. In N. K. Denzin & Y. S. Lincoln (Eds.), *Handbook of qualitative research* (2nd ed., pp. 509–535). Thousand Oaks, CA: Sage.

Cheng, A. (2006). Understanding learners and learning in ESP genre-based writing instruction. *English for Specific Purposes, 25,* 76–89.

Cho, S. (2004). Challenges of entering discourse communities through publishing in English: Perspectives of nonnative speaking doctoral students in the United States of America. *Journal of Language, Identity and Education, 3,* 47–72.

Clifford, J. (1986). Introduction: Partial truths. In J. Clifford & G. E. Marcus (Eds.), *Writing culture: The poetics and politics of ethnography* (pp. 1–26). Berkeley, CA: University of California Press.

Connor, U. (2002). New directions in contrastive rhetoric. *TESOL Quarterly, 35,* 493–510.

Creswell, J. W. (2003). *Research design: Qualitative, quantitative, and mixed method approaches* (2nd ed.). Thousand Oaks, CA: Sage.

Crotty, M. (1998). *The foundations of social research: Meaning and perspective in the research process.* London: Thousand Oaks, CA: Sage.

de Larios, J. R., Manchon, R. M., & Murphy, L. (2006). Generating text in native and foreign language writing: A temporal analysis of problem-solving formulation processes. *Modern Language Journal, 90,* 100–114.

Deleuze, G., & Guattari, F. (1987). *A thousand plateaus: Capitalism and schizophrenia* (B. Massumi, Trans.). Minneapolis: University of Minnesota Press.

Denzin, N. K., & Lincoln, Y. S. (2000). Introduction: The discipline and practice of qualitative research. In N. K. Denzin & Y. S. Lincoln (Eds.), *Handbook of Qualitative Research* (2nd ed., pp. 1–29). Thousand Oaks, CA: Sage.

DePew, K. E., & Miller, S. K. (2005). Studying L2 writer's digital writing: An argument for post-critical methods. *Computers and Composition, 22,* 259–278.

Evans-Pritchard, E. E. (1962). *Essays in social anthropology.* Oxford: Oxford University Press.

Faigley, L. (1994). *Fragments of rationality: Postmodernity and the subject of composition.* Pittsburgh: University of Pittsburgh Press.

Flowerdew, L. (2004). An integration of corpus-based and genre-based approaches to text analysis in EAP/ESP: Countering criticisms against corpus-based methodologies. *English for Specific Purposes, 24,* 321–332.

Gebhard, M. (2004). Fast capitalism, school reform and second language literacy practices. *Modern Language Journal, 88,* 245–265.

Geertz, C. ([1966]1973). *The interpretation of cultures.* New York: Basic Books.

Glaser, B., & Strauss, A. (1967). *The discovery of grounded theory.* Chicago: Aldine.

Glesne, C., & Peshkin, A. (1992). *Becoming qualitative researchers: An introduction.* New York: Longman.

Goffman, E. (1959). *The presentation of self in everyday life.* Garden City, NY: Doubleday.

Goldschmidt, W. (2001). Historical essay. A perspective on anthropology. *American Anthropologist, 102,* 789–807.

Grabe, W. (2001). Notes toward a theory of second language writing. In T. Silva & P. K. Matsuda (Eds.), *On second language writing* (pp. 39–57). Mahwah, NJ: Erlbaum.

Greckhamer, T., & Koro-Ljungberg, M. (2005). The erosion of a method: Examples from grounded theory. *International Journal of Qualitative Studies in Education, 18,* 729–750.

Halliday, M. A. K. (1973). *Explorations in the functions of language.* New York: Elsevier.

Halliday, M. A. K. (1978). *Language as social semiotic.* London: Edward Arnold.

Hammersley, M., & Atkinson, P. (1983). *Ethnography, principles in practice.* London: Tavistock.

Harkin, P., & Schilb, J. (1991). *Contending with words: Composition and rhetoric in a postmodern age.* New York: Modern Language Association of America.

Hayes, J. R. (2006). New directions in writing theory. In C. A. McArthur, S. Graham & J. Fitzgerald (Eds.), *Handbook of writing research* (pp. 28–40). New York: Gulford Press.

Heath, S. B. (1983/1996). *Ways with words: Language, life, and work in communities and classrooms.* Cambridge, MA: Harvard University Press.

Holliday, A. (2004). Issues of validity in progressive paradigms of qualitative research. *TESOL Quarterly, 38,* 731–734.

Hyland, K. (2002). Authority and invisibility: Authorial identity in academic writing. *Journal of Pragmatics, 34,* 1091–1112.

Hyland, K. (2003). Genre based pedagogies: A social response to process. *Journal of Language, Identity and Education, 12,* 17–29.

Hyon, S. (1996). Genre in three traditions: Implications for ESL. *TESOL Quarterly, 30,* 693–722.

Kamberelis, G., & Dimitriadis, G. (2005). *On qualitative inquiry: Approaches to language and literacy research.* New York: Teachers College Press; National Conference on Research in Language and Literacy.

Katznelson, H., Pepigan, H., & Rubin, B. (2001). What develops along with the development of second language writing? Exploring the "by-products." *Journal of Second Language Writing, 10,* 141–159.

Kern, R., & Schultz, J. M. (2005). Beyond orality: Investigating literacy and the literary in second and foreign language instruction. *Modern Language Journal, 89,* 381–392.

Kobayashi, H., & Rinnert, C. (2002). High school students' perceptions of first language literacy instruction: Implications for second language writing. *Journal of Second Language Writing, 11,* 91–116.

Labov, W., & Waletzky, J. (1967). Narrative analysis: Oral versions of personal experience. In J. Helm (Ed.), *Essays on the verbal and visual arts* (pp. 12–44). Seattle: University of Washington Press.

Lantolf, J. P. (1996). Second language theory building: Letting all the flowers bloom! *Language Learning, 46,* 713–749.

Lantolf, J. P., & Pavlenko, A. (2001). (S)econd (L)anguage (A)ctivity theory: Understanding second language learners as people. In M. P. Breen (Ed.), *Learner contributions to language learning: New directions in research* (pp. 141–158). London: Longman.

Lather, P. (2006). Paradigm proliferation as a good thing to think with: Teaching research in education as a wild profession. *International Journal of Qualitative Studies in Education, 19,* 35–57.

Lather, P., & St. Pierre, E. A. (2005, June). Postpositivist new paradigm inquiry. Athens, GA: University of Georgia.

Lave, J., & Wenger, E. (1991). *Situated learning: Legitimate peripheral participation.* New York: Cambridge University Press.

Lazaraton, A. (1995). Qualitative research in applied linguistics: A progress report. *TESOL Quarterly 29,* 455–472.

Leibowitz, B. (2005). Learning in an additional language in a multilingual society: A South African case study on university level writing. *TESOL Quarterly, 39,* 661–681.

Leontiev, A. (1981). The problem of activity in psychology. In J. V. Wertsch (Ed.), *The concept of activity in Soviet psychology.* Armouk, NY: M.E. Sharpe.

Li, X. (2005). Composing culture in a fragmented world: The issue of representation in cross-cultural research. In P. K. Matsuda & T. Silva (Eds.), *Second language writing research: Perspectives on the process of knowledge construction* (pp. 121–131). Mahwah, NJ: Erlbaum.

Lyotard, J. F. (1984). *The postmodern condition: A report on knowledge* (G. Bennington & B. Massumi, Trans.). Minneapolis: University of Minnesota Press.

Maguire, M. H., & Graves, B. (2001). Speaking personalities in primary school children's L2 writing. *TESOL Quarterly, 35,* 561–593.

Marcus, G. E., & Fischer, M. (1986). *Anthropology as cultural critique.* Chicago: University of Chicago Press.

Matsuda, P. K. (2003). Process and post-process: A discursive history. *Journal of Second Language Writing, 12,* 65–83.

Matsuda, P. K. (2005). Historical inquiry into second language writing. In P. K. Matsuda & T. Silva (Eds.), *Second language writing research: Perspec-*

tives on the process of knowledge construction (pp. 33–46). Mahwah, NJ: Erlbaum.

Merriam, S. B. (1998). *Qualitative research and case study applications in education.* San Francisco: Josey-Bass.

Miles, M. B., & Huberman, A. M. (1994). *Qualitative data analysis: An expanded sourcebook* (2nd ed.). Thousand Oaks, CA: Sage.

Myers, J. L. (2001). Self-evaluations of the "stream of thought" in journal writing. *System, 29,* 481–488.

Nikolov, M. (2006). Test-taking strategies of 12-and 13-year old Hungarian learners of EFL: Why whales have migraines. *Language Learning, 56,* 1–51.

Ochs, E., & Capps, L. (2001). *Living narratives: Creating lives in everyday storytelling.* Cambridge, MA: Harvard University Press.

Parks, S. (2001). Moving from school to the workplace: Disciplinary innovation, border crossing and the reshaping of a written genre. *Applied Linguistics, 22,* 405–438.

Parks, S., Huot, D., Hamers, J., & Lemonnier, F. H. (2005). "History of theatre" web sites: A brief history of the writing process in a high school ESL language arts class. *Journal of Second Language Writing, 14,* 223–258.

Piantanida, M., Tananis, C. A., & Grubs, R. E. (2004). Generating grounded theory of/for educational practice: The journey of three epistomorphs. *International Journal of Qualitative Studies in Education, 17,* 325–346.

Prior, P. (2006). A sociocultural theory of writing. In C. A. McArthur, S. Graham & J. Fitzgerald (Eds.), *Handbook of writing research* (pp. 54–66). New York: Guilford Press.

Rajagopalan, K. (2004). The philosophy of applied linguistics. In A. Davies & C. Elder (Eds.), *Handbook of applied linguistics* (pp. 397–420). Malden, MA: Blackwell.

Ramanathan, V. (2002). *The politics of TESOL education: Writing, knowledge, critical pedagogy.* New York: RoutledgeFalmer.

Ramanathan, V., & Atkinson, D. (1999). Ethnographic approaches and methods in L2 writing research: A critical guide and review. *Applied Linguistics, 20,* 44–70.

Roca de Larios, J., Manchon, R. M., & Murphy, L. (2006). Generating text in native and foreign language writing: A temporal analysis of problem solving formulation processes. *Modern Language Journal, 90,* 100–114.

Schultz, K. (2006). Qualitative research on writing. In C. A. McArthur, S. Graham & J. Fitzgerald (Eds.), *Handbook of writing research* (pp. 357–373). New York: Guilford Press.

Silva, T. (2005). On the philosophical bases of inquiry in second language writing: Metaphysics, inquiry paradigms and the intellectual zeitgest. In P. K. Matsuda & T. Silva (Eds.), *Second language writing research: Perspectives on the process of knowledge construction* (pp. 3–16). Mahwah, NJ: Erlbaum.

Silva, T., & Leki, I. (2004). Family matters: The influence of applied linguistics and composition studies on second language writing studies- past, present and future. *Modern Language Journal, 88,* 1–13.

Steinman, L. (2005). Writing life 1 in language 2. *McGill Journal of Education, 40*(1), 65–79.

Swales, J. (1990). *Genre analysis: English in academic and research settings.* New York: Cambridge University Press.

Swales, J. M. (1998). *Other floors, other voices: A textography of a small university building.* Mahwah, NJ: Erlbaum.

Tannenbaum, M. (2003). The narrative of language choice: Writers from ethnolinguistic minorities. *Canadian Modern Language Review, 60,* 7–26.

Teachers of English to Speakers of Other Languages, I. (2006). TESOL Quarterly Research Guidelines. Retrieved May 10, 2006, from http://www.tesol.org/s_tesol/seccss.asp?CID=476&DID=2150.

Tedlock, B. (2000). Ethnography and ethnographic representation. In N. K. Denzin & Y. S. Lincoln (Eds.), *Handbook of qualitative research* (pp. 455–486). Thousand Oaks, CA: Sage.

Van Maanen, J. (1988). *Tales of the field: On writing ethnography.* Chicago: University of Chicago Press.

Wang, L. (2003). Switching to first language among writers with differing level of second language proficiency. *Journal of Second Language Writing, 13,* 347–375.

Wang, M.-f., & Bakken, L. L. (2004). An academic writing needs assessment of English-as-a-Second-Language clinical investigators. *Journal of Continuing Education in the Health Professions, 24*(3), 181–190.

Wang, W., & Wen, Q. (2002). L1 use in the L2 composing process: An exploratory study of 16 Chinese EFL writers. *Journal of Second Language Writing, 11,* 225–246.

Weigle, S. C., & Nelson, G. L. (2004). Novice tutors and their ESL tutees: Three case studies of tutor roles and their perceptions of success. *Journal of Second Language Writing, 13,* 203–225.

White, R. (2001). Adapting Grice's maxims in the teaching of writing. *ELT Journal, 55,* 62–69.

Wortham, S. (2001). *Narratives in action: A strategy for research and analysis.* New York: Teachers College Press.

Yoon, H., & Hirvela, A. (2004). ESL student attitudes towards corpus use in L2 writing. *Journal of Second Language Writing, 13,* 257–283.

Young, R. F., & Miller, E. R. (2004). Learning as changing participation: Discourse roles in ESL writing conferences. *Modern Language Journal, 88,* 519–535.

Zhu, W. (2004). Faculty views on the importance of writing, the nature of academic writing and teaching and responding to writing in the disciplines. *Journal of Second Language Writing, 13,* 29–48.

Znaniecki, F. (1934). *The method of sociology.* New York: Farrar & Reinhart.

6 Cleaning up the Mess: Perspectives from a Novice Theory Builder

Christine Tardy

I begin with a caveat: I consider my own research and theory practices to be neither ideal nor expert-like. My first attempts at qualitative research were only eight years ago, and I've only very recently come to acknowledge my work as "theory building," so I consider myself to be more of a novice than an expert in this area; it is, therefore, from this novice perspective that I approach this chapter. Specifically, I will explore the practice of theory building first by tracing my own process of "coming to theory" through qualitative research. Second, I will discuss the relationship between qualitative research and theory building more broadly.

DISCOVERING QUALITATIVE RESEARCH

My first exposure to doing empirical research was as a master's student in a TESOL program in the early 1990s. I took a required course on basic statistics and research design, and I was fascinated by it. Concepts like validity, reliability, and operationalization made sense to me; my peers and I came to see case studies as primarily anecdotal and mostly useless—not that we read very many of them. How could you possibly learn anything from a sample size of one, or even four, I thought? At this point in time, I equated the term "research" with quantitative empirical studies. Through controlled research designs, such studies allowed us to make generalizations. Generalizations, in turn, could help someone (not me) develop theories.

It is worth noting that at this point I used the term "theory" as a catch-all phrase for "research-driven explanations of complex phenomena." *Theory* encompassed language acquisition theory, syntactic theory, theories of language teaching, theories of reading and writing, and so on. (Of course, there were also social theories, mostly by people with French names, but these seemed to have little relevance to me at that point in time.) While I did acknowledge the importance of teacher theory, I saw this as largely distinct from scholarly theory, which seemed quite removed from my own classroom experiences.

After completing an MA-TESL, I became an EFL teacher. Teaching ESP and EAP writing courses overseas, I had come to see genre as a key concept in specialized writing and genre-based pedagogy as an effective approach to teach specialized writing courses. Still, I found myself constantly wondering what students retained after leaving my classes. During this time, I read an article by Sunny Hyon in *TESOL Quarterly* (Hyon, 1996), which provides an overview of current orientations to genre theory. In the conclusion, Hyon outlines future research directions for genre studies. Here, she notes that "little work has actually investigated the impact of genre-based pedagogy in the classroom" (p. 714) and calls for ESL researchers to conduct both controlled experiments and case studies to learn more about student genre learning. This call for research caught my eye, as it seemed to articulate the very questions that I struggled with as a teacher. As I shifted my focus from full-time teaching to returning to graduate school, I began my doctoral program with research questions ready to explore:

- How do advanced second language writers learn disciplinary genres in the classroom?
- What resources do they draw upon as they learn these genres?

I want to emphasize here that I began with questions because I believe this exemplifies my own theory-building paradigm that guided my dissertation research. Many of my peers in graduate school described their dissertations as "theoretical," or they developed new theories through their research (whether it was empirical, archival, or hermeneutic). But I was intimidated by the idea of theory building as a graduate student, and I certainly never considered theory as the starting point—or even the end point—of my research. Instead, my focus was on designing and carrying out a sound research study.

Although I still understood theory primarily as being derived from empirical study, one important shift in my thinking had already occurred: I no longer saw *quantitative* research as the only way to study a problem. Because I was interested in questions like *how* and *why*, and because I didn't want to control all of the messy realities that influence writing, I realized early on that I needed to study a small number of writers in close detail. Qualitative research—case studies, in particular—provided the perfect method for looking at the types of intricacies I was interested in. A qualitative research approach would allow me to explore a local context, identify unanticipated phenomena and influences, understand the processes of events and actions, and develop causal explanations (Maxwell, 1996)—all research purposes that appealed to my goals and interests.

I carried out my first case study as a pilot for my dissertation research, using interviews, text analysis, and classroom observation. For four months, I followed three international students as they participated in an ESL writing class, wrote their assignments, and carried out their other graduate work. A few months after I had collected my data, I began to analyze it—this, of course, was not an ideal way to go about the process. At this later point, I identified all of the things that I should have asked about or should have collected but did not. I realized (both through the data and some reading I was doing at the time) that learning disciplinary writing was not at all limited to the classroom context; I needed to know more about what was going on outside of the classroom. But all was not lost: The study nudged me into new directions. I realized that in order to understand genre learning, I first needed to understand genre *knowledge*. I had been led to new research questions:

- What it is that writers learn when they learn genres?
- How do they learn these things?

I had no answers to the second question yet, but I did have some initial answers to the first question of what do writers learn. I saw them learning stylistic features, layout, patterns of organization, content to include or exclude, and the disciplinary practices for carrying out genres. Then I noticed in one transcript a writer speaking about learning "some tricks" for writing a grant proposal. He explained that there were things that writers did to make their work look better than it was. He didn't know what these were, or how to do it himself, but he had some awareness that this was a part of what academics in his field of engineering did. This pointed me toward another dimension of learning genres—the rhetorical element. Little did I know, I was starting to try to understand this somewhat amorphous concept of "genre knowledge."

FORMING THEORY

As I worked with my pilot study data, I also went back to my readings. How was genre knowledge described theoretically? How was it operationalized in empirical work? Next, I began preparing my dissertation proposal. I brought together what I had learned about genre knowledge through both my pilot study and the work I had read. In the prospectus, I wrote:

> Assuming the theoretical dimensions of genre outlined above, such knowledge must encompass (inter-) textual and social dimensions that change over time. On the most salient level, this is knowledge of textual form, including elements such as text organization, disciplinary terminology, or citation practices. But genre knowledge extends beyond knowledge of form to knowledge of content (Berkenkotter & Huckin, 1995; Bhatia, 1999; Johns, 1997). This less visible knowledge requires writers to understand the discourse community's ideologies and discursive practices. Content knowledge also requires writers to understand a text's rhetorical timing, surprise value, or *kairos,* including a sense of how a text may be received at a given time within a given community. Another dimension of genre knowledge seems to be a shared understanding of genre membership. Expert users may, for example, share a knowledge of the generic name (Johns, 1997) or may recognize prototypes or exemplars of the genre (Paltridge, 1997; Swales, 1990).

At this point, my discussion of genre knowledge was nothing resembling a new or expanded theory, but was instead a rather simple (even simplistic) synthesis of other scholars' ideas. I relied heavily on citations and couched my own ideas in those of established writers.

As I began turning toward the dissertation research, my relationship with theory became more complicated. As a typical graduate student, I read whatever I could get my hands on: any empirical or theoretical work related to disciplinary writing, genre, graduate student writing, or advanced ESL writing was on my list. As I read, I took notes, trying to sort out the salient variables, the key findings, the methodologies, and the theories. I created a kind of spreadsheet that helped me sort out these dimensions and identify patterns. This classification was an important part of my early theory building, leading me to understand concepts in particular ways and to consider relationships among a variety of local studies.

At the same time, I was beginning to carry out my own empirical work. Through my reading and preliminary research, I had formulated (more) new research questions, focused particularly around the notion of *genre knowledge*:

- How do advanced L2 writers learn disciplinary genres in classroom and non-classroom contexts over time?
- How does their genre knowledge change?
- What influences those changes?

I mapped out a set of methods that I felt would help me answer my questions. Genre and text analysis gave me a means for following changes in writers' texts over time. Content analysis of oral interview transcripts helped me identify changes in the writers' declarative knowledge of genres at different points in time. Intertextual tracing allowed me to locate links between changes in the writers' declarative or procedural genre knowledge, discussions about genres in the writing classroom, feedback and advice on writing they received from instructors and mentors, and other texts that the writers encountered. At the time, I had no name for the theoretical (or ideological) paradigm that I was working within, but I recognize it now as critical rationalism, or what Silva (2005) refers to as humble pragmatic rationalism—"*humble* reflecting the limits of one's knowledge and *pragmatic* in the sense of a pluralistic and eclectic approach that accommodates different worldviews, assumptions, and methods in an attempt to address and solve specific problems in particular contexts" (p. 9).

Soon, I set out to begin the real study. I found four multilingual graduate students willing to participate in my research. I met these writers every three or four weeks to collect their writing and discuss it with them. After my interviews, I diligently transcribed every word of every recording, highlighting passages as I typed as a reminder to return to them. I looked in particular at how the writers spoke about different genres, what they seemed to know, what they didn't seem to know.

I also collected their writing. I looked for how they demonstrated their knowledge of these different genres. What did they seem to know about genre form, for example, as demonstrated in their written texts? What rhetorical moves did they use or not use? How did their writing change over time within one genre? How did it resemble the other texts that they encountered?

Before I knew it, I had collected, quite literally, piles of data, which I somehow had to make sense of (see Figure 1). During the first few months of data collection, I thought carefully about coding, hoping to identify categories early on that I could continue to use throughout the two-year study. I began using a coding software program (ATLAS. ti) that promised to help "uncover the complex phenomena hidden in your data in an exploratory way," therefore providing "aid in generating social theory" (Scientific Software Development, 1997). Exactly what I needed!

Figure 1. Piles of transcripts and participants' writing. Photograph by the author.

The program works like a database of sorts. Researchers can load any electronic text (e.g., transcripts, writing, field notes) into what is called a "hermeneutic unit." These texts can include transcripts, writing, or even observation notes. My own process was to read through the texts and generate coding categories based on what seemed interesting or salient. For example, I could code in terms of the text type (e.g., CV, conference abstract, research article), in terms of the genre knowledge that is being drawn upon (e.g., knowledge of disciplinary content, form, readers), or in terms of the sources of genre knowledge (e.g., classroom instruction, collaboration, feedback). The software can also count the codes so you can see how many times you have used each one, giving you a sense of the relative frequency or infrequency of a given category. The coding interface is illustrated in Figure 2.

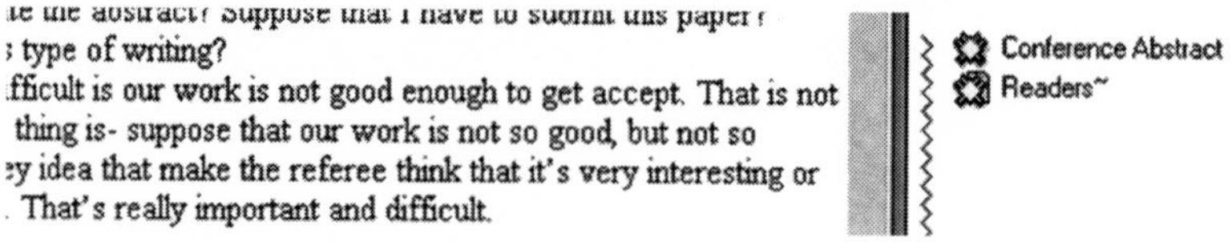

Figure 2. Example of a coded transcript using qualitative research software.

The very process of coding is of course a highly interpretive one, influenced by the researcher and the research context, among many other factors. Still, the software helped me make the process a little more orderly and was particularly helpful when I felt "stuck" or at a loss for making sense of my data. The software can also generate a list of all of the quotes in the data coded within one category. I could sub-categorize this list by writer or by genre, and I could also see what other codes co-occurred with a given category (see Figure 3). Reading through these lists of quotes helped me identify patterns and track longitudinal changes.

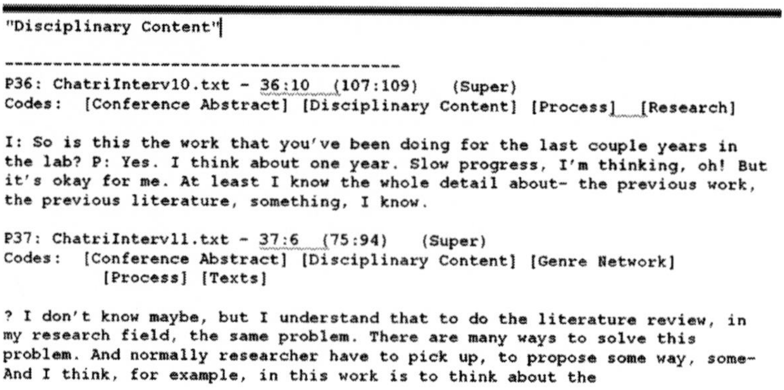
"Disciplinary Content"

P36: ChatriInterv10.txt - 36:10 (107:109) (Super)
Codes: [Conference Abstract] [Disciplinary Content] [Process] [Research]

I: So is this the work that you've been doing for the last couple years in the lab? P: Yes. I think about one year. Slow progress, I'm thinking, oh! But it's okay for me. At least I know the whole detail about- the previous work, the previous literature, something, I know.

P37: ChatriInterv11.txt - 37:6 (75:94) (Super)
Codes: [Conference Abstract] [Disciplinary Content] [Genre Network] [Process] [Texts]

? I don't know maybe, but I understand that to do the literature review, in my research field, the same problem. There are many ways to solve this problem. And normally researcher have to pick up, to propose some way, some- And I think, for example, in this work is to think about the

Figure 3. Partial list of quotes coded as "Disciplinary Content" for one participant.

Of course, these neat and tidy "scientific" tools obscure the messy reality of qualitative research. Categorizing other people's words and actions is not an objective process in any sense—and this fact was not lost on me at all. For instance, it was impossible to truly begin with a "blank slate." Like it or not, my readings, pilot study, and classroom teaching already had me thinking of particular categories to look for as I scoured my data. Although I tried not to "impose these categories on my data," my attention was more attuned to certain things, so these appeared more "salient" to me.

My coding categories were also evolving as I worked. In some cases, my categories were influenced by readings or discussions that led me to see certain trends or patterns. Surely, my reading of *Writing and Identity* (Ivanič, 1998) and *Writing Games* (Casanave, 2002) led me to be more attuned to issues of identity. In other cases, an unexpected issue, such as "exigency," arose so frequently that I could no longer ignore it. These new categories then joined my older categories so that I soon had a long list of codes. These codes could further be grouped into "families," such as Elements of Genre Knowledge, Sources of Genre Knowledge, or Strategies for Knowledge Building. The software had become a tool for me—helpful for identifying trends and patterns, but at times too rigid in its characterizations of these writers' stories.

After eight months of data collection and ongoing analysis, I began writing up the methodology chapter of my dissertation. This process required me to re-examine my codes and to identify trends and relationships, perhaps larger-order categories. First, I determined the dimensions of genre knowledge that I had identified in the transcripts, the field notes, and the writers' texts. But of course this wasn't sufficient. Because I was working with writers who were in many cases novices, they were not likely to hold the same genre knowledge as experts. Therefore, I needed to identify elements of genre knowledge that were *not* present in my data; this sent me back to my readings and my own experiences as a writer and a teacher of writing. Soon, I had refined my categories, creating a table that very neatly presented four dimensions of genre knowledge as major coding categories, along with some of the sub-codes that demonstrated this knowledge in my data (see Table 1). It looked good, but did it work?

Table 1. Coding Scheme of Genre Knowledge Dimensions, from Tardy (2004).

Major Coding Category	Sub-codes	Descriptions
Formal Knowledge	Format/Structure	discourse and lexico-grammatical conventions; format; layout
	Content	content to be included/excluded
	Modality	modes of writing and reading (e.g., paper vs. screen)
Procedural Knowledge	Process	how to accomplish the intended action; composing process
	Reading	how/where/why/when the text is read
	Distribution	manner in which the text is distributed to/received by others
	Genre Network	other genres linked to the text
Rhetorical Knowledge	Purpose/Intended Action	the writer's purpose in writing the text; the intended action that the text hopes to achieve
	Context	the specific context in which the text will be read, distributed, and evaluated; values and ideology of the context
	Sociopolitics	the social and political dimensions of the context that govern interactions that surrounding the genre
	Readers	the readers and their purpose(s) in reading the text; what they value/expect to see in the text
	Writer	the unique positioning of the writer (e.g., linguistic proficiency, professional status) vis-à-vis the context
Subject-Matter Knowledge	Disciplinary Subject-Matter	Subject-matter content

In my first foray into sharing these ideas, I received important comments. "How do you separate formal and rhetorical knowledge?" someone asked. "I'm not sure," I answered, "but these writers do when they first encounter a genre." I pointed to an example from the writing classroom that I had observed. As writers first approached new genres, they tended to learn *form* somewhat distinctly from rhetorical elements or subject matter or procedures. But for expert writers, these boundaries did seem more artificial. One of my committee members advised that I describe my dimensions of genre knowledge as "a heuristic" that did not necessarily hold "any sort of epistemic reality." This helped, temporarily giving me a way to mediate the need to categorize with the acknowledgement that the categorization was really just a cleaned up version of reality.

But the problem had not been resolved. In fact, the boundaries of my coding categories (what was becoming, in fact, my "model" of genre knowledge) deteriorated as my data collection continued into year two. After about 16 months of data collection, I watched one of my participants compose multiple research articles within a short span of a few months. As I read through his transcripts, scribbling in the paper margins and coding electronically on my computer, I noticed an interesting change. In my earlier coding analysis, I had typically assigned just one or two categories of genre knowledge to a quotation. But in these later transcripts, I found myself piling on the categories. In other words, within one quote, the writer demonstrated multiple types of genre knowledge; process knowledge, disciplinary content knowledge, and format and structural knowledge were all integrated in the ways that this writer talked about his research writing at this point in time.

When I first noticed this trend, I was frustrated. Did this mean that my codes were useless and I would need to start over? Then I had a kind of epiphany. Perhaps the breakdown of my categories was actually *interesting* rather than problematic. Perhaps it was the case that the categories "worked" to describe *novice* genre writers but the boundaries between them were useless (or at least of little use) as writers gained expertise. I thought back to another project I had done, studying grant writers, and I remembered how experienced grant writers were unable to separate out knowledge of proposal form from the procedures or the rhetoric or even the subject matter (Tardy, 2003). These categories had become one blurry mass of genre knowledge for them. Perhaps it was the case, I thought, that this blurring of knowledge domains is part of the genre learning process. At the early stages, writers distinguish among these different generic dimensions. As in the information-processing model of second language acquisition, writers cannot focus on everything, so they focus on only one or two things. Second language writers—particularly in the writing classroom—often focus on form. With repeated practice and experience, the form becomes "automatic" or "tacit." The writer can then focus on other genre dimensions, which may restructure his/her knowledge of form, but will eventually integrate with it. The end result—expertise—is a complicated, richly layered knowledge of genre. I looked back at my data from the previous 20 months. The idea seemed to make sense; it seemed to describe the changes I was seeing. As a visual learner, I created a diagram to illustrate my model of this process (see Figure 4). Suddenly, the ideas in my head had a structure. It was tangible—something I could easily describe and share. It began to take on a kind of reality. It *looked* like a model. That model also contributed to part of a larger understanding that I had built of this complex phenomenon.

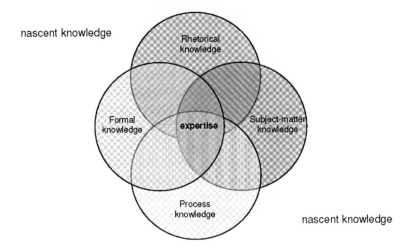

Figure 4. Model of building genre knowledge, from Tardy (2009). Reprinted with permission.

What I didn't realize until after my dissertation defense was that I had in fact already dove into theory building. Throughout my research—even before I began it—I had gradually constructed a theory of how writers build genre knowledge. It is not a predictive theory, nor is it a particularly expansive one, limited as it is to advanced multilingual writers; nevertheless, it is a theory. That is, it provides a framework or a model for describing a complicated process, it is based on both empirical research and hermeneutic research, and it relies on the process of categorizing—and, thus, simplifying—complex phenomena.

COMING TO TERMS WITH THEORY

It is only in the past couple of years that I've come to view theory as less intimidating. I no longer see it solely as a "data-driven explanation" but instead as a kind of working knowledge. Such knowledge is developed through an integration of our experiences as writers and writing teachers, our scholarly influences, our own studies, our colleagues' studies, and our unpacking of other theories and concepts. So even though I still feel the need to emphasize my novice-ness, I can now finally describe myself as a theory builder.

The theory building process which I have shared here began, in one sense, with my teaching. Then, my classroom experience led me to certain readings, which led me to the research, which led to a theory. But this is not a linear process at all. The theory—that is, my understanding of what genre knowledge is and how it is learned—was evolving as I was teaching, reading, designing and carrying out my study, and writing up and sharing my work. My working theory shaped my research, leading me to ask certain questions and not others, leading me to see certain trends and not others, leading me to read certain pieces of the literature and not others. It seems to me now that the entire process of carrying out a qualitative study reflects the process of theory building. This process requires grounding ideas in prior research and theory, categorizing phenomena, and building models or narratives that explain or simplify details, perhaps leading to new or modified theories.

So why did it take me so long to characterize my work as theory building? When I look back at this process now, I see two reasons. First, it was so chaotic—far more so than I could even describe it within the constraints of this chapter—and so full of uncertainty that it seemed far removed from the elegant theories that I had read. Throughout my research, I remember constantly asking myself whether I was just "making things up" and seeing what I wanted to see. Surely, *real* theories were more unambiguous, I thought.

Second, as a graduate student, I felt unprepared to propose a *theory*. I was comfortable designing, carrying out, and reporting on a study, but I was unsure how one really goes about building theory through research, much less qualitative research. Graduate courses on research generally allow students to design and carry out their own study. Even if the project is small, students gain hands-on practice, and they see research as something that they can do—in fact, something that they must do. In contrast, graduate courses on *theory* tend to focus on reading and understanding theories developed by others. There was an intimidating aura around "theory building"—something that Matsuda (2003) also chronicles in his reflections on his own professional growth. Theories are presented as the basis of current or historical scholarly thought in the discipline, generally written by the "big names," and often in language that is difficult for newcomers to grasp. As a student, I was never asked to *do* theory in the same way that I was asked to *do* research. With time, however, theory has become something I see as "doable," another stage in attempting to understand particular aspects of the world we observe and participate in. I now see that research and theory share a great deal in common, as both impose order, lending coherence to the very messy, even unruly, realities of human activity.

References

Casanave, C. P. (2002). *Writing games: Multicultural case studies of academic literacy practices in higher education.* Mahwah, NJ: Erlbaum.

Hyon, S. (1996). Genre in three traditions: Implications for ESL. *TESOL Quarterly, 30,* 693–722.

Ivanič, R. (1998). *Writing and identity: The discoursal construction of identity in academic writing.* Philadelphia: John Benjamins Publishing Company.

Matsuda, P. K. (2003). Coming to voice: Publishing as a graduate student. In C. P. Casanave & S. Vanderick (Eds.), *Writing for scholarly publication: Behind the scenes in language education* (pp. 39–51). Mahwah, NJ: Erlbaum.

Maxwell, J. A. (1996). *Qualitative research design: An interactive approach.* Thousand Oaks, NJ: Sage.

Scientific Software Development. (1997). *ATLAS.ti short user's manual.* Berlin, Germany: Sage.

Silva, T. (2005). On the philosophical bases of inquiry in second language writing: Metaphysics, inquiry paradigms, and the intellectual zeitgeist. In P. K. Matsuda & T. Silva (Eds.), *Second language writing research: Per-*

spectives on the process of knowledge construction (pp. 3–15). Mahwah, NJ: Erlbaum.

Tardy, C. M. (2003). A genre system view of the funding of academic research. *Written Communication, 20,* 7–36.

Tardy, C. M. (2004). *Exploring the interactions between writing instruction and disciplinary practice: Pathways of four multilingual writers.* Unpublished doctoral dissertation, Purdue University.

7 A Reconsideration of Contents of "Pedagogical Implications" and "Further Research Needed" Moves in the Reporting of Second Language Writing Research and Their Roles in Theory Building

Doug Flahive

While some readers may interpret my comments below as critical, I believe fair and constructive criticism is an unequivocal litmus test for optimism about the potential for change. It is from this optimistic perspective that these comments are offered. While my specific focus in this chapter is on second language writing research, I consider this field a subset of the more expansive area of second language teaching and learning research. Therefore, I cite a broader, more inclusive selection of studies outside of and within the field of second language writing as I develop my rationale for changes in the reporting of research not only in second language writing but also in related subfields of second language acquisition.

Through the data reported in this chapter, I hope to initiate a professional conversation regarding the need for change in conventions used to report research in our field of inquiry and to offer specific suggestions regarding the nature of these changes. My focus is on the contents of two moves which have become largely ritualized in the reporting of second language studies: Pedagogical Implications (PIs) and Further Research Needed (FRNs). My reasons for drawing attention to the need for revisions in the contents of these Moves are motivated by my role as a teacher-educator, where I consistently attempt to highlight the importance of theory-based research to bring about improvements in language teaching. My suggestions are also motivated by my desire to see the field of second language writing continue to mature in ways consistent with sound principles of social science inquiry.

I begin by describing the activities which I use to nurture a spirit of critical inquiry in my students with respect to the place of theory, research, and practice in their current and, more importantly, in their future professional lives. In the second portion of this chapter, I present a series of brief summaries of my professional experiences and research projects to give readers a sense of how I arrived at where I am or, more realistically, where I was in when this chapter was written, regarding my views of the role theory, research, and practice.

Next, I move to a presentation of an evaluation checklist to assess research studies along with a broad classification of four different types of research. Finally, I move to a corpus of studies drawn from the flagship journal of second language writing, the *Journal of Second Language Writing*. In this section are found examples of the two moves found in the title of this chapter, Pedagogical Implications and Further Research Needed. It is by drawing readers' attention to current status of these two moves and the interrelationships between them that I hope producers of second language research may become more aware of how significantly altering the contents of these moves has the potential to make their research more pedagogically relevant to teachers and more useful to researchers and theorists.

MY ROLE AS A TEACHER-TRAINER

Being involved in teacher-training for nearly three decades, I have been continually challenged by the chronic resistance of both students and veteran English language teachers regarding the importance of theory and research and their potential role in informing second language pedagogy. Having first witnessed this resistance as a beginning graduate student, and later confronting it in successive cohorts of graduate students in the M.A. program in which I teach, my need to address and mitigate this resistance has evolved into both a personal and professional challenge. I have few illusions about transforming the majority of my students into lifelong critical consumers and producers of pedagogically based classroom research. More realistically, through a few relatively transferable classroom procedures I have developed over the years, I believe I have somewhat legitimized the role of theory and research in the minds of my students, at least until they have secured their degrees and move on with their careers.

In the teaching of my classes, in my responsibilities as a mentor of student research, and in my own research, I emphasize the theory-research-practice relationship in a multiplicity of ways, but with one consistent theme. This theme, simply put, is that literally everything we do as teachers is theoretically motivated. I point out that this theoretical motivation begins with our selection of a textbook to use in a language teaching class, the sequencing of activities we implement in classes, and even through our organization of syllabi.

I further emphasize that it is the informed teacher who understands these theoretically motivated underpinnings of pedagogy and who can explicitly describe them, granted in highly metaphorical terms. (I suspect some practitioners have minimal interest in these under-pinnings.) Once I have made my agenda explicit, I then move to my largely inductive pedagogical practices. In most of my classes, I begin with a hands-on analysis of learner texts. With SLA, for instance, we examine textbooks designed to teach grammar. In L2 Vocabulary De-velopment, it is exercises which focus on vocabulary building. In an L2 Reading and Writing seminar, I have students assemble an eclectic collection of reading textbooks, writing textbooks and those which emphasize reading-to-write. Some texts reflect expressivist perspec-tives; others display more formalist/cognitivist views of literacy devel-opment. For many, we see an eclectic mix of both.

Working with different texts, either individually or in pairs, we complete a series of activities designed to deconstruct the implicit the-oretical assumptions found in these learner textbooks. We then syn-thesize these analyses through a listing and subsequent grouping of theoretical teaching and learning assumptions. Our initial listing is an eclectic mixture of theories drawn from linguistics, psycholinguistics, and educational psychology. As the courses proceed, we frequently re-visit these listings and attempt to fit the labels found in the research literature to as many items on the list as we are able. Following this labeling, we then try to determine whether a specific sequencing or classroom activity was or was not in any way supported by relevant research. In working through this activity, I reaffirm my own beliefs that language teaching textbooks are unambiguous illustrations of applied theory and feel that by the end of this exercise my students guardedly buy into these beliefs.

What they also eventually induce is the eclecticism of the theories embedded in pedagogical materials. As a consequence, they also discover that any notions of some encompassing Macro theory of language learning and/or teaching pundits may speculate about or attempt to visualize by means of intersecting circles and boxes with strategically placed uni- and bi-directional arrows may be, as Schumann (1983) long ago pointed out, best viewed as works or art rather than science. (See Grabe and Kaplan [1996] for a more contemporary work of computer-assisted artistry relevant to second language writing.)

Then, we turn to research studies. While it sometimes takes considerable effort to tease out implicit theories embedded in pedagogical texts, theories become somewhat more explicit in research studies, a point I will return to in the latter portion of this chapter. To build and strengthen this link between research and practice, I direct students to an array of journals to either identify research studies that illustrate the issue under discussion or select from a list of studies I have pre-selected for their investigations. It is navigating this problematic symbiosis among theory, research, and practice which forms the focus of the next section.

MACRO AND MICRO THEORIES FROM THE PERSPECTIVE OF RESEARCH EXEMPLARS

I readily concede that for me the prospect of embracing some grand or Macro theory was largely short-circuited by a project on which I based my first professional presentation back in the late 1970s. Using an early version of a General Linear Model (GLM), I mined a rich data base at the Center for English as a Second Language (CESL) at Southern Illinois University, where I was employed as a graduate assistant. These files included a range of demographic and language proficiency data related to students who had completed their English language training prior to enrolling in university classes. Once my coding and matrix manipulation was complete, 22 percent of the variability in my criterion variable, scores on the Michigan Test of English Language Proficiency, was accounted for by my predictors. For me, this was a disappointing result until I began to read "theoretically based" award-winning research studies in SLA where 5 percent of the variance was accounted for. I observed in another study, published in a prestigious SLA journal, a researcher offering explicit pedagogical recommendations on the basis of 4 percent explained variance.

Although my initial study using the GLM was disappointing, this approach in which one posits a criterion variable and tries to build a model to account for the variability in a specific criterion measure has been a way for me to connect many of the disparate strands of second language research. After reading Spolsky (1989), I found further confirmation of my regression-based view of theory in SLA. Grabe's (2001) resurrection and proposed extension of Spolsky to the potential development of an L2 theory of writing further confirmed my GLM perspective.

As I view the Spolsky or Grabe proposals with their specified "Conditions," I see a collection of micro theories, each potentially useful in helping to explain the conditions for learning a second language or, in the case of Grabe's proposal, for developing a specific subset of language proficiency, namely writing. While Spolsky's "Conditions" proposal might possibly be of some limited use with subjects sampled from a relatively homogeneous cohort of refugees recently migrated to Israel and placed in a controlled language learning setting, the Grabe extension of Spolsky strikes me as stretching the parameters of plausibility, largely because of the indeterminate nature of the dependent variable, "learning to write" or "attained writing proficiency." Further complicating the Conditions proposals is the mix of what I term hard and soft variables. Age and short-term memory I consider " hard" variables. Motivation and learning style variables, which are largely based on questionnaire results, I consider "soft." My 22 percent study was based largely on hard data. More about the problems with soft variables as I discuss Flahive and Dahlman (2003).

Limited as GLM modeling may be, it is the most satisfactory procedure I have come up with to date in terms of forming for me a somewhat unifying framework of a highly disparate "field" of inquiry as opposed to a discipline, a distinction indirectly made in Swales (1990) in his defining of the characteristics of a "discourse community." The GLM model also minimizes the art work I referred to earlier. It involves the selection and measurement of the relevant predictor and criterion variables, and you have a working model. Naturally, the selection of variables would need to be justified by theoretical underpinnings.

Criterion = Variable 1 + Variable 2 + Variable 3 . . . . . . + Variable 17 + Error (The unaccounted for variance)

In viewing theoretical proposals, I'm not overly concerned whether what they propose can result in a "true" encompassing theory and subsequent model of second language learning or second language writing. Like many approaches to theorizing in our field, Krashen for example, such speculation is extremely useful in that it promotes productive professional discussions which may lead to research that may result in pedagogical improvement or, at the very minimum, the classroom exploration of interesting theoretically motivated pedagogical techniques.

As I mentioned above, I regularly integrate journal articles into my discussion of theory and pedagogy. Research studies provide the bridge between these two. However, for more years than I care to recall, my students and I used to basically cherry-pick research studies to fit the discussion of the relevant model that served as the focus for a particular issue. At times, an older study or two would fit into a topic better than more recent ones. Sometimes a more recent one would provide a useful synthesis of prior research and offer results which extended older findings into a newer domain. Research studies were for me an eclectic repository of insights with varying degrees of pedagogical and field-extending usefulness. I paid relatively little attention to the fact that sometimes older studies were far superior in design and execution than newer ones. I also noted that some poorly designed studies offered elaborate pedagogical recommendations while some of the better ones barely mention potential implications. The obligatory "more research is needed" became a classroom joke. We could only guess at what the researchers meant by "more."

My uncritical mining of the body of second language research literature took on an increasingly critical focus beginning with a study conducted by Balloffet (1996) and a subsequent study by Flahive and Dahlman (2003). Finally, in Flahive (2004), it was through a historical examination of the topics and types of second language writing research which led to my focus on PIs and FRNs, hence, this chapter. Each of the three studies was motivated by different factors. Each contributed to the shaping of my views as to the need for change in both the reporting and interpreting of research. Below are brief overviews of the projects.

The theoretical underpinnings of the Balloffet study were Swales (1988, 1990) and an assortment of feminist authors. In Swales (1988), he chronicles the evolution and increasing sophistication of the *TESOL*

Quarterly. Among the many variables he noted was the relative number of female authors, which increased from 26 percent in 1968 to 70 percent in 1986. With this in mind, we then looked at the widely cited and used CARS Model (Swales 1990). As we know, the first of three Moves he identifies in research paper introductions consists of what he terms "Establishing a Territory." The second Move, which became the focus of our investigation, is termed "Establishing a Niche." The third and final Move is labeled "Occupying the Niche." Within the second Move, Swales identifies four possible options or Steps. (See the bottom of Table 1 for a brief description of these options.) After discussing the writings of a number of feminist authors who highlighted differences between male and female authored discourses, we hypothesized that there would probably be more counterclaiming, namely attempting to demonstrate the viability of an alternative hypothesis, in the research studies conducted by men than women.

To test this working hypothesis that males were more likely to "Create a Niche" by Counter-claiming than females, we systematically analyzed three flagship journals: *The TESOL Quarterly, Language Learning,* and *The Modern Language Journal.* We selected research articles from the following years: 1980, 1985, 1990, and 1995. Initially, we identified 156 studies which fit our category of research. I later added studies from 2000 and increased the total to 177. My addition did not alter our initial findings

First, the male versus female hypothesis turned out to be a nonstarter. However, the so-called law of unintended consequences was operational. Data presented in Table 1 are self-explanatory. Over two-thirds of the studies either fill a "gap" or "continue a tradition." Scientific procedures such as "falsification" are limited to well-meaning discussions in SLA textbooks such as Larsen-Freeman and Long (1993) and seldom become the catalyst for follow up research. If I were to characterize the research culture of second language studies based upon our findings, I would say it is one of finding something new to investigate, as opposed to spending the requisite time in rigorously examining and helping to strengthen previous results. This is particularly troubling to someone who is attempting to use results to promote pedagogical innovation. It was a re-analysis of these and other data that contributed to the views leading to the latter portion of this chapter.

Table 1. Research articles from 1980 through 1995 found in *TESOL Quarterly* (*TQ*), *Language Learning* (*LL*), and the *Modern Language Journal* (*MLJ*)

Journal	# of RAs	1A Counter Claim	1B Gap	1C Raise Question	1D Continue Tradition	Other
TQ	61		26	7	12	16
LL	62		31	9	15	7
MLJ	54		24	1	11	18
Total	177		82	17	38	41
			45%	9%	21%	23%

Numbers and letters A-D are taken from Swales (1990, p.141). To these we added a fifth category: Other.

In the *Niche* study, we neither focused on any particular type of research nor did we focus on specific research topics. However, in a later study where research types and topics were the focus (Flahive & Dahlman 2003), my rethinking of the topic of theory, research, and pedagogy took a decidedly more critical turn. We initiated our research by examining trends in individual difference research with the purpose of selecting one which could be easily operationalized within the context of a foreign language class. We also added a metalinguistic variable, formal knowledge of English grammar, to assess the impact of these variables on success in a foreign language class, in this case three classes of second-semester German. In this classroom-based study, we were building a mini-GLM model with the purpose of selecting the fewest possible variables which would account for the greatest amount of variance in final test scores.

This need to find both a trendy and easily operationalizable variable resulted in a selective, systematic search of the Individual Difference (ID) research from 1981–2000. We re-examined the journals I mentioned above and added *Studies in Second Language Acquisition*. Within our 1981–2000 parameters we located every article in the target journals whose focus was individual difference research. Results are found in Table 2.

Table 2. Individual difference studies from *TESOL Quarterly, Language Learning,* the *Modern Language Journal,* and *Studies in Second Language Acquisition*

Individual difference variables 1981-1990	Individual difference variables 1991-2000
Motivation 8 (3)	Anxiety 17 (7)
Strategies 8 (2)	Age 2
Field Independence/Dependence 7 (7)	Aptitude 11 (5)
Age 5	Motivation 10 (5)
Anxiety 5 (1)	Gender 9
Aptitude 5 (2)	Field Independence/ Dependence 6 (6)
Atitude 5 (2)	Strategies 6 (1)
Gender 4	Attitude 3 (1)
Total 47 (17)	Total 64 (25)

What this table illustrates is not only the number of studies of IDs published in the 20 years the study includes, but also the number of studies in parentheses ( ) where the researcher included a measure of language proficiency. For example, from 1981–1990 we located 8 studies whose central focus was Motivation. Of those, only 3 included some measure of English language proficiency. The rest focus on either questionnaire data only or procedures as to how questionnaires were developed or modified.

Recognizing the fact that research without synthesis is simply gossip, we then conducted a meta-analysis of those studies where a measure of language proficiency was included and found that Anxiety was the ID which accounted for the greatest amount of language proficiency. In our analysis, Anxiety produced a mean correlation with language proficiency of (.45) with a range from a minimum of .20 to a maximum of .60. Motivation resulted in a mean of (.24) with a range from .17 to .56. Field independence/dependence research resulted in a mean of (.39) with a range of .07 to .75. Ultimately, we selected Anxiety to include in our study for two reasons: the highest mean correlation and the narrowest range.

What proved to be even more instructive was the relative instability of the Individual Difference constructs. While the Grabe and Spolsky Conditions proposals posit several categories of ID variables such as ability, learning style preferences, attitudes, and motivation, these types of variables demonstrate a high level of cross study variability and hence may be of limited usefulness in theory/model building. Note the study completed by Masgoret and Gardner (2003). In their meta-analysis of research conducted by Gardner and associates which included 75 independent samples with 10,489 subjects, Masgoret and Gardner found in a subset of 55 samples, where motivation and grades were correlated, obtained correlations ranging from .03 to .55. We also have a more practical issue for model or theory building in second language writing, namely how few studies second language writing researchers have undertaken in the area of individual differences.

What I concluded from the two studies is the following: researchers basically accumulate data with little criticism of previous research and studies which focus on collecting data on a specific set of variables, individual differences, display an uncomfortable level of variability. Add to this how few studies have been undertaken in the L2 writing literature whose primary focus is IDs, and we do not have a very optimistic picture of the theory, research, practice continuum which I believe is critical if research is to have any relevance to practicing teachers.

Now to the data that will demonstrate the range of "micro" theories that have been the focus of second language writing research for the past two and a half decades. In a survey I conducted (Flahive 2004), I examined the following journals: *TESOL Quarterly (TQ)*, *Language Learning (LL)*, *The Modern Language Journal (MLJ)*, and *Journal of Second Language Writing (JSLW)*. My initial focus was on all L2 writing articles. I then determined the number of articles which I considered "research" articles, classified them according to research type, and tabulated the number of times these topics were investigated. (A brief description of this classification system is seen in the following section.) A listing and frequency of topics is seen in Tables 3 and 4. As Table 3 indicates, this survey began in 1976 and is ongoing. Table 3 displays the findings from the *TQ, LL,* and *MLJ*. Table 4 lists the results for *JSLW*.

Table 3. Topics of second language writing research found in *TESOL Quarterly, Language Learning, and the Modern Language Journal* 1976–2004

1976-85	1986-95	1996-2004
Text analysis (5)	Evaluation (6)	Text analysis (4)
Processes (3)	Processes (5)	Prompts/tasks(4)
Error evaluation (3)	Feedback /revision (4)	Processes (4)
Feedback/revision (2)	Individual differences	Evaluation (3)
T-Units (2)	Text analysis	Individual differences (2)
Evaluation	Prompts/tasks	Feedback/revision (2)
Sentence combining	Reading/writing	Transfer
Individual differences		
Total 18	Total 19	Total 20

Table 4. Research topics from the Journal of Second Language Writing: 1992–2005

1992-1997	1998-2005
Feedback/revision (18)	Feedback/revision (18)
Text analysis (8)	Text analysis (8)
Evaluation (6)	Transfer (3)
Processes (6)	Processes (2)
Prompts/tasks (4)	Plagiarism (2)
Plagiarism	Evaluation
Sentence Combining	

As one familiar with second language writing research can probably anticipate, far and away the most frequent research topic was response to essays by either teachers or by peers within the context of "group work." In the first six years of its publication, *Journal of Second Language Writing* published eighteen such articles. Since 1998 the number has added another eighteen. These figures do not include the various "debates" which have been the focus of a series of stimulus-response papers extolling or condemning the relative merits of error correction.

The evaluation of compositions has also been a constant through the years of my survey, although the numbers have been significantly reduced in recent years no doubt because of the appearance of a journal whose primary focus is writing assessment, *Assessing Writing*. We also see a major focus on text analysis, most of these consisting of contrasts between and among different types of texts be they comparisons of different genres or comparisons of learner texts versus texts produced by more advanced writers. These topics offer researchers a nearly endless range of possible combinations. Whether such open-ended research has any genuine usefulness or applicability beyond specific teaching-learning contexts in which they were conducted, I will leave for others to debate. As the tables also demonstrate, a number of topics such as plagiarism, dictionary use, and an old favorite, sentence combining, had their bright shinning moment in the research sun and never reappeared. In my professional lifetime, I have witnessed the rise, fall, and quiet burial of a multiplicity of topics ranging from EFTU (Error-Free T-Units) to sentence combining. Relatively short attention spans among researchers seem to be something of a constant through the years.

For my purposes here, I believe attempting to build upon what currently exists in the form of research topics into any type of descriptive model of L2 writing offers model builders serious challenges. Clearly, many of the topics which form the focus of L2 writing research are embedded in larger issues. Clearly, the topic of error correction is not really about error correction, but a superficial manifestation of deeper issues regarding the role of grammar and explicit grammar instruction in second language teaching and learning.

The efficacy of group work, the focus of well over a dozen studies in the 1990s in *JSLW*, whose theoretical beginnings can be traced to Vygotsky (1978), makes little mention of his theories. Equally challenging are current trends in writing research in both first and second languages where more narrative, story-telling genres are displacing more quantitative approaches. Empirical evidence of this shift is presented later in this chapter. Johanek (2000) offers a number of interesting insights to explain this preference for narrative forms of inquiry among compositionists with substantive suggestions for alternative, more inclusive approaches.

To this point, I have not raised the question of evaluating the quality of research studies on which pedagogical suggestions have been made. Nor have I mentioned the relative numbers of the different types of research studies found in the literature. This next section presents a brief evaluation metric, a classification system along with two illustrations of its use and a look at trends in second language writing research. It is these trends which I find a bit problematic in trying to promote the theory, research, practice continuum/cycle in the context I described earlier.

EVALUATION METRICS, TYPES AND TRENDS

As I mentioned earlier, pedagogical applications along with calls for further research have become part of textual conventions the reporting of second language research. Certainly pedagogical application is even more relevant in the case of second language writing, given its pragmatic goals, than in other types of second language research. Equally important is the need to build upon prior research, especially in areas where better studies conducted a decade of two earlier are sometimes of higher quality than recently published research. (I conduct these analyses in the confines of my classroom since I do not believe a public forum is an appropriate venue of such critiques.)

Below are criteria borrowed and adapted from a range of sources including *TESOL Quarterly,* a document published under the auspices of the Board of Scientific Affairs (BSA) of the American Psychological Association (Wilkinson 1999), whose focus is on establishing guidelines for the reporting of inferential statistical data, and Thompson (1993). Since I take liberties with Thompson's analyses of biochemistry articles, I highly recommend her study to those genuinely interested in the comprehensive reporting of research. Those criteria marked with a double asterisk (**) I regard as important as does the *TESOL Quarterly,* which, since 1991, "requires" this information in the reporting of studies submitted to the *Quarterly.* Those marked with a single asterisk (*), I feel are also important. Those which are unmarked may be important in some studies, but in general, are not that critical. Below is a list of criteria with explanations found in Appendix A.

Table 5. Criteria for evaluating research articles

---

1. Reliable, valid instrumentation**

2. Consistency in alpha level selection and reporting

3. Inclusion of all descriptive statistics**

4. Justification of statistical test(s)**

5. Indication that assumptions of the statistical test were met**

6. Complete source tables**

7. Confidence intervals

8. Effect size

9. Eta or omega squared computations

10. Practical versus statistical significance*

11. Agree/disagree with prior studies

12. Discrepancies in the data

13. Perplexing issues in interpretation

14. Extension of current models/theory

15. Explicit focus for future research

16. Specificity with respect to pedagogical implications

Clearly Items 1–9 relate to statistically based data. While I could expand this list and incorporate some of the suggestions for the evaluation of qualitative studies such as those found in Richards (2004), I am uncomfortable with the level of subjectivity of these metrics and leave it to others to develop appropriate metrics.

These metrics obviously need to be accompanied by a system of classification of research articles since not all apply to all types of research. This naturally raises the question of what constitutes a "research" article. With this in mind, papers which offer pedagogical advice to teachers, non-statistical research syntheses, and position papers do not, in my view, qualify as research. I then group research articles into four categories with brief descriptors (Table 6).

Table 6. Schema for classifying writing research articles

Type 1. Descriptive	
	Ethnographic Studies
	Case Studies
	Questionnaire
	Writing Processes
Type 2. Text Analysis	
	Source Comparisons
	Corpus Comparisons
	Scoring Studies
Type 3. Independent Variable Testing	
	Correlation/Regression Studies
	Causal/Comparative Studies
Type 4. Experimental	
	Quasi
	True

Table 7. Research Articles (RAs) *TESOL Quarterly,* 1985 (TQ 85)

Source: TQ 85	RA Type	1	2	3	4	5	6	7	8	9	10	11	12	13	14	15	16
27-58	3 B	/	–	–	–	–	–	–	–	–	–	/	–	–	–	/	/	/
79-102	1 B	–	–	–	–	–	–	–	–	–	–	–	–	–	–	–	+
103-123	3 B	+	–	+	–	–	+	–	–	–	–	+	–	–	+	–	+
137-151	3 B	+	–	+	+	–	–	–	–	–	–	+	–	–	–	–	+
229-258	1 C	+	–	+	–	–	–	–	–	–	–	–	–	–	+	–	+
283–301	3 C	+	–	+	/	–	+	–	–	+	–	+	–	–	–	–	+
317–334	4 O	+	–	–	–	–	–	–	–	–	–	–	–	–	–	–	+
335–351	2 B	/	–	–	–	–	+	–	–	–	–	+	–	–	–	–	+
455–474	3 B	/	–	+	–	–	–	–	–	–	–	+	/	+	+	–	+
497–513	3 B	/	/	+	+	+	+	–	–	–	–	–	–	–	–	–	+
535–556	3 C	+	–	+	+	+	+	–	–	–	–	+	–	–	–	–	+
557–584	4 C	+	–	+	+	+	+	–	–	–	–	+	–	–	–	–	+
673–688	2B	/	/	/	/	/	/	–	–	/	/	–	–	–	–	–	/
689–702	3 D	+	–	–	–	–	–	–	–	–	–	+	–	+	–	–	+
727–752	4 B	+	–	–	–	–	+	–	–	–	–	–	–	–	–	–	+
765–781	2 B	+	–	–	/	–	+	–	–	+	–	–	–	–	–	–	+

Descriptive studies:	2	Complete source tables: 8/16 (50%)
Correlation studies:	3	
Causal/Comparative studies:	8	
Hypothesis testing studies:	3	

To illustrate the use of this metric for purposes of this chapter, I selected research studies found in *TESOL Quarterly* in the years 1985 and 1995. Using the criteria above, I developed a grid to evaluate "research" articles found in the *Quarterly* in 1985 and 1995 (Tables 7 and 8). (These data are part of a larger study in which research articles found in *TESOL Quarterly, Language Learning, Studies in Second Language Acquisition,* and *The Modern Language Journal* were selected and evaluated via the metric at five-year intervals beginning in 1980 and

Table 8. Research Articles (RAs) *TESOL Quarterly,* 1995 (TQ 95)

Source: TQ 95	RA Type	1	2	3	4	5	6	7	8	9	10	11	12	13	14	15	16
33–54	1 D	/	/	+	/	/	/	/	/	/	/	/	/	/	+	–	+
55–85	4 B	+	–	+	–	–	+	–	–	–	–	–	–	–	–	–	+
107–131	1 B	/	–	+	–	–	–	–	–	–	–	+	–	–	+	–	+
235–260	1 B	/	/	/	/	/	/	/	/	/	/	/	/	/	/	/	+
261–297	2-3 B	+	–	+	+	–	–	–	–	–	–	–	–	–	+	–	+
299–322	1 D	/	/	+	+	/	/	/	/	/	/	/	/	/	/	/	/
325–343	3 O	/	/	–	–	–	–	/	/	/	/	/	/	/	+	/	/
345–373	1 B	/	/	/	/	/	/	/	/	/	/	/	/	/	/	/	+
473–504	1 B	/	/	/	/	/	/	/	/	/	/	/	/	/	/	/	/
505–537	1 B	/	/	/	/	/	/	/	/	/	/	/	/	/	/	/	/
539–568	1 B	/	/	/	/	/	/	/	/	/	/	/	/	/	/	/	/
635–661	1 C	/	/	/	/	/	/	/	/	/	/	/	/	/	/	/	/
663–686	3 C	+	–	–	+	–	+	–	–	–	–	+	–	–	–	–	+

Descriptive studies:	9	Complete source tables: 2/5 (40%)
Correlation studies:	1	
Causal/Comparative studies:	2	
Hypothesis testing studies:	1	

concluding in 2005.) *TESOL Quarterly* published guidelines for the reporting of the results of statistical research. A few words of explanation regarding the tables below I believe are necessary.) The left hand column indicates the pages of the source article. The next column indicates the Research Article type using the 1–4 classification scheme as described above.

The letters B, C, D, and O, also in the second column, are drawn from the CARS Model Described Earlier. The (+) indicate that the specific feature should be and was included. The (–) indicates the selected feature should and was not included. The (/) indicates the specific metric was not relevant. Included in Tables 5 and 6 are two samples from this extensive study. Note the trend reflected in the 10 year interval of the two samples. The most obvious is the shift from quantitative to qualitative research.

I include these more inclusive tables of all L2 research to highlight the fact that second language writing, which as I stated earlier, is a subset of the broader field of second language research and clearly reflects this qualitative trend. Note the change between 1985, where 2 descriptive studies were published, to 1995 where the number increased to 9. Causal/comparative and genuine experimental studies experienced a corresponding drop from 11 to 3. (Of additional note is the fact that despite the 1991 guidelines which specify full disclosure of statistical data, this is still not consistently done.)

As I stated earlier, the data presented here are representative overviews drawn from more comprehensive projects. Now to a graphic follow-up of my comments regarding the shift to more qualitative approaches in second language writing. Two illustrations are offered. One is based upon data from the *The Modern Language Journal* and the second drawn from second language writing research published in *Written Communication,* a journal whose primary focus is the writing of native speakers but ironically has published more second language writing research articles than publications whose focus is on second language development such as *Studies in Second Language Acquisition* and *Language Learning.* Here, once again, trends are evident. These data a drawn from a larger project where we examine trends in research types through the perspective offered by Haswell (2005), where he notes the relative decline in research which he calls RAD: replicable, additive, and data-based. Complete data are seen in Flahive and Ehlers-Zavala (2006).

In *The Modern Language Journal* (Figure 1), in the 1980–85 time period, 1 descriptive study and 4 experimental studies were published. In the 2001–05 period, 3 descriptive and no experimental studies

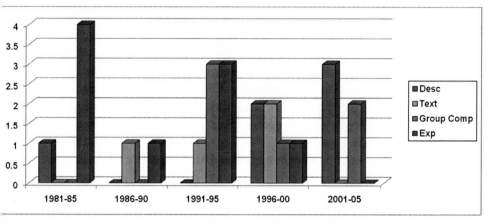

Figure.1. Trends in L2 writing research in *Modern Language Journal.*

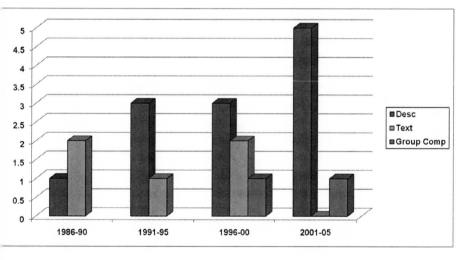

Figure 2. Trends in L2 writing research in *Written Communication*

were published. In *Written Communication* (Figure 2), descriptive studies have gone from 1–3 to 3–5 in the 5 year increments studied. Tendencies presented here reflect those in the larger study from which these two graphs are drawn.

To summarize the data presented in the previous three sections of this chapter: studies accumulate with little effort to critically test the results of previous studies, constructs involving individual differences seem to vary widely, reported research studies sometimes fail to exhibit a high level of scientific rigor, and recent trends in writing research suggest a tendency to toward more descriptive, qualitative studies and away from more experimental varieties of research. The evaluation metric is offered so as readers may decide for themselves the relative quality of specific studies. Obviously, none of the data presented above suggests optimism for those interested in or engaged in theory building or for those of us who are attempting to relate theory based research to pedagogy.

Finally, in the presentation of these data, I hope that the readers do not take my findings as being in any way conclusive, but will systematically reexamine these data and other data sources through the use or adaptation of the analytic tools I have illustrated. Naturally, all the frameworks are subject to any types of modification that might enhance their usefulness. Now we move to the analysis of PIs and FRNs as seen in second language writing research.

Pedagogical Implications and Further Research Needed Moves

As I presented data above, my approach was comprehensive within pre-selected, limited contexts. Clearly my sampling of journals was selective. My selection of topics was limited to research found in those journals. Whether of not my sampling was reflective of larger fields of inquiry is an empirical question just as in the case of any empirical research where sampling is employed. For this final portion of this chapter, I will employ similar procedures in my selection of topics and types of research. My broad focus will be on the study of feedback. Note the list of references which appear below. One cannot help but note the impressive number of studies devoted to the study of responding to student texts. In the classification system, which is found at the top of the listing of the references from the *JSLW*, I have attempted to sort these studies into categories. Clearly, the two which stand out are those which focus on teacher generated error correction (EC) and those which focus on peer-group feedback (G). Those marked (TF) are studies where feedback is the focus but there is generally an interplay between form and content feedback. Those marked with an (O) are more concerned about the topic of feedback than by offering specific information concerning types of feedback.

I will divide my illustrations of PIs and FRNs into two parts: the first portion will examine the evolution of one subtopic of feedback, namely error correction. Here I begin with the classic study conducted in 1986 by Robb, Ross and Shortreed, and use it as a metric by which to judge more contemporary studies on error correction. The second will look at the topic of group work with a specific focus on revision. Here I use a different set of criteria. They are found at the bottom of Table 10. My focus will be on one journal, the *Journal of Second Language Writing*. Once again, I offer snapshots in the hopes that researchers will engage in further explorations of the issues the data raise.

Table 9. Empirical/Experimental studies of the efficacy of error-correction

Study	Subjects	Design	Duration	Treatments Described	Pre-Post Task
Robb, Ross & Shortreed (1986)	134 Japanese EFL	4-groups	8 months	Yes	Yes

PI: Could not demonstrate value of error correction and suggested that teachers attend to other matters.

FRN: No mention

| Ferris et al. (1997) | 47 Adv ESL | 3-groups | 2 semesters | Yes, but no differential treatment | Yes |

PI: Feedback schema might be useful for teachers. Adjust feedback to students' needs.

FRN: Try suggested feedback method in differing contexts with differing levels of learners.

| Ashwell (2000) | 50 Japanese EFL | 2-groups counter-balanced | 7 months | Yes | Yes |

PI: Students may not have been ready for the experimental task demands. Ultimately, teachers need to facilitate revising skills in students.

FRN: Multiple design problems. Issues of reliability and the fact that the experimenter was also the principal investigator confounded results of the study.

Study	Subjects	Design	Duration	Treatments Described	Pre-Post Task
Fazio (2001)	5th graders (46 majority, 66 minority)	2 groups random assignment	4 months	Yes	Yes

PI: Generally error correction is ineffective, but possibly because of student inattentiveness.

FRN: Differing learning environments and differing classroom orientations need to be considered.

Chandler (2003)	36 "East Asians"	2 groups	10 weeks	Yes	Yes

PI: Improvement on all measures including accuracy.

FRN: No critical assessment of findings.

Bitchener et al. (2005)	53 migrants	4 groups	12 weeks	Yes	Yes

PI: Improvement on selected target structures. No improvement on others.

FRN: Compare treatable vs. non treatable errors with varied feedback options.

Note: All studies employed quasi-experimental designs.

Table 10. Studies of Group Work

Study	Subjects	Design	Measure of Effectiveness	Theory	RAD Replicable, Aggregate, Data-Driven
Nelson & Murphy (1992)	4 ESL	1	N	N	R

PI: Include teacher as part of group; shift group membership; training of members of group. Researchers were vague as to what type of training was done.

FRN: More research on the factors mentioned in PIs.

Stanley (1992)	31 ESL	4	Y	N	RD

PI: Training in peer editing appears to work; Training takes time.

FRN: Not mentioned

Mangelsdorf & Schlumberger (1992)	60 ESL	1	N	N	RD

PI: None

FRN: Need to take decontextualized task into classroom with real peers; Examine interaction between classroom context and peer review stances

Study	Subjects	Design	Measure of Effectiveness	Theory	RAD Replicable, Aggregate, Data-Driven
Hedgcock & Lefkowitz (1992)	30 NS Learners	4	Y	Y	RD

PI: Peer oral revision works as well as teacher commentary; verbalization may promote "noticing" and hence facilitate revision

FRN: Samples used may not have been equal. No suggestions for follow up research.

Connor & Asenavage (1994)	8 ESL	2	Y	N	RD

FI: Long-term effects are difficult to assess. Need to clarify what students need to focus on; More extensive training. Comments could be made prior to review session. Prior experience needs to be taken into account. Teacher involvement is important

FRN: Use of think-aloud protocols and their effect on revision might be useful to give teachers a clearer picture of decision-making strategies as well as the relative importance students give to comments by peers and teachers.

Zhang (1995)	81 "Asian" subjects	1	N	N	RD

PI: None. Suggestion that "imported" L1 theories may not be relevant/useful to L2 writing contents, specifically with students from "Asian" cultures.

FRN: Study underway to examine the differential effects of differing types of feedback.

Carson & Nelson (1996)	11 ESL	1	N	N	RA

PI: Chinese students reluctant to criticize peer writing.

FRN: How does gender impact peer group behavior? Would indirect criticism be understood by learners with differing communication styles?

Villamil & De Guerro (1996)	54 ESL, L1 Spanish	1	N	Y	—

PI: Peer work gives students an opportunity for students to explore their limitations and potential.

FRN: Follow up quantitative study to explore impact of revisions on writing quality.

Study	Subjects	Design	Measure of Effectiveness	Theory	RAD Replicable, Aggregate, Data-Driven
Nelson & Carson (1998)	5 ESL (3 Chinese, 2 Spanish)	1	N	N	RA

PI: Peer work not really useful when problems not specifically identified. Cultural differences exist.

FRN: Compare usefulness of teacher versus peer responses.

Berg (1999)	46 ESL	4	Y	N	RD

PI: Peer response can be useful given the fact that training is essential.

FRN: Look at differences between trained and untrained negotiations. Determine which portions of training program were differentially effective. Is there a washback effect on students' own writing?

Paulus (1999)	11 ESL	4	Y	N	RD

PI: Commentary by teacher is more important than peer commentary.

FRN: Teacher as researchers may have influenced results. Limited inter-rater reliability.

Tsui & Ng (2000)	27 secondary EFL	Mixed	N	N	RD

PI: Oral and written feedback useful to students. Teachers need to share responsibility with students.

FRN: None

* Designs are described in Table 2. Measure of effectiveness indicates whether writing actually improved. Theory indicates whether a brief mention was made of Vygotsky. RAD indicates whether the study was replicable, the findings were aggregate, namely building upon prior studies to either confirm or disconfirm previous findings, and whether the research resulted in quantifiable data.

PIS AND FRNS IN TEACHER FEEDBACK RESEARCH

Given the fact that the topic of feedback and a subset of this topic, error correction, are among the most widely researched topics in second language writing research, it is only appropriate that I highlight studies whose focus is feedback/error correction for my analysis of PIs and FRNs. In order to avoid being accused of taking gratuitous cheap shorts directed toward specific studies, I will observe the chronological perspective of the earlier studies I cited and limit my focus to those found in the journal where the majority of recent studies of this topic are found, the *Journal of Second Language Writing*.

While there are many differences in the experimental designs and measurements of dependent variables among researchers who conduct error correction research, the one constant is the citing of Robb, Ross and Shortreed (1886). The study included an N size of 134 allocated to 4 treatment groups. The four treatments were reasonably well described and the instructor variable reasonably controlled. The study took place over a period of 8 months. Dependent variables were explicitly delineated. Explanation of results was totally consistent with findings. The only glaring weakness was the absence of a No-treatment control group.

What struck me about this study was the scientific detachment of the researchers. In both the design and reporting of the findings, researchers appeared to have little personal stake in the possible outcomes of the study. With the design of this study which I used to extract comparable categories, I present an overview of studies with a similar focus taken chronologically from the *JSLW*. These EC studies are found in Table 9 with brief samples taken from PIs and FRNs included in the Table. Table 9 summarizes five studies which appeared during the years of this study. Each has been conducted in a different setting with highly divergent L2 learners. Each employs a wide range of independent and dependent variables. None makes mention of theoretical underpinnings related to second language acquisition. I am assuming here that clearly issues related to second language acquisition are implicated in responding to student errors. Of note is the fact that we find as many "commentaries" in the *JSLW* related to the relative value of error correction as we do studies that examine its effectiveness. These are the entries marked EC-C.

When I create these "overviews" of a specific topic of research for my students, such as the ones found in Tables 9 and 10, I remind them of the fact that despite assurances from self-appointed pundits that second language studies is a "maturing" field, true maturity can only come through a focus on theoretically based research and a healthy amount of self-criticism. One-shot, atheoretical studies such as we find filling the pages of second language research journals offer little to energize the practices of teachers or little to promote the field as one where important research is taking place.

Would not a process where a researcher builds upon a previous study with a view toward controlling for the uncontrolled variables in the initial study add a needed degree of scientific rigor to current research practices? Given the information presented on Table 9, it would be relatively easy to conclude that several of the studies would serve as "pilot" studies and not publishable research findings.

Instead of these flawed "dangling data collections efforts," why not begin with the initial study and, in the same manuscript, do a follow up, more tightly controlled study to both strengthen and possibly broaden the generalizability of the findings. Would it not also be useful to start a study with a sample size which could be minimally generalizable instead of pointing out sample size limitations? Proponents of "power analysis" have been advocating this since Cohen (1987). Then, only after two to three related studies were completed would the researcher(s) submit the article for publication. If this sounds familiar to those of us who read psycholinguistic journals, this is what I am also suggesting for the reporting of L2 research in general and L2 writing in particular.

Table 10 provides brief overviews of "group work" studies. Given the dates of these studies, I believe we could look back at the 90s as the "golden age" of group work. What I found interesting about this line of research was the notable non-mention of the theoretical underpinnings provided by the work of Vygotsky (1986). It would seem clear to anyone with a nodding familiarity with his work of the central notion of "scaffolding." Without this potential for scaffolding, would not the use of group work with relatively homogeneous clusters of students seem highly problematic? The reader is invited to examine the original studies to see whether or not I am being overly critical in suggesting that the theoretical underpinnings for group work were basically left out of the initial designs of many of these studies.

Now back to where I began, to my role as a teacher-trainer attempting to integrate research and theory into pedagogical practice. In writing up pedagogical implications, would not a brief mention of the theoretical underpinnings of the study be useful? Would not a pointing out of the possible limitations related to specific teaching/ learning contexts be equally useful? Instead of pointing out the methodological flaws of a one-shot effort, wouldn't the cumulative results to two to three integrated studies be more pedagogically and theoretically useful?

I end with several questions relevant to the issues I have raised. While we all recognize the value of our private micro theories in the absence of a generalized macro theory, shouldn't the explicit testing of these clearly delineated micro theories be the focal point of every research effort we undertake? Although the term "theory" has been affixed to an eclectic array of terms, how may of these terms lend themselves to testable hypotheses? Within the field of second language writing, how many of the topics that researchers have addressed can be considered theoretically motivated? Is there a discernable trend away from theoretically motivated research to more anecdotal reports of what is taking place in specific teaching/learning contexts?

References

Balloffet, S. (1996). *Gender approaches to research.* Unpublished master's thesis, Colorado State University, Fort Collins, Colorado.

Cohen, J. (1987). *Power Analysis* (revised). Hillsdale, NJ: Erlbaum.

Flahive, D., & Ehlers-Zavala, F. (June, 2006). Tracing writing epistemologies in flagship journals. Paper presented at the annual meeting of the American Association of Applied Linguisitics, Montreal, Canada.

Flahive, D. (April, 2004). Ways of knowing in second language writing research. Paper presented at the annual TESOL Convention, Long Beach, CA.

Flahive, D., & Dahlman, A. (April, 2003). A meta-analysis of individual difference research in second language acquisition research. Paper presented at the annual TESOL Convention, Salt Lake City, Utah.

Flahive, D., & Balloffet, S. (April, 1997). Finding a niche in second language acquisition research. Paper presented at annual meeting of the American Association of Applied Lingustics, Orlando, Florida.

Grabe, W. (2001). Toward a theory of second language writing. In T. Silva and P.K. Matsuda (Eds.) *On Second Language Writing* (pp..39–57) Mahwah, NJ: Erlbaum.

Grabe,W., & Kaplan, R. (1996). *Theory & Practice of Writing.* Harlow, UK: Addison Wesley Longman.

Haswell, R. (2005) NCTE/CCCC's recent war on scholarship. *Written Communication, 22*(2), pp. 198–223.

Johanek, C. (2000). *Composing research: A contextualist paradigm for rhetoric and composition.* Logan, UT: Utah State University Press.

Larsen-Freeman, D., & Long, M. (1993) *An introduction to second language acquisition research.* New York: Longman.

Masgoret, A.-M., & Gardner, R.C. (2003). Attitudes, motivation, and second language learning: A meta-analysis of studies conducted by Gardner and associates. *Language Learning, 53*(1) pp. 123–163.

Richards, K. (2003). *Qualitative inquiry in TESOL.* New York: Palgrave MacMillan,

Robb, T, Ross, S., & Shortreed, I. (1986). Salience of feedback on error and its effect on EFL writing quality. *TESOL Quarterly, 20,*(1), 83–95.

Schumann, J. (1983). Art and science in second language acquisition research. In M.Clarke & J. Hanscombe (Eds.), *On TESOL'82: Pacific perspectives on language learning and teaching* (pp.107–124). Washington, DC: Teachers of English to Speakers of Other Languages.

Spolsky, B. (1989). *Conditions for second language learning.* New York: Oxford University Press.

Swales, J. (1990). *Genre analysis.* New York: Cambridge University Press.

Swales, J. (1988). 20 years of the *TESOL Quarterly. TESOL Quarterly, 22*(1), 151–163.

Thompson, D.(1993). Arguing for experimental "facts" in science: A study of research article results in biochemistry. *Written Communication, 8*(1), 106–128.

Vygotsky, L.S. (1978). *Mind in society: The development of higher psychological processes.* (A. Kozulin, Rev. Trans., Ed). Cambridge MA: Harvard University Press.

Wilkinson, L. (1999). Statistical methods in psychology journals: Guidelines and explanations. *American Psychologist 54*(8), 594–604.

FEEDBACK REFERENCE ADDENDUM

Revision/feedback-focused studies found in *The Journal of Second Language Writing 1992–2000.* (EC = major focus on error correction; EC-C = commentary about usefulness of EC, G = group work, FT = teacher feedback O = other, not fit into major categories)

Ashwell, T. (2000). Patterns of teacher response to student writing in a multiple-draft composition classroom: Is content feedback followed by form feedback the best method? *Journal of Second Language Writing, 9* (3), 227–257. (EC)

Berg, E. C. (1999). The effects of trained peer response on ESL students' revision types and writing quality. *Journal of Second Language Writing, 8*(3), 215–241(G)

Bitchener, J., Young, S., & Cameron, D. (2005). The effects of different types of corrective feedback on ESL student writing. *Journal of Second Language Writing, 14*(3), 191-.205. (EC)

Brock, M. N. (1993). Three disk-based text analyzers and the ESL writer. *Journal of Second Language Writing, 2*(1), 19–40. (O)

Carson, J.G., & Nelson, G.L. (1994). Writing groups: Cross-cultural issues. *Journal of Second Language Writing, 3*(1), 17–30. (G)

Carson, J.G. & Nelson, G.L. (1996). Chinese students' perceptions of ESL peer response group interaction. *Journal of Second Language Writing, 5*(1), 1–19. (G)

Chandler, J. (2003). The efficiency of various kinds of error feedback for improvement in the accuracy and fluency of L2 student writing. *Journal of Second Language Writing, 12*(3), 267–296. (EC)

Chandler, J. (2004). A response to Truscott. *Journal of Second Language Writing, 13*(4), 345–348. (EC-C)

Conrad, S.M., & Goldstein, L.M. (1999). ESL student revision after teacher-written comments: Text, contexts, and individuals. *Journal of Second Language Writing, 8*(2), 147–179. (EC)

Connor, U., & Asenavage, K. (1994). Peer response groups in ESL writing classes: How much impact on revision? *Journal of Second Language Writing, 3*(3), 257–276. (G)

Fazio, L.L. (2001). The effect of corrections and commentaries on the journal writing accuracy of minority and majority language students. *Journal of Second Language Writing, 10*(4), 235–249. (EC)

Ferris, D.R., Pezone, S., Tade, C.R., & Tinti, S. (1997). Teacher commentary on student writing: Descriptions & implications. *Journal of Second Language Writing, 6*(2), 155–182. (EC)

Ferris, D. (1999). The case for grammar correction in L2 writing classes: A response to Truscott. *Journal of Second Language Writing, 8*(1), 1–11. (EC-C)

Ferris, D., & Roberts, B. (2001). Error feedback in L2 writing classes: How explicit does it need to be? *Journal of Second Language Writing, 10*(3), 161–184. (EC)

Ferris, D.R. (2004). The "grammar correction" debate in L2 writing: Where are we, and where do we go from here? (and what do we do in the meantime . . . ?) *Journal of Second Language Writing, 13*(1), 49–62. (EC-C)

Goldstein, L.M. (2004). Questions and answers about teacher written commentary and student revision: Teachers and students working together. *Journal of Second Language Writing, 13*(1), 63–80. (G)

Hedgcock, J., & Lefkowitz, N. (1992). Collaborative oral/aural revision in foreign language writing instruction. *Journal of Second Language Writing, 1*(3), 255–276. (G)

Hedgcock, J., & Lefkowitz, N. (1994). Feedback on feedback: Assessing learner receptivity to teacher response in L2 composing. *Journal of Second Language Writing, 3*(2), 141–163. (O)

Hyland, F. (1998). The impact of teacher written feedback on individual writers. *Journal of Second Language Writing, 7*(3), 255–286. (TF)

Hyland, F., & Hyland, K. (2001). Sugaring the pill: Praise and criticism in written feedback. *Journal of Second Language Writing, 10*(3), 185–212. (TF)

Jacobs, G.M., Curtis, A., Braine, G., & Huang, S.Y. (1998). Feedback on student writing: Taking the middle path. *Journal of Second Language Writing, 7*(3), 307–317.

Johns, A. (2004) Searching for answers: Response. *Journal of Second Language Writing, 13*(1) 81–85. (O)

Lee, I. (2004). Error correction in L2 secondary writing classrooms: The case of Hong Kong. *Journal of Second Language Writing, 13*(4), 285–312. (EC)

Mangelsdorf, K. & Schlumberger, A. (1992). ESL Student response stances in a peer-review task. *Journal of Second Language Writing, 1*(3), 235–254. (G)

Nelson, G.L. & Murphy, J.M. (1992). An L2 writing group: Task and social dimensions. *Journal of Second Language Writing, 1*(3), 171–193. (G)

Nelson, G., & Carson, J.G. (1998). ESL Students' perceptions of effectiveness in peer response groups. *Journal of Second Language Writing, 7*(2), 113–131. (G)

Paulus, T.M. (1999). The effect of peer and teacher feedback on student writing. *Journal of Second Language Writing, 8*(3), 265–289. (G)

Phinney, M., & Khouri, S. (1993). Computers, revision, and ESL writers: The role of experience. *Journal of Second Language Writing, 2*(3), 257–277. (O)

Polio, C., Fleck, C., & Leder, N. (1998). "If I only had more time": ESL Learners' changes in linguistic accuracy on essay revisions. *Journal of Second Language Writing, 7* (1), 43–68. (O)

Porte, G.K. (1997). The etiology of poor second language writing: The influence of perceived teacher preferences on second language revision strategies. *Journal of Second Language Writing, 6*(1), 61–78. (O)

Stanley, J. (1992). Coaching student writers to be effective peer evaluators. *Journal of Second Language Writing, 1*(3), 217–234. (G)

Truscott, J. (1999). The case for "the case against grammar correction in L2 writing classes": A response to Ferris. *Journal of Second Language Writing, 8*(2), 111–1220. (EC-C)

Truscott, J. (2004) Evidence and conjecture on the effects of correction: A response to Chandler. *Journal of Second Language Writing, 13*(4), 337–343. (EC-C)

Tsui, A.B.M., & Ng, M. (2000). Do secondary L2 writers benefit from peer comments? *Journal of Second Language Writing, 9*(2), 147–170. (G)

Villamil, O.S. & de Guerrero, M.C.M. (1996). Peer revision in the classroom: Social-cognitive activities, mediating strategies, and aspects of social behavior. *Journal of Second Language Writing, 5*(1), 51–75. (G)

Weigle, S.C. & Nelson, G.L. (2004). Novice tutors and their ESL tutees: Three case studies of tutor roles and perceptions of tutorial success. *Journal of Second Language Writing, 13* (3), 203–225. (O)

Williams, J. (2004). Tutoring and revision: Second language writers in the writing center. *Journal of Second Language Writing, 13*(3), 173–201. (0)

Yates. R., & Kenkel, J. (2002). Responding to sentence-level errors in writing. *Journal of Second Language Writing, 11*(1), 29–47. (0)

Zhang, S. (1995). Reexaming the affective advantage of peer feedback in the ESL writing class. *Journal of Second Language Writing, 4*(3), 209–222. (G)

Zhang, S. (1999). Thoughts on some recent evidence concerning the affective advantage of peer feedback. *Journal of Second Language Writing, 8*(3), 321–326. (G-C)

Zhu, W. (2001). Interaction and feedback in mixed peer response groups. *Journal of Second Language Writing, 10*(4), 251–276

Appendix A

1. Reliable, valid instrumentation.** All studies which explore differences require a measurable dependent variable. It could be a global measure of language proficiency. It could be something more specific such as a limited range of target linguistic structures whose acquisition is measured by a test designed specifically for the study. You can be reasonably sure that if the reliability coefficient for the instrument is not reported, it hasn't been calculated. Since reliability is related to the number of test items, you should be suspicious of measurements of the dependent variable with fewer than 20 items. A reliability level of .70 or less should lead readers to question results. Reliability levels in the low .90s are about as good as it gets in attempting to measure the constructs in our field.

2. Consistency in alpha level selection and reporting. The selection of an alpha level is a cost/benefit decision made by the researcher. Given the fact that few studies state "a priori" alpha levels, a formality largely limited to theses and dissertations, we can assume that researchers simply report what a computer printout indicates, even $p < .000$. It would be something of a scientific breakthrough if researchers would simply report significance levels at .05 or .01 and eliminate the rhetorical intensifiers such as "very," "highly," and on more than one occasion, "extremely" before the word "significant." Statistical significance should be looked upon as a binary concept, either the obtained value exceeds the critical or tabled value or it does not, and hence the statistical test resulted in a significant or non- significant result.

3. *Inclusion of all descriptive statistics**.* Here simple means and standard deviations with ranges and, if appropriate, maximum possible score. It might be also useful to mention whether the test produced "outliers," scores that went beyond group tendencies. It would not be inappropriate to exclude outliers from the analysis if this procedure were pointed out to the reader.

4. *Justification of Statistical Test(s)**.* Over two decades ago, a number of statisticians were predicting the demise of the use of ANOVAS in research. Their suggested substitute was the General Linear Model. Their reasoning is that the same information regarding the role of independent variables in predicting outcomes could be presented in a more transparent manner. Although some statistical packages have transitioned to GLM, ANOVAs still are ubiquitous in applied linguistics research. In many studies, data can be analyzed in more than one way. It would be a refreshing change if these options were discussed in the research.

5. *Indication that assumptions of the statistical test were met**.* Parametric tests require homogeneous variances. Once again, these tests are available on all statistical packages. Regression studies assume that predictor variables are not highly correlated.

6. *Complete source tables**.* For ANOVAs this should include the Between, the Within and the Total Sum of Squares. This information makes it possible for the reader to compute eta or omega squared statistic.

7. *Confidence intervals.* In a world of less than precise operationalization of constructs and hence measurement instruments, confidence intervals provide an additional useful measurement. In a prediction model, the range of the predicted variable gives a reader a useful metric by which to evaluate the strength of the model.

8. *Effect size*.* This allows the reader to determine the relative importance of significant findings. In recent years, *Language Learning* has

required researchers to publish effect sizes. Unfortunately, other publications in the field have not followed *Language Learning's* lead. For a simple, somewhat biased measure of effect size, the following formula is adequate.

$$d = \frac{\text{Mean}_{\text{Experimental}} - \text{Mean}_{\text{Control}}}{\text{SD}_{\text{Control}}}$$

$$= \frac{32-27}{2}$$

$$= 2.5$$

If the experimental group obtains a mean of 32, and the mean of the control is 27 with a SD of 2, the effect size would be 2.5. This measure is a unit normal distribution with a mean of 0 and a standard deviation of 1. So the effect size of d = 2.5 would be considered very large.

ES estimates for d = .20 for a small effect
.50 for a medium effect
.80 for a large effect

So an effect size of less than one standard deviation is considered large. Be wary of reported effect sizes that are overly large. Consider the treatment given the Controls. Could they better have been labeled the "Benign Neglect" group?

For correlation studies, the effect size is the simple *r*.

ES estimates for r = .10 for small
.30 for medium
.50 for large

9. *Eta or omega squared computations**. Simply divide the Sums of Squares found in the Independent variable(s) by the total Sum of Squares for the omega squared. This is an oversimplified but useful index of the variance accounted for.

10. *Practical versus statistical significance***. This is a determination where the researcher and the reader may have differences. Given the information regarding effect size, variance accounted for, as well as a number of non-statistical considerations, the reader is in a relatively good position to make an informed critical judgment as to the practical importance of a finding. We may have a case of a researcher high-

lighting the theoretical or pedagogical importance of a finding where a mere 5 percent of the variance is accounted for. A critical reader may come to a different conclusion.

11. *Agree/disagree with prior studies**. Here, simply look for a discussion of agreement or disagreement with prior findings. Naturally, if the researcher has conducted similar studies and the research study you are reading has similar results, you will certainly be informed. If there are no prior similar studies, there is not much to discuss.

12. *Discrepancies in the data.* It would be difficult to predict what these might be for any particular study. Certainly there could be outliers as mentioned above. Distributions could be bi-modal—that is, two different distributions.

13. *Perplexing issues in interpretation**. In my discussion with researchers, these are common but never reported. It goes to the fiction that research studies are to be simply objective reporting of unmitigated scientific truth. Discussing perplexing issues would be of great benefit to those reading the study whose purpose would possibly be an attempted replication. These discussions would also be of benefit for future researchers in the field who would be apprised to the realities of research.

14. *Extension of current models/theory**. Here we have a need for researchers to transition from the little picture of a specific study to the larger mosaic of a possibly more abstract theoretical model of learning or teaching and just where this particular study might fit into a bigger picture.

15. *Potential for falsification**. If the researcher is confident in the findings, a few suggestions as to how the findings might be falsified might be instructive. On the other hand, if a study does not have the potential for falsification, is it really good research?

16. *Pedagogical implications**. Whether justified or not, pedagogical implications appear to be a necessity in language learning research. If the researcher feels it is necessary to include the mention of pedagogical implications, it is incumbent on that researcher to discuss the issue in some depth rather than a patronizing mention.

8 Beyond Texts: A Research Agenda for Quantitative Research on Second Language Writers and Readers

Dudley W. Reynolds

Discussions of how research translates into theory frequently address the impact of methodologies and epistemologies (Ortega, 2005b; Silva & Leki, 2004). Smagorinsky (2006a), for example, links recent advances in composition theory to research that relies on more than just "the traditions of the hard sciences" (p. 4). It can be argued, however, that even in its infancy second language writing research is already characterized by a healthy mix of methodologies borrowed from our diverse disciplinary ancestors (Silva & Leki, 2004). Moreover, as a number of educational researchers have recently argued (Eisenhart & DeHaan, 2005; Hostetler, 2005; Ortega, 2005a; Siegel, 2006), discussions of methodology and epistemology must not be allowed to sidetrack discussions of what we know and what we value. As a means of keeping the focus on how second language writing research models what we know and value, the following discussion limits its scope to a single methodological orientation—quantitative research. It will be argued that at a time when political authorities around the world are equating quantitative approaches with "scientifically based research" (National Research Council, 2002; "No Child Left Behind Act," 2001), it is of crucial importance to consider not only the findings of such research but also the questions it asks, the variables it considers, and the relations it investigates.

Another way of phrasing the central question of this chapter is, how does quantitative research on second language writing operationally define the object of its inquiry? I would argue that the phrase "second language writing" refers to something akin to an enterprise. It is the process of writers embedded in cultures and societies using a language that is not their first to engage with tasks, ideas, instruction, and potential readers to produce texts that engender affective reactions. Clearly there are a multitude of entities and potential relations in this gloss. Second language writing is—and should be depicted as—a complex entity. The way in which our research designs model this enterprise is therefore of crucial importance precisely because of their implications for conceptions of reality.

Quantitative research is frequently criticized for essentializing complex entities as variables and then further simplifying them by characterizing relations between only those entities identified as variables. Thus a study that compares the length of papers written by students in a core university composition class for nonnative speakers with the length of papers written by students in a general core composition class risks the trivialization of both the learning goals for those classes and the identities of the students in them. As teachers, we rarely comment on paper length, and we also know that when it comes to writing quality a native/nonnative dichotomy is only one of many potential influences. To be fair, however, numerous studies have shown paper length to be a good predictor of affective reader judgments (Wolfe-Quintero et al., 1998), and it is possible to include measures of effect size that will indicate how much of the differences in paper length we have and have not explained.[1] Thus, I am not really concerned here about trivialization through the use of variables to represent constructs or the limitations of statistical inferencing.

I am more concerned about the reality implicit in the design of this hypothetical study. I am concerned that it prioritizes the written product as the goal and ultimate measure of a writing class. I am concerned that there is no chance to see how the native/nonnative distinction stacks up against how many years of L2 education the students had and in which educational systems and whether they were asked to summarize, compare, or critique. On a larger scale, I am concerned that this type of setting is much more likely to be studied than a group writing activity in an MBA program, consulting sessions in a writing center, or the job application review process for an adult immigrant. One reason I am concerned is because educational policy makers, faced with increasing demand in an era of limited resources, want something they refer to as "scientifically based research"—research that prioritizes quantitative measurement over qualitative interpretation and experimental or quasi-experimental designs over exploratory and case study designs (Kamil, 2004; National Research Council, 2002; Slavin, 2003). I am concerned about the view of reality we give these policy makers.

Because my concerns too need to be grounded in a picture of reality, I have undertaken a study of the focus and stance towards knowledge-building represented in quantitative second language writing research published between 2001 and 2005. The principal questions addressed by the study are:

1. What is the relative distribution of quantitative, qualitative, and mixed-method approaches to inquiry?

2. Among studies employing quantitative measures (solely or as part of a mixed-method design), what is the relative distribution of studies where the variable(s) in focus measured attributes of writing, writers, readers, or multiple entities?

3. Among studies employing quantitative measures (solely or as part of a mixed-method design), what is the relative distribution of studies whose purpose is descriptive, hypothesis-testing, exploratory, and case study?

METHOD

Selection of Journals and Articles

Using lists of journals published as part of the 2004 TESOL Research Agenda (Borg, Curtis, Davison, Han, Reynolds, & Scovel, 2004) and Smagorinsky's recent overview of composition studies (2006a), 15 applied linguistic and composition journals were identified as likely to include empirical studies related to second language writing. They comprised one journal solely dedicated to the field (*Journal of Second Language Writing*), five journals oriented towards applied linguistics in general (*Applied Linguistics, Canadian Modern Language Review, Language Learning, The Modern Language Journal, System,* and *TESOL Quarterly*), two specialized journals within applied linguistics (*Journal of English for Academic Purposes* and *World Englishes*), three assessment journals (*Assessing Writing, Language Assessment Quarterly,* and *Language Testing*), and three composition journals (*Journal of Basic Writing, Research in the Teaching of English,* and *Written Communication*).[2]

To select articles for inclusion in the study's database, the table of contents of each issue with a publication year in the period 2001–2005 (N = 265) was reviewed. Where the title indicated a possibility that the article might deal with second language writing, the abstract (and if necessary, the article itself) was then reviewed to decide whether it presented empirical research related to individuals writing in a second language, their texts, and/or their readers' reactions. Theoretically-oriented literature reviews as well as empirical studies where the data were associated exclusively with first language writers (e.g., studies describing target genres) or multilingual writers' published texts (e.g., novels by a world English speaker) were excluded. Out of approximately 1290 articles published in the journals during this period, 133, or roughly 10 percent, were identified as meeting the criterion for inclusion.[3]

ANALYSIS

Each article in the database was coded for the method of inquiry and, if it was determined to be using quantitative measures, then the entities it put into focus and the purpose of the study. All codings were done by the author and generally required a review of the method, analysis, and results sections of the article unless the abstract was sufficiently explicit to obviate the need for this.

Method of Inquiry

Three method categories were identified: qualitative, quantitative, and mixed. The distinction between qualitative and quantitative rested on whether numerical measures of the data were used as a primary justification for the interpretations presented.[4] Mixed studies employed both quantitative and qualitative data assessments.

Focus Entities

Identification. The entities in focus in a study are the object(s) of its description. Identification of the focus entity was clearest in studies where the distribution of a single variable was being described. In studies with dependent and independent variables, the dependent variable(s) constituted the focus entity. Although explanatory or independent variables are usually studied for the significance of their relation to the dependent variable(s), the positioning of the entities implicit in the two labels suggests that the dependent measure is what learning to write should affect. In exploratory studies using procedures such as factor analysis or cluster analysis, the variable used as input to the procedure (e.g., survey responses or frequency of linguistic structures) was identified. In studies relying solely on correlations (e.g., Helms-Park & Stapleton, 2003), all variables were considered to be focus entities.

Coding. Once the entities were identified, each study was coded for whether it focused on: 1) writing, 2) writers, 3) readers, or 4) multiple categories.

1. Writing. Two types of studies focusing on writing were identified. The first relied on measures of textual characteristics including fluency, accuracy, and/or development (for a comprehensive listing, see Wolfe-Quintero et al., 1998), discourse features (e.g., K. Hyland, 2003), linguistic features (e.g., Jarvis et al., 2003), and/or ratings of textual traits such as voice (e.g., McCarthey et al., 2005). The other type of writing study focused on ratings of writing quality (e.g., Schoonen et al., 2003). Although such ratings are technically the product of readers and often stand-in for a writer's general composing ability, they are usually based on single texts and are used to distinguish between the texts as opposed to the readers.

2. Writers. These studies relied on measures derived from think-aloud protocols (e.g., Wang, 2003), attitudinal surveys (e.g., Stapleton, 2005), and tests of cognitive abilities (e.g. Snellings et al., 2004).[5]

3. Readers.[6] Two types of reader-focused studies were identified in the data. The first relied solely on measures derived from reader reactions either in the form of written feedback (e.g., F. Hyland & K. Hyland, 2001) or comments produced as part of think-aloud protocols (e.g., Cumming et al., 2002). The second type relied on measures of readers directly interacting with writers (e.g., Zhu, 2001).

4. Multiple. This category included studies such as Sasaki's (2004) longitudinal investigation of changes in the writing and writer

behavior of Japanese learners of English or Liu and Sadler's (2003) descriptive reporting of comments made by peer reviewers and subsequent changes to texts in technology- and non-technology-mediated classrooms.

Study Purpose

Finally, each article was also categorized according to whether its primary purpose was *descriptive, hypothesis-testing, exploratory,* or *exploration through case study* design.[7] Broadly construed, the goal of empirical research is to either establish or discover relations. Descriptive and hypothesis-testing studies seek to establish pre-determined relations as real or unreal, whereas exploratory and case studies emphasize discovery of new relations. Categorization of study purpose was based on any stated research questions and the presentation of the results.

1. *Descriptive.* In these studies, the distribution of the data across a range of categories is reported. The selection of categories and the data's assignment to them is determined by the researcher. An example of this type of study is K. Hyland's (2003) description of the characteristics of English dissertation acknowledgments written by graduate students in Hong Kong.

2. *Hypothesis-testing.* In contrast to descriptive studies where the relations are simply identified by the researcher, hypothesis-testing studies rely on statistical procedures usually involving significance testing to verify assumed relations. Thus Elder, Knoch, Barkhuizen, and von Randow (2005) posit that providing raters with feedback on how much they agree with other raters will increase intragroup consistency, and they use changes in scores derived from a multifaceted Rasch analysis to verify the assumption.

3. *Exploratory.* Exploratory studies also rely on statistical procedures but not strictly to verify assumptions. They may use techniques such as exploratory factor analysis, cluster analysis and discriminant analysis (e.g., Jarvis et al., 2003), which seek to find relations among very large data sets, or structural equation modeling (e.g., Schoonen et al., 2003), which works to find the best model for how a complex set of variables is related.[8] They may also use combinations of statistical procedures. Esmaeili

(2002), for example, explored relations between content knowledge, writing performance and reading performance using differences between test scores as well as the distribution of different test strategies to identify relations in both the testing process and products.

4. *Case study.* In contrast to the three other categories, the label "case study" reflects the type of data being analyzed more than the purpose of the study. Nevertheless, case studies are separated out as a special type of exploratory research because they exploit the richness of detail possible with a limited data set to suggest relations that may not be readily apparent with more macro-level analyses. They are distinguished by the reporting of findings for individual entities (be they people, papers, or interactions) as a basis for general conclusions. Thus, Williams (2004) uses measures derived from the interaction between writing consultants and five English as a second language writers along with quality ratings of the students' texts to suggest, for example, that a relation exists between what gets talked about in the consulting session and what the students change in their papers.

RESULTS

The first research question addresses the relative distribution of qualitative, quantitative, and mixed-method studies in the database of 133 articles presenting empirical second language writing research. A breakdown of studies by journal is shown in Table 1. Findings indicate a relatively balanced distribution of qualitative (n = 58, 44) and quantitative studies (n = 60, 45%) with a much smaller percentage of mixed-method studies (n = 15, 11%). Two journals, *Journal of Basic Writing* and *Research in the Teaching of English* published only qualitative studies related to second language writing in this period.

Table 1. Empirical Research Appearing in Surveyed Journals 2001–2005

Journal	Issues Surveyed	Empirical Studies	Mixed Method	Quantitative Methods	Qualitative Methods
Applied Linguistics	20	6	0	3	3
Assessing Writing	9	11	4	3	4

Journal	Issues Surveyed	Empirical Studies	Mixed Method	Quantitative Methods	Qualitative Methods
Canadian Modern Language Review	21	5	0	2	3
Journal of Basic Writing	10	2	0	0	2
Journal of English for Academic Purposes	18	7	0	2	5
Journal of Second Language Writing	20	42	3	20	19
Language Assessment Quarterly	8	3	1	2	0
Language Learning	20	5	1	4	0
Language Testing	20	9	1	4	4
Modern Language Journal	20	7	2	3	2
Research in the Teaching of English	20	2	0	0	2
System	20	13	3	5	5
TESOL Quarterly	20	5	0	2	3
World Englishes	19	5	0	3	2
Written Composition	20	11	0	7	4
TOTAL	265	133	15	60	58

Findings for the second research question regarding the focus of the 75 articles that use quantitative measures or a mixture of quantitative and qualitative measures are presented in Table 2. As indicated by the last column of the table, over half of the studies focus on writing (n = 39, 52%). Of these studies the majority describe textual characteristics (n = 26). The next most common foci are writers (n=14, 19%) and multiple components (n = 14, 16%). The least common foci are reader reactions and interactions (n=8, 11%). Interestingly 6 of the 8 reader studies employed a mixture of quantitative and qualitative approaches.

With respect to purpose, 62% (37/60) of purely quantitative studies involve testing hypotheses about relations between entities. Less common are descriptive (10/60, 17%) and exploratory (9/60, 15%) studies, and case studies that rely solely on quantitative measures are very rare (4/60, 7%). Among the 15 mixed method studies, however, case studies are the most common type (n = 6) followed by hypothesis-testing (n = 5) and exploratory (n = 3) studies with only one descriptive study.

As a whole, these findings suggest that, while there is a healthy balance of second language writing researchers using quantitative and qualitative methods, there are relatively few studies that combine the two approaches to inquiry. Furthermore, in research using purely quantitative approaches, there is a definite bias towards foregrounding the understanding of writing over writers or what happens when readers interact with writers or their writing. Finally, the majority of research conducted with quantitative measures seeks to establish categories and *a priori* relations identified by the researchers, either through verification of hypothesized relations or simply reporting their distributions. There is very little use of quantitative approaches to establish new categories, whether through exploratory statistical approaches or case studies.

Discussion

What do these observed distributions mean? Part of the bias towards writing and hypothesis-testing may derive from the disciplinary history of the researchers conducting it. Silva and Leki (2004) argue that, while second language writing studies draws theory from both applied linguistics and composition studies, the use of empirical research to support that theory (as opposed to hermeneutic or dialectic inquiry) is much more characteristic of applied linguistics. If the people conducting empirical second language writing research are applied linguists by training, then perhaps that explains the emphasis on predicting and understanding written language as opposed to the internal dimensions of the individuals who produce it or who interact with it. It is interesting to note in this regard that, within applied linguistics—or more specifically, second language acquisition studies—individual differences in language learning (e.g., Dewaele, 2005; Robinson, 2002) is a relatively recent topic of inquiry that may serve as a useful direction for future second language writing research.

Table 2. Distribution of Focus Entities and Study Designs across Methodologies

	Quantitative				Mixed				
	Descriptive	Exploratory	Hypothesis	Case Study	Descriptive	Exploratory	Hypothesis	Case Study	
WRITING									
Characteristics	3	2	19	2					26
Quality	1	5	7						13
WRITER									
Writer	4	1	6			2		1	14
READER									
Reactions			1		1	1	3	1	7
Interactions				1					1
MULTIPLE									
Multiple	2	1	4	1			2	4	14
Total	10	9	37	4	1	3	5	6	75

If we look also at a standard guide for conducting quantitative research in applied linguistics, such as Hatch and Lazaraton's *The Research Manual: Design and Statistics for Applied Linguistics,* we find that the dominant paradigm is the experimental (or quasi-experimental) study that relies on hypothesized models. Only one of eighteen chapters deals with procedures that "give us a way of *discovering* factors that underlie language proficiency (and, hopefully, language learning) and ways of testing the relationships among them (Hatch & Lazaraton, 1991, p. 489; emphasis added)."[9] Admittedly, characterizing current research as biased is less optimistic than Leki, Cumming, and Silva's (2006) recent overview of topics covered in twenty years worth of qualitative as well as quantitative second language writing research. Their review heralds both the methodological diversity of the field and the advances made in our understanding of "issues in pedagogy and assessment, [c]ontextual factors influencing ESL writers in academic contexts, [and] [c]haracteristics of L2 writers, writing processes, and texts" (p. 142). The scope of the present review is purposefully limited, however. It focuses only on quantitative research, published in a few select journals, and during only a five-year period. The goal is to show what someone interested in the short run and possibly from outside the field sees. The review presented here evaluates our research not in terms of its findings but in terms of what we seem to be dedicating our time and energy to. Thus, the question asked here has not been *"what makes a difference?"* but rather, the arguably more basic questions, *"what are we trying to make a difference in?"* and *"how willing are we to consider a range of possibilities?"*

RESEARCH AGENDA FOR QUANTITATIVE RESEARCH
ON SECOND LANGUAGE WRITING

If our research is primarily looking for factors that predict texts of a certain type or quality, then the implicit—and sometimes explicit—message is that the teaching and learning of writing is primarily about producing better texts as output. Notwithstanding North's (1984) admonition that it's the writer, not the writing, that we are trying to improve, this may not seem very problematic. Indeed, my own research has sought to identify factors that predict a range of textual characteristics (Reynolds, 1995, 2001, 2002, 2005). I believe that it is important to understand the ways that texts vary linguistically with respect to multiple variables, including tasks, writer characteristics such as educational background and language proficiency, and judgments of writing quality. Nevertheless, I also believe that it is extremely important to realize that no single linguistic feature, such as nominal usage, will make or break a text; rather, it is a confluence of linguistic features that shape texts and affect readers. In short, my research has led me to appreciate the complexity of the contexts and interactions that produce texts.

Thus, I am not arguing that we need to stop doing the kind of research that I have spent my academic life doing, simply that we need to consider carefully the complexity of its design. Approximately 23 percent (17/75) of all the quantitative studies reviewed here did nothing more than evaluate differences in texts one condition at a time (i.e. they used procedures such as t-tests, ANOVAs, and Chi-squares to evaluate the significance of differences in frequencies or means of textual characteristics or quality ratings with respect to single variables such as native/nonnative or with feedback and without feedback). They did not show how those textual characteristics might be the product of differential learner characteristics interacting with task variables to accommodate distinct audiences.

This is problematic at the very least because we now live in an era when no second language writer shall be left behind, and the dominant paradigm for assessing progress is short-term, usually pre-course/post-course accountability measures produced as part of quasi-experimental designs. As writing teachers, we know that consistently observable changes in writing take time. Numerous longitudinal and meta-analysis studies confirm this (Bangert-Drowns et al., 2004; Boulton-Lewis et al., 2004; Curtis & Herrington, 2003; Gleason, 2000; Haswell, 2000; Ortega, 2003; Sommers & Saltz, 2004; Sternglass, 1997). When the weight of our research represents ability primarily in terms of written texts that vary in relation to single factors, we are setting ourselves up for failure in the arena of public accountability.

Moreover, by passively failing to explore the psyche of the writer and the variability of readers and the complexity of interaction we are missing out on things we should be discussing in composition classes and in our textbooks. As Leki, Cumming, and Silva (2006) lay out, we know a considerable amount about characteristics of writers that predict "a high level of L2 writing ability" (p. 152). We know a lot less about factors that predict those characteristics and how we might influence them.

For example, Cheng (2004) recently reported an exploratory study identifying constructs associated with writer anxiety. In another exploratory study, Esmaeelii (2002) examined relations in and among strategies used by L2 writers under different testing conditions. These are good, insightful studies. Both sought to identify relevant constructs before validating them and both identified a range of measures as their domain for exploration. Now, we need additional studies exploring factors like writer motivation and the interaction between strategy use and personality variables. Then, we need more studies such as Lee's (2005) that explore how multiple positive and negative psychological variables interact with each other and with writing performance. We also need to investigate the effects that teaching may have on these psychological variables, and whether or not those effects might provide alternatives to essay tests as ways of measuring short-term development.[10]

Finally, we need more research that explores the interaction between readers and writers, especially the kinds of interactions that occur in contexts other than formal assessment. We need studies of reactions to job application letters by adult immigrants and studies of how the focus of consulting sessions relates to the background of the participants, their training, and their previous experiences together (for an initial foray into this area, see Williams, 2004).

These may sound like questions better suited to qualitative investigations than quantitative measurement because of their complexity, but they are in fact asking about measurable constructs. When we take on complex research designs that require multiple methods of inquiry as well as multivariate analyses and exploratory procedures of the quantitative data, we communicate a very public message about the complexity of learning to write and the expertise that teachers need. In the words of Robert Slavin (2003), a leading proponent of experimental designs as a tool for educational reform: "The new policies that base education funding and practice on scientifically based, rigorous research have important consequences for educators. Research matters" (p. 12).

NOTES

1. Unfortunately, too many studies of this type only include tests for the significance of the differenc, while ignoring the magnitude of the effect.

2. As noted by Silva and Leki (2004), the major composition journals, most notably *College English* and *College Composition and Communication*, "would seem to have a de facto ban on publishing empirical research reports" (p. 9). They list *Research in the Teaching of English* and *Written Communication* as exceptions to this generalization, however.

3. It is interesting to cross-reference this percentage with Haswell's (Haswell, 2005) recent criticism of a wide-scale lack of published "replicable,

aggregable, and data supported" studies of U.S. post-secondary composition in general.

4. This criterion is not meant to imply that qualitative research should be defined or characterized as the absence of quantitative measures. See Harklau (this volume) for a fuller discussion of the epistemology of qualitative research.

5. There were no examples of empirical studies using key-stroke logging technology such as that illustrated by Lindgren and Sullivan (2002). Had there been any they would have been coded as writer focused.

6. Although many of the studies in this category deal with teacher comments on student papers, they are coded under the more inclusive term "reader."

7. Educational researchers including those involved in the debate over scientifically based research (e.g., Eisenhart & DeHaan, 2005; Lomas, 2004; Slavin, 2003) frequently categorize study designs as "experimental" or "observational," with the distinction resting on whether or not a treatment condition can be identified in the data. In the scheme used for this study, hypothesis-testing equates with experimental. Because a large number of second language writing studies deal with naturally–occurring "treatments" (e.g., course enrollment, culture of birth, the teacher's feedback preferences), however, it was felt that "experimental" would be a misnomer.

8. It might be argued that structural equation modeling is an hypothesis testing procedure since it starts with a proposed model that is then evaluated for goodness of fit. The decision was made to categorize it as exploratory, however, because it is generally assumed that the model is a starting point and that it may undergo various revisions until the best one is found.

9. Dörnyei's recent research guide (2007) presents a much more balanced treatment of quantitative, qualitative, and mixed-methods procedures and suggests that the bias in the field may be changing.

10. Leki, Cumming, and Silva (2006) underscore this need for more research on effective teaching.

REFERENCES

Bangert-Drowns, R. L., Hurley, M. M., & Wilkinson, B. (2004). The effects of school-based writing-to-learn interventions on academic achievement: A meta-analysis. *Review of Educational Research, 74*(1), 29–58.

Borg, S., Curtis, A., Davison, C., Han, Z. H., Reynolds, D., & Scovel, T. (2004). 2004 TESOL research agenda. Retrieved on May 31, 2006 from http://www.tesol.org/s_tesol/sec_document.asp?CID=236&DID=2924.

Boulton-Lewis, G. M., Marton, F., & Lewis, D. C. (2004). A longitudinal study of learning for a group of indigenous Australian university students: Dissonant conceptions and strategies. *Higher Education, 47*(1), 91–112.

Cheng, Y. S. (2004). A measure of second language writing anxiety: Scale development and preliminary validation. *Journal of Second Language Writing, 13*(4), 313–335.

Cumming, A., Kantor, R., & Powers, D. E. (2002). Decision making while rating ESL/EFL writing tasks: A descriptive framework. *Modern Language Journal, 86*(1), 67–96.

Curtis, M., & Herrington, A. (2003). Writing development in the college years: By whose definition? *College Composition and Communication, 55*(1), 69–90.

Dewaele, J.-M. (2005). Investigating the psychological and emotional dimensions in instructed language learning: Obstacles and possibilities. *Modern Language Journal, 89*(3), 367–380.

Dörnyei, Z. (2007). *Research methods in applied linguistics.* Oxford, U.K.: Oxford University Press.

Eisenhart, M., & DeHaan, R. L. (2005). Doctoral preparation of scientifically based education researchers. *Educational Researcher, 34*(4), 3–13.

Elder, C., Knoch, U., Barkhuizen, G., & von Randow, J. (2005). Individual feedback to enhance rater training: Does it work? *Language Assessment Quarterly, 2*(3), 175–196.

Esmaeili, H. (2002). Integrated reading and writing tasks and ESL students' reading and writing performance in an English language test. *Canadian Modern Language Review, 58*(4), 599–622.

Gleason, B. (2000). Evaluating writing programs in real time: The politics of remediation. *College Composition and Communication, 51*(4), 560–588.

Haswell, R. H. (2000). Documenting improvement in college writing: A longitudinal approach. *Written Communication, 17*(3), 307–352.

Haswell, R. H. (2005). NCTE/CCCC's recent war on scholarship. *Written Communication, 22*(2), 198–223.

Hatch, E., & Lazaraton, A. (1991). *The research manual: Design and statistics for applied linguistics.* Boston: Heinle & Heinle.

Helms-Park, R., & Stapleton, P. (2003). Questioning the importance of individualized voice in undergraduate L2 argumentative writing: An empirical study with pedagogical implications. *Journal of Second Language Writing, 12*(3), 245–265.

Hostetler, K. (2005). What is "good" education research? *Educational Researcher, 34*(6), 16–21.

Hyland, F., & Hyland, K. (2001). Sugaring the pill: Praise and criticism in written feedback. *Journal of Second Language Writing, 10*(3), 185–212.

Hyland, K. (2003). Dissertation acknowledgements: The anatomy of a Cinderella genre. *Written Communication, 20*(3), 242–268.

Jarvis, S., Grant, L., Bikowski, D., & Ferris, D. (2003). Exploring multiple profiles of highly rated learner compositions. *Journal of Second Language Writing, 12*(4), 377–403.

174   Reynolds

Kamil, M. L. (2004). The current state of quantitative research. *Reading Research Quarterly, 39*(1), 100–107.

Lee, S.-Y. (2005). Facilitating and inhibiting factors in English as a foreign language writing performance: A model testing with structural equation modeling. *Language Learning, 55*(2), 335–374.

Leki, I., Cumming, A., & Silva, T. (2006). Second-language composition teaching and learning. In P. Smagorinsky (Ed.), *Research on composition: Multiple perspectives on two decades of change* (pp. 141–169). New York: Teachers College Press.

Lindgren, E., & Sullivan, K. P. H. (2002). The LS graph: A methodology for visualizing writing revision. *Language Learning, 52*(3), 565–595.

Liu, J., & Sadler, R. W. (2003). The effect and affect of peer review in electronic versus traditional modes on L2 writing. *Journal of English for Academic Purposes, 2*(3), 193–227.

Lomas, R. G. (2004). Whither the future of quantitative literacy research? *Reading Research Quarterly, 39*(1), 107–112.

McCarthey, S. J., Guo, Y.-H., & Cummins, S. (2005). Understanding changes in elementary Mandarin students' L1 and L2 writing. *Journal of Second Language Writing, 14*(2), 71–104.

National Research Council. (2002). *Scientific research in education.* Washington, D.C.: National Academy Press.

No Child Left Behind Act of 2001, Pub. L. No. 107–110. Washington, DC: GPO.

North, S. M. (1984). The idea of a writing center. *College English, 46*(5), 433–446.

Ortega, L. (2003). Syntactic complexity measures and their relationship to L2 proficiency: A research synthesis of college-level L2 writing. *Applied Linguistics, 24*(4), 492–518.

Ortega, L. (2005a). For what and for whom is our research? The ethical as transformative lens in instructed SLA. *Modern Language Journal, 89*(3), 427–443.

Ortega, L. (2005b). Methodology, epistemology, and ethics in instructed SLA research: An introduction. *Modern Language Journal, 89*(3), 317–327.

Reynolds, D. W. (1995). Repetition in nonnative speaker writing: More than quantity. *Studies in Second Language Acquisition, 17*(2), 185–209.

Reynolds, D. W. (2001). Language in the balance: Lexical repetition as a function of topic, cultural background, and writing development. *Language Learning, 51*(3), 437–476.

Reynolds, D. W. (2002). Learning to make things happen in different ways: Causality in the writing of middle-grade English language learners. *Journal of Second Language Writing, 11*(4), 311–328.

Reynolds, D. W. (2005). Linguistic correlates of second language literacy development: Evidence from middle-grade learner essays. *Journal of Second Language Writing, 14*(1), 19–45.

Robinson, P. (Ed.). (2002). *Individual differences and instructed language learning.* Amsterdam: J. Benjamins.

Sasaki, M. (2004). A multiple-data analysis of the 3.5-year development of EFL student writers. *Language Learning, 54*(3), 525–582.

Schoonen, R., Gelderen, A. v., Glopper, K. d., Hulstijn, J., Simis, A., Snellings, P., et al. (2003). First language and second language writing: The role of linguistic knowledge, speed of processing, and metacognitive knowledge. *Language Learning, 53*(1), 165–202.

Siegel, H. (2006). Epistemological diversity and education research: Much ado about nothing much? *Educational Researcher, 35*(2), 3–12.

Silva, T., & Leki, I. (2004). Family matters: The influence of applied linguistics and composition studies on second language writing studies—past, present, and future. *Modern Language Journal, 88*(1), 1–13.

Slavin, R. E. (2003). A reader's guide to scientifically based research. *Educational Leadership, 60*(5), 12–16.

Smagorinsky, P. (2006a). Overview. In P. Smagorinsky (Ed.), *Research on composition: Multiple perspectives on two decades of change* (pp. 1–14). New York: Teachers College Press.

Smagorinsky, P. (Ed.). (2006b). *Research on composition: Multiple perspectives on two decades of change.* New York: Teachers College Press.

Snellings, P., Van Gelderen, A., & De Glopper, K. (2004). Validating a test of second language written lexical retrieval: A new measure of fluency in written language production. *Language Testing, 21*(2), 174–201.

Sommers, N., & Saltz, L. (2004). The novice as expert: Writing the freshman year. *College Composition and Communication, 56*(1), 124–149.

Stapleton, P. (2005). Using the web as a research source: Implications for L2 academic writing. *Modern Language Journal, 89*(2), 177–189.

Sternglass, M. S. (1997). *Time to know them: A longitudinal study of writing and learning at the college level.* Mahwah, NJ: Erlbaum.

Wang, L. (2003). Switching to first language among writers with differing second-language proficiency. *Journal of Second Language Writing, 12*(4), 347–375.

Williams, J. (2004). Tutoring and revision: Second language writers in the writing center. *Journal of Second Language Writing, 13*(3), 173–201.

Wolfe-Quintero, K., Inagaki, S., & Kim, H.-Y. (1998). *Second language development in writing: Measures of fluency, accuracy, and development* (No. 17). Manoa, HI: Second Language Teaching and Curriculum Center, University of Hawaii at Manoa.

Zhu, W. (2001). Interaction and feedback in mixed peer response groups. *Journal of Second Language Writing, 10*(4), 251–276.

9 Ideology and Theory in Second Language Writing: A Dialogical Treatment

A. Suresh Canagarajah

In this article, I consider the charge that ideologies are an imposition on writing practice. I narrate the experience of a multilingual student and a writing teacher to show how ideological explanations provide an important orientation toward understanding textual conflicts and creative options. In order to develop this perspective, I will challenge other stereotypes about ideologies (i.e., that they are deliberately constructed for purposes of social control and that they inculcate an illusory view of social life). I demonstrate how ideologies are always already there in social practice, that their manifestation is both unconscious and material, and that they can enable a deeper understanding of social life and human agency for textual/discursive change.

Part i: The Writing Teacher's Dilemma

MIN[1]: I faced a conflict when I read a Malaysian Chinese student's essay one day. I found that Ling was using an unconventional verb construction very consistently. The construction was "can able to." What was puzzling was that the related modals "can" and "may" were used with their conventional meaning. It appeared therefore that the student was using the new construction with a meaning not conveyed by the other available modals. The following are some examples which explain my confusion:

> "As a Hawaiian native historian, Trask *can able to* argue for her people."

> "Most of the new universities' students are facing new
> challenges like staying away from family, peer pres-
> sure, culture shock, heavy college work, etc. I *can* say
> that these are the "obstacles" to success. If a student
> *can able to* approach each situation with different per-
> spectives than the one he brought from high school,
> I *may* conclude that this student has climbed his first
> step to become a 'critical thinker.'"

It seemed to me that Ling had a mental grammar that was different from mine and that of standard English. I was convinced that I
shouldn't mark this verb construction as incorrect, but talk first and
find out the meaning ascribed by Ling.

CRITIC: Come on! Are you forgetting that this is an ESL student?
Are you saying that you will accept any lame excuse given by any linguistically handicapped student to justify an error? Just send her to the
writing center for grammar treatment!

MIN: I am glad I didn't send Ling to the writing center. As I spoke to
her, I realized that we shouldn't assume every unconventional usage
of our ESL students to be an unconscious error. Some are conscious
strategies for creative expression. First of all, I found that in Ling's
first language "can" and "be able to" have interchangeable meanings.
However, Ling showed with the help of her *Random House Dictionary*
that "can" has an additional meaning of "have permission to" that is
not connoted by "be able to" in English. Therefore, Ling had constructed "can able to" to connote "ability from the perspective of the
external circumstances." This construction was an alternative to the
individual transcendence and personal power connoted by "be able
to." It was also an alternative to the fatalism and deference to authority
connoted by "may." It emerged that Ling wanted to steer clear of the
American "can do" attitude of individual agency. She also wanted an
alternative to the fatalism of her native community. She had personally overcome the barriers set by her family and community to migrate
to the U.S. for education. It is this desire to resist external constraints
to develop an earned agency that she wanted to convey through her
neologism. She was struggling to find a different modal unavailable in
the language to express her specific meaning. It is this orientation to

power that Ling saw in native American historian Trask and first-year students in college she was writing about.

AUTHOR: What is instructive about this example is that even grammar can be ideological. Many writing teachers think of grammar as value-free, abstract features at the deep structure of language, untouched by sociopolitical concerns.[2] We read social meanings readily into other rhetorical features such as voice, tone, and style, but consider grammar as too abstract and technical to carry ideological meanings. However, for Ling, the choice of the modal positions her in competing ways toward social constraints and the ability to exercise one's human agency. Even more instructive is the fact that these ideological insights arise from writing practice. Her discomfort is experienced at the most basic level as a struggle for meaning and expression. The grammatical conflict for Ling is not motivated by any "critical thinking" reading, lectures, or exercises given by the teacher. Ling realizes that ideological considerations are intrinsic to writing. They are not imported into writing from outside. Good writing, for Ling, is dependent on negotiating satisfactorily her positioning towards social constraints through the choice of a suitable modal. The process of negotiating this language conflict generates some interesting ideological insights for Ling on how written expression is implicated in power difference.

CRITIC: Can we keep politics out of this? Can't we address this as a mere struggle for expression? Should we politicize everything?

AUTHOR: This is a choice all instructors face: we can limit writing practice to a consideration within the boundary of the text or situate writing in the widest social context. My feeling is that we cannot adequately address the challenges and conflicts students face within the bounds of the text. Writing is social practice, involving communication of meaning to readers, representing the identity of the author, performing acts such as changing opinions or recommending social action of some sort. For Ling, the choice of a modal is not eventually a problem of finding the most grammatical way of saying something; it is also a problem of saying something about herself, motivating her readers (first year students, in one essay) to act in certain ways, and promoting an alternative interpretation on her subject (i.e., the activity of historian Trask in another essay). Implicit in this conflict is another:

whether Ling should fit her expression to available form or challenge and expand the form to suit her desired meaning. Such conflicts in writing practice often demand ideological explanations. They can be explained, named, and interpreted with greater clarity when we connect them to ideological conflicts—either personally experienced by the author or hidden in social processes.

The reason why we should address these conflicts explicitly as ideological is more importantly because ideologies can be unconscious. Ling doesn't discuss her rhetorical conflict as explicitly ideological. Ideologies are experienced often as personal, mental, or psychological. This is especially because ideologies are most effective when they are internalized. Since much of the ideological negotiation, conflict, and repositioning is experienced at the most personal level, it is important for teachers to make ideologies explicit when they are manifested as a choice of grammar or struggle for expression. This orientation goes against the stereotype that ideologies are consciously formulated, as in political manifestoes, and can be addressed when they are encountered in their explicit form in a separate activity at a later point. The fact that ideologies are already part of social life, including writing and language use, is not always recognized.[3]

CRITIC: Hello! Are we forgetting something here? This student is Chinese! Aren't all third world students always political and biased? They just live and breathe politics.

Read the lead story in the *Chronicle of Higher Education* (Monaghan, 2006): American professors find that Chinese students are dogmatic and narrow-minded. They know nothing but ideology! Ideologies are a problem only for some writers.

AUTHOR: There are other ways to explain why multilingual students might be especially sensitive to ideological conflicts in writing. If writing practice is embedded in social practice (as I mentioned before), the conflicts multilingual students experience in their everyday life will generate ideological reflection. The tensions between their vernacular and the global language of English, cultural conflicts between the local and the global, and economic disparities—all experienced at the most personal level—can develop a sensitivity to politics. Ling's struggle to seek higher education against the wishes of her family and community is rife with conflicts motivated by gender, ethnicity, and tradition. Her personal struggles motivate the choice of her unique modal to convey "ability from the perspective of the external circumstances."

This doesn't mean that multilingual students don't have reason to be unreflective or to suppress their ideological tensions in order to play it safe and get a good grade. Nor does this mean that students from dominant communities don't experience social tensions of their own. Though Anglo-American students in Min's class didn't see any problems in using "can" and "be able to" as being interchangeable in meaning, it is not impossible to find Anglo-American students coming with a different social practice holding a different position on such questions. Differences in social practice may explain why students may or may not display greater ideological awareness.

PART 2: RESPONDING TO THE DILEMMA

CRITIC: So what are you going to do about this unusual modal? Don't say you are going to accept an incorrect grammatical usage? Some people will do anything for politics! Are you going to write a new dictionary with brand new modals?

MIN: No, I didn't accept the peculiar usage of the student. What arose from writing practice, I turned into pedagogical practice. I presented to other students in the class the dilemma experienced by Ling. Engaging students with the linguistic and rhetorical options they have and exploring the meaning potential in these choices are more effective in encouraging critical thinking than any lecturing or preaching on politics. I was amazed by the depth of the discussion when I posed these ideological considerations as encountered in writing practice. Many multilingual students didn't see "can" and "be able to" as interchangeable in meaning. They explored other ways in which Ling's desired meaning can be captured. Some suggested "may be able to." Others suggested adding an "if" clause to "be able to." Still a few mavericks suggested using "can able to" with a parenthetical explanation (or with a footnote). In discussing these options, students not only developed a sensitivity to the ideological implications of grammar, they also developed a richer stock of vocabulary. However, the choices were taken up differently by students according to their expressive needs and social position. Ling opted to adopt "may be able to" as she was concerned about being grammatically correct even as she expressed her agency. A Vietnamese student, Tranh, on the other hand, opted to use "can" and "be able to" interchangeably because their connotations of agency inspired modes of resistance and individual empowerment that were a corrective to the fatalism of his own community

AUTHOR: I am fascinated how writing practice not only generates ideological conflicts but also provides diverse alternatives. A discussion of the above kind as a straightforward grammar lesson or theoretical lecture may not have generated the critical reflection and creativity it did. There are good reasons why writing practice affords more agency for ideological resistance. The creativity of language affords possibilities for resistance, as we can see in the many alternatives proffered by the students. Even the rhetorical modalities and textual spaces of writing may afford creativity for resistance. The suggestion to use parentheses or footnotes exploits rhetorical and textual ways out of any restrictive influences of standard language.

It is important to realize, however, that the empowering alternatives students come up with are also ideological. The alternative against the grammatical impositions of restrictive ideology is not transcendence to an ideology-free discourse. The preferred alternatives of the students are themselves ideological. It is simply that the alternatives are perceived by students to represent ideologies that are more empowering. This realization goes against certain popular stereotypes about ideologies. People think of ideologies as only coercive. They also think of ideologies as false consciousness, reductive, illusory, or distorting.[5] However, in Min's example we see ideologies as also explanatory or enlightening. As students understand their grammar alternatives as holding different meaning potential, they also gain insights into the ideological implications behind their choices.

CRITIC: Not so fast, Mr. Ideologue! How do you explain the Vietnamese student? He opted for the standard usage and sympathizes with the dominant community's perspective. He's my man! He doesn't let himself become stupid because of ideology!

AUTHOR: Tranh's choice shows that the choice of a suitable language and the ideological implications of these choices are based on the social positioning of the students. Tranh's experiences and needs are different from Ling's. While Ling still faces constraints from her family and community in addition to the conflicts from her gender identity, Tranh is interested in making a break from what he perceives as the fatalistic worldview of some members of the community he has left behind in fleeing to the United States. He finds the volitionism of the "can do" philosophy liberating and, even, practicable. However, what is important is that Tranh doesn't choose his modal unthinkingly. The choice derives from a probing classroom discussion. Even standard language can be used with critical thinking for empowering purposes. Tranh's example shows that individual grammar items don't have rigid ideological meanings attached to them. They gain their meaning in relation to the social positioning and rhetorical purposes of the users.

CRITIC: A cop out! I thought the whole point of this article is to give us the rules for ideologically-informed teaching. I have the chart ready for you to fill in:

GRAMMAR		IDEOLOGY
may	=	
can	=	
be able to	=	
may be able to	=	
can able to	=	

AUTHOR: No, we can't come up with rules like this. There is no one-to-one relationship between a grammatical item and an ideological meaning. Writers have to adopt the more demanding but creative process of negotiating ideological meaning in grammar in relation to their social positioning, rhetorical objectives, and expressive needs. Min's classroom discussion where students explore the implications of different grammatical choices goes a long way towards cultivating such negotiation skills.

CRITIC: Okay, Mr. Karl Marx! Are you saying that the whole point of this exercise is having a great classroom discussion? I am surprised how conservative you are? No implications for social structure, power relations, "base"—practice?!

MIN: Wait a minute. You haven't listened to my full story. There are already implications for practice when you think about the new grammatical awareness that feeds into the revised versions of these students.

Furthermore, after the class discussion the unusual modal became a newly coined phrase we shared throughout the term. Students referred to "can able to" as an inside joke at opportune moments. This eventuality mimics the slow process of language and discursive change. What is considered a nonstandard item or erroneous use becomes standardized when it serves social purposes for language users. What arises from the writing practice of Ling goes on to affect the language practice of the students. We know of other examples in discourse and communication that are slow but significant. These changes originated probably in the same way—through subtle moods of discomfort, minor gestures of breaking the rules, small acts of resistance. The ideological considerations that motivate these acts have initiated serious changes in rhetorical and educational practice—i.e., new genres or writing in the academy (such as multivocal essays), the inclusion of first person pronouns in scholarly writing, the representation of students' own voices, ethical research practices, and multicultural curricula in schooling.

PART 3: PROFESSIONAL IMPLICATIONS

CRITIC: Okay! How do I become an ideologically informed writing teacher? I am ready for the reading list! Spell it out, Philosopher! With whom shall I start? Who is more fashionable?

Derrida?
Foucault?
Althusser?
Bourdieu?
Giroux?
Aronowitz?

or do you want the classics?

Karl Marx?
Machiavelli?
Weber?
Raymond Williams?

and what about the wannabes?

Benesch?
Pennycook?
Kubota?
Canagarajah?

AUTHOR: I don't think this is the best strategy to prepare ourselves for critical teaching practice. There is always a gap between the reading we do and the challenges we encounter in our writing classrooms. Therefore, it is much better to start from practice. We can address the ideological conflicts for our students much more effectively if we start from the dilemmas that arise from writing process and classroom life. To do this, we must develop a different orientation to teaching. Our teaching has to become more reflective: we must cultivate a tolerance for error, a sensitivity to students' struggles, and a willingness to listen to others and appreciate conflicting positions. Our attitudes may have to change as well: we must develop the humility to learn from students, the open mindedness to consider alternative perspectives, and an imagination to consider new possibilities. Such an orientation will enable us to be alert to the teachable moments that arise from students' writing practice.

CRITIC: Are you kidding? You are telling me that Min and you would have discussed the ideological issues here with absolutely no knowledge of these theorists?

AUTHOR: Reading can certainly help. It can help to name ideologies, explain the options better, and interpret the social motivations behind writing dilemmas. So a person can not only name the dilemma between *may* and *can* for Ling as a dilemma between volitionism and determinism, for example. Reading can help explain how and why students from other communities might bring a different cultural and ideological perspective on American college writing. However, it is good to start from practice. Instructors will find that practice provides a context for our reading. It can even motivate further reading. The reading I have enjoyed has always been spurred by the need to understand the conflicts I have faced in my teaching or writing. The need to explain the complexities in writing or teaching practice charges our reading with a lot of significance.

CRITIC: Are you saying that we can adopt a neutral stance and engage in classroom discussion without adopting an ideological position of our own? Out with it. Which ideology do you want me to promote in my class? It's okay, you can tell me!

Marxism?
Feminism?
Structuralism?
Poststructuralism?
Postmodernism?
Critical Race Theory?
Contact Zone Perspective?
Postcolonialism?
Post Marxism?
Post Feminism?

AUTHOR: Although it is impossible not to hold an ideological position of our own—whether it is consciously held or not—we must adopt a healthy detachment towards ideological paradigms. This is because all ideologies—even liberatory ones—are partial and partisan. They speak to the interests of specific social groups; they explain certain areas of social life and leave out others. This is partly because everyday life and social practice are much more complex than ideologies. So, even liberatory ideologies have limitations. We see how postcolonialism is beginning to be critiqued as the thinking of migrant middle class intellectuals in the West, and doesn't speak to the experiences of many marginalized social groups in the periphery. On the other hand, even repressive ideologies have empowering possibilities. For example, capitalism was empowering to the middle class in relation to feudalism, which favored the birthright of aristocracy. As we perceive ideologies from changing historical and geographical contexts, we will realize their limits. Therefore, our primary commitment is to empowering and ethical practices in the local contexts in which we work. When we approach our work this way, we'll find that practice helps us critique ideological paradigms. Practice can even help us reconstruct paradigms, developing more ethical and empowering discourses for our students and ourselves.

MIN: That's precisely what emerged from my experience. The grammar problem faced by Ling posed some uncomfortable questions for multiculturalism. Although this was treated as a fashionable "PC" (politically correct) ideology, it became apparent that it was also limited in many ways. Ling's question—if she could be bold enough to engage with the grammar of a language to express her difference—made me realize that multiculturalism permitted us to express our cultures and identities as long as we contained our differences for the sake of the whole. Ling could be different as long as she worked within the legitimized structures of language and rhetoric. This is analogous to what goes on in multicultural communities—you can be different as long as your difference doesn't make others uncomfortable or strain the framework of the whole.

Part 4: Theory/Ideology Connection

CRITIC: So what composition theory accommodates such a perspective? Which theory are you promoting here? Which theory should I adopt for an ideologically informed teaching? What about the following list?

Superior Theories	Evil Theories
Critical Linguistics	Current-Traditional Theory
Social Process Theory	Process Theory
Critical Discourse Analysis	Expressive Theory
Contact Zone Model	Genre Theory
Critical EAP	ESP/ EAP
Critical Contrastive Rhetoric	Contrastive Rhetoric

AUTHOR: Well, the only difference in what you cynically label superior theories is that they are more explicit about issues of power. The composition theories in the other column don't address power or consider it irrelevant to writing instruction. Still, we have to be critical of the theories in the first column as well. All theories, including critical ones, are partial and partisan. They orientate to power according to the interests of specific social groups. Let's remember what we said about ideologies. The same points apply here for writing theories:

- practice demands theory for meaning and significance
- theory informs practice
- but practice is more complex than theory
- practice can critique theory
- practice helps reconstruct existing theories
- we need to unpack theories which claim to be objective, neutral, absolute
- we must use theories critically and reflectively

So, for example, even product oriented models have liberatory potential. Compared to the elitism of the previous classical orientations to rhetoric—which assumed that one had to be aware of Ciceronian rhetorical principles in order to be a good communicator—current/traditional paradigm holds that good writing is all about the practical skills of getting a well-made text together. Of course, in the process of defining writing as a practical skill, it ignored the social context, among other things. Similarly, even critical theories have to be critiqued.

MIN: That's precisely what happened in my case. My classroom experience led me to critique what was then a fashionable model: contact zone pedagogy. While contact zone perspective values multicultural readings and discussions to facilitate border crossing, it didn't address issues at the more fundamental level of grammar. Ling's dilemma helped me question the hands off approach to standard language and grammar. The questions I asked writing theories twelve years ago, motivated by my classroom practice, still reverberate in composition journals. Such is the power of practice over theory that Ling's case is an excellent example of practice in search of a theory. Consider publications like the following that continue Ling's question to this day:

Elbow, P. (1999). Inviting the mother tongue: Beyond "mistakes," "bad English," and "wrong English." *JAC, 19*(2), 359–388.
Horner, B. & Trimbur, J. (2002). English only and U.S. college composition. *College Composition and Communication, 53,* 594–630.
Canagarajah, A. S. (2006). The Place of world Englishes in composition: Pluralization continued. *College Composition and Communication, 57*(4), 586–619.

AUTHOR: It is for such reasons that I adopt the tool box approach to writing theories. I pick and choose theories to explain specific areas of writing practice. I am not fully committed to any of them. I have the detachment to critique and reconstruct them if the complexities of practice demand a different theory.

PART 5: A REFLECTIVE CONCLUSION

CRITIC: Wait a minute, Mr. Ideologue! If everything is ideological, why should we accept the positions you present? Isn't your theory partial and partisan as well? Keep your damn ideology to yourself!

AUTHOR: You are right. My position is also value-ridden, motivated by my social background and experience. Nothing is neutral or objective. I cannot appeal to reason or logic to claim a superior status for the position I am advocating. Eventually, it is only ethical consideration that can help us decide if we should adopt a position or not. We have to ask ourselves what positions are fair, humane, caring, affirming, and empowering. Though these values are subjective, we have to negotiate them according to our different social positioning. To facilitate an open and frank conversation, I must see that I provide spaces for multiple perspectives, even for criticism, against my own position. Hence the writing of this article as a multi-vocal essay, where three parties take turns speaking. The adoption of a narrative—based on Min's experience, but further embellishing her original study with names for her students and personal voice for the teacher—will enable readers to develop other interpretations to this experience.

CRITIC: You mean you just used me all this time to make your argument persuasive? You made me utter strawman arguments to strengthen your own position? How democratic and ethical is that?

AUTHOR: I acknowledge that I cannot claim neutrality even though I make alternate positions available. It is still I who is the author of this article. However, this is the fundamental paradox we face in all social activity. In teaching, we are always experimenting with instructional practices to accommodate alternate perspectives (adopting student-driven or collaborative learning environments) while we exert our teacherly authority to set up these activities. Or, while we offer opportunities for critical practice in classrooms, we still have to adopt an ideological position of our own all the time. In writing, while we have to develop a thesis of our own, we are always pushing against textual, rhetorical, and linguistic boundaries to offer multiple perspectives, encourage civil discourse, and expand readers' awareness. The same applies to our negotiation of power. Though we will always have inequality in social life, we constantly struggle to create a more democratic environment, working within power relations to initiate progressive changes. It is this paradox that charges our writing and teaching practice with so much meaning and significance: we are always pushing against established forms and conventions to create richer meaning, egalitarian relations, humane values.

CRITIC: Paradox? Blah, blah, blah . . . ! Why can't we just get back to writing—pure and simple—as we always knew it? Why can't we get back to teaching as we know it—and tell those dumb kids what they need to know? Give me practice—without all this ideological rubbish!

MIN: Remember: nothing ideological like practice!

AUTHOR: I thought the point of your story was "nothing practical like an ideology?"

NOTES

1. Min's narrative (that I have reconstructed here) is based on her article that recounts this experience. See Lu, 1994.

2. This view is often implied rather than consciously adopted. For example, the treatment of error in the influential book by Ferris and Hedgecock (1998) isn't informed by the social context of writing or the ideological implications of students' grammatical choices. I offer a reinterpretation of the constructs introduced by Ferris and Hedgecock to show how grammatical choices of students are shaped by their creative and critical objectives in writing (in Canagarajah, 2002, pp.48–57). What is unconventional in the established grammar system can be agentively renegotiated to seem rhetorically appropriate for the objectives of the author.

3. For example, John Swales (1990) explains that his reason for leaving out ideological considerations about academic discourse in his book "rests on a pragmatic concern to help people, both nonnative and native speakers, to develop their academic communicative competence" (p. 9). He assumes that ideological issues are an "extra," extraneous to the more basic concerns of writing. The statement conveys the impression that these issues are separable and ideologies can be left for later when students have the competence or the need to address them. To give another example, in his influential book on values in language teaching, Bill Johnston assumes that ideologies are not already implicit in language teaching when he argues: "At heart, teaching for me is not about political interests. It is about the teacher-student relation and about the nurturing of learning" (p.70).

4. The position of textbook writer Robert O'Neil against my discussion of his book exemplifies this attitude. He argues that I am imposing an ideological reading into his presumably neutral characters and narratives. He goes on to argue that such ideological readings and pedagogical proposals lead to distorting students' perspectives and causes needless social conflict. I give space to his criticism in his own voice in my book (see Canagarajah, 1999, pp. 100–101). The assumption that ideologies are coercive is also reflected in Johnston's (2003) argument against critical pedagogy. He asks critical teachers: "How do you decide when your values should override those of your students or the alleged values of their cultures?" (p.73), implying that an ideologically motivated teaching would impose extraneous values on students. He further states: "Democracy, freedom, and social change are all terribly important, but for the great majority of us the real business of life can and must go on regardless, whatever our political context. The alternative view—that until equality among all people is achieved we must devote ourselves above all to the struggle for social change—strikes me as being a bleak prospect indeed, and one that denies the richness and profound humanity of relation, including the teacher-learner relation, as it is played out in whatever circumstances it has found itself" (p.71). Johnston assumes that power relations are not part of the "real business of life." He also assumes that engaging with power denies the richness of life, presumably reducing life to simple categories or distinctions.

REFERENCES

Canagarajah, A. S. (2002). *Critical academic writing and multilingual students*. Ann Arbor: University of Michigan Press.

Canagarajah, A. S. (1999). *Resisting linguistic imperialism in English teaching*. Oxford, UK: Oxford University Press.

Ferris, D., & Hedgcock, J. S. (1998). *Teaching ESL composition: Purpose, process, and practice*. Mahwah, NJ: Erlbaum.

Johnston, B. (2003). *Values in English language teaching*. Mahwah, NJ: Erlbaum.

Lu, M. (1994). Professing multiculturalism: The politics of style in the contact zone. *College Composition and Communication, 45*(4), 442–458.

Monaghan, P. (2006, May 19). Open doors, closed minds? Collaborations and confrontations accompanying a growing Chinese presence in American academe. *Chronicle of Higher Education*. Retrieved June 2, 2006, from http://chronicle.com/weekly/v52/i37/37a01401.htm

Swales, J. (1990). *Genre analysis*. Ann Arbor: University of Michigan Press.

10 Critical Approaches to Theory in Second Language Writing: A Case of Critical Contrastive Rhetoric

Ryuko Kubota

The field of second language writing is roughly situated at the crossroads of composition studies and applied linguistics. While composition studies has increasingly been influenced by post-foundational critical inquires such as cultural studies, feminist studies, and critical pedagogies (Fulkerson, 2005), the field of applied linguistics, especially teaching English to speakers of other languages, has also made a critical turn during the last two decades or so (Canagarajah, 2006; Kumaravadivelu, 2006; Pennycook, 2004). Research in applied linguistics has increased the amount of inquiry into such topics as linguistic imperialism, language policy and planning, issues of gender, class, race, and sexual identities, native speaker supremacy, and so forth. As with critical pedagogies, inquiry fields have adopted the term *critical* as seen in critical applied linguistics (Pennycook, 2001), critical English for academic purposes (Benesch, 2001), and critical language testing (Shohamy, 2001). However, the term *critical* can have different meanings to different people, posing an important question of how to apply a critical approach to theory in second language writing. This chapter explores how conceptual principles of what is critical within applied linguistics can apply to contrastive rhetoric, an inquiry area in need of a critical approach. Reflecting on some concrete examples of small-scale studies, this chapter will also explore how different political and theoretical underpinnings within critical approaches can inform different approaches to research focus.

CRITICAL APPROACHES TO APPLIED LINGUISTICS

The term *critical* can mean different things depending on the theoretical stance within an inquiry. It could be used in the context of the neoliberal educational agenda to improve individual students' thinking and achievement or the postcolonial project to critique and recast canonical knowledge and master narratives (Luke, 2004). It could refer to cognitive and academic skills as in the phrase "critical thinking" (see Atkinson, 1997) or social, political, and ideological inquiry into language use in relation to power as seen in critical discourse analysis (CDA) (see Fairclough, 1995; Kress, 1990; Wodak, 1996). In some cases, merely investigating linguistic practices in sociocultural contexts or in relation to social categories, such as gender, class, and ethnicity could be considered as critical when it challenges the paradigm of scientific objectivism and universalism. In contrast, the critical in critical applied linguistics, which is influenced by intellectual traditions of cultural studies, including postmodernism, poststructuralism, and postcolonial studies, problematizes the social relations that inform the use and interpretation of language and aims to use the analysis for social critique and transformation. As such, it "raises more critical questions to do with access, power, disparity, desire, difference, and resistance" (Pennycook, 2004, p. 797).

These different approaches to the critical in applied linguistics can be categorized into the following four forms: (1) critical thinking, (2) social relevance (focus on social categories and contexts), (3) emancipatory modernism (ideology critique as seen in CDA), and (4) problematizing practice (critical applied linguistics informed by post-foundational thought) (Pennycook, 2001, 2004). These varied understandings of *critical* represent theoretically and politically different stances. For example, teaching to be critical as a thinking skill is concerned with cognitive understanding of individuals and can easily be co-opted by positivism and the politically conservative establishment, whereas the focus on social contexts is often based on liberal pluralism and the conceptual framework of constructivism. The critical approach to analyzing texts as in CDA scrutinizes and uncovers unequal relations of power that structure and reproduce social practices and relations. Yet, as Pennycook (2001; 2004) critiques, based on a neo-Marxist scientific approach to linguistic analysis, CDA's ideology critique implies the existence of an alternative objective truth to replace ideology as a false consciousness or a misled understanding of reality. While critical analysis of texts represented by CDA seems to occupy a large domain within critical approaches to applied linguistics, the fourth approach—critical applied linguistics as problematizing practice—is influenced by postmodern, poststructuralist, and postcolonial intellectual orientations that are skeptical about the pursuit of objective truths and are committed to problematizing power, knowledge, and discourse. It also explores how identities and agencies are performed through language and how the plurality of meanings can be achieved in social, educational, and political contexts (Pennycook, 2004). This approach, however, has a danger of falling into relativism, approving all views as equally valid, or endorsing another dogmatic commitment to a single perspective. Thus, advocates of this approach emphasize the importance of situated ethics and constant self-reflection through problematizing all versions of knowledge, including the ones supporting critical applied linguistics.

Critical applied linguistics can be applied to the field of second language writing, and the field would benefit from its application especially to an inquiry into cultural difference in rhetorical organizations(i.e., contrastive rhetoric) for several reasons. First, classification and descriptions of rhetoric based on cultural differences tend to produce and reinforce cultural stereotypes or essentialism, creating the dichotomous us-versus-them paradigm which has increasingly been critiqued as problematic in the age of globalization (Kubota & Lehner, 2004; Spack, 1997). Second, such cultural essentialism directly affects groups of teachers of learners not only in classroom instruction (e.g., composing texts, responding to texts, constructing cultural and linguistic identities) but also on wider issues of text production and curriculum development which feed into the essentialist discourse. Third, in spite of many researchers' efforts to dismantle cultural essentialism, the discourse of cultural difference in rhetoric epitomized by the doodles by Kaplan (1966) persists in both academic and public spheres. Fourth, while cultural essentialism has negative effects in many domains, the poststructuralist plurality of meanings and postcolonial appropriation of language as resistance can provide a different perspective on the cultural uniqueness of rhetoric. These trends and points of view justify the usefulness of applying critical applied linguistics to contrastive rhetoric research.

Critical Contrastive Rhetoric

Contrastive rhetoric is a contested area of inquiry that has presented pedagogical implications to second language writing. In recent years, there has been an attempt to rename the field as intercultural rhetoric in order to pay closer attention to the social, situational, and genre-specific nature of written texts and to the dynamic and hybrid, rather than static and homogeneous, nature of culture (Atkinson, 2004; Connor, 2002, 2004). However, a mere focus on the diverse nature of rhetoric would not move the inquiry beyond liberal pluralism. Pushing the inquiry to a more critical direction would require questioning how power, knowledge, and discourse are implicated in the formation of cultural rhetoric and scrutinizing the ways in which the rhetoric is described and classified.

Around the time of the shift from contrastive rhetoric to intercultural rhetoric, I collaborated with Al Lehner to propose critical contrastive rhetoric, an inquiry approach that incorporates postmodern, poststructuralist, and postcolonial critiques of culture and language in investigating the organization of written discourse in cross-cultural contexts (Kubota & Lehner, 2004). In this theoretical work, we aimed to reconceptualize cultural difference in rhetoric through examining unequal relations of power between languages, discursive construction of knowledge about ideal rhetoric, colonial construction of cultural dichotomies manifested in commonly accepted images of languages (e.g., logical vs. emotional, direct vs. indirect), and rhetorical plurality brought about by diaspora and cultural and linguistic hybridity. When put into practice, critical contrastive rhetoric affirms the plurality of rhetorical forms and students' identities in L1 and L2 writing, while problematizing taken-for-granted cultural knowledge about rhetorical norms and allowing writing teachers to recognize the complex web of rhetoric, culture, power, discourse, and resistance within which they conduct classroom instruction and respond to student writing.

While theorizing a new approach to contrastive rhetoric is an abstract intellectual exercise, actually conducting a study based on the theoretical framework involves alignment of the interpretation of findings with the framework, which is not always straightforward. One example is my own recent data-based research on critical perspectives on contrastive rhetoric. I collaborated with Ling Shi to investigate rhetorical patterns of opinion texts that appear in junior high school (or middle/intermediate school) L1 language arts textbooks published in mainland China, Japan, Canada, and the United States. Our first study (Study 1) examined junior high school language arts textbooks published in mainland China and Japan and investigated the types of writing instructions and the rhetorical patterns of texts containing the author's opinion (Kubota & Shi, 2005). Although we did not frame our chapter specifically in the critical contrastive rhetoric paradigm, we raised some critical questions about cultural representation. Our second study (Study 2) examined middle school language arts textbooks published in Canada and the United States with a focus similar to Study 1 (Shi & Kubota, 2007). However, in the peer review process for publication, some reviewers' comments compelled us to shift our frame from contrastive rhetoric to rhetorical analysis within genre studies. Nevertheless, we have maintained some critical analysis of the results based on critical contrastive rhetoric.

Both studies focused mainly on texts illustrating opinion or argumentative writing because such texts are considered to be more difficult to write than other text types such as narratives and thus require explicit teaching. Due to many methodological limitations, generalizations cannot be made. Nonetheless, reflecting on the results of these studies would help us understand how different interpretations are aligned with different theoretical and political orientations within the critical approaches to applied linguistics delineated above. In the following section, I will briefly summarize each study.

STUDY 1 (KUBOTA & SHI, 2005)

This study examined L1 language arts textbooks commonly used in junior high schools (grades 7, 8, and 9) in mainland China and Japan (one textbook series for each country) in order to identify (1) what kinds of instruction for writing are provided for all text types,[1] and (2) how reading materials illustrating opinion writing are rhetorically structured. We found that these textbooks instruct students to follow a direct and linear pattern in opinion writing, represented by such descriptors as "good organization and paragraphing," "clarity," "effective supporting details and counter opinions," and "main point placed at the beginning." There was no mention of the four-unit style that has often been identified as a culturally specific pattern (e.g., Hinds, 1983, 1990; Maynard, 1998; Tsao, 1983), underscoring the need to view such cultural representations critically (Kubota, 1997; Cahill, 2003).

In our analysis, all of the 22 essays with an author's opinion demonstrated a three-unit organizational structure of introduction, body (with supporting details and a logical connection between ideas), and conclusion, paralleling a general structure that often characterizes English texts. All of the sample essays in the Japanese textbooks presumably written by student authors presented an opinion in the introduction. However, unlike the prototypical English organization, none of the main point statements that appear in the introduction included a preview statement to forecast the content and organization of the supporting details. This shed light on culturally situated interpretations of deductive patterns (Shi, 2002). In addition, a small number of texts exhibited a structure that might be interpreted as a quasi-inductive pattern in which arguments supporting the conclusion are only loosely connected to the main idea placed in the conclusion (Hinds, 1990). This interpretation partly derived from the difficulty of assigning a single text type to opinion texts in Japanese. That is, almost half of the Japanese opinion texts that we identified with this pattern were in the informational (expository) mode with the author's view on the topic added at the end of the text. This suggested that in learning to read and writing in L1 at school, students are exposed to many structures, not just the prototypical rhetorical patterns or conventions suggested in the textbook. This led to the question of whether English texts to which young L1 English writers are exposed align with instructions for writing opinion texts in English.

STUDY 2 (SHI & KUBOTA, 2007)

To explore that question, we examined middle school language arts textbooks adopted in British Columbia, Canada and in North Carolina, the United States and investigated whether or not the prescriptive conventions for linear and deductive English rhetoric are actually identified in the rhetorical organizations of texts. As mentioned earlier, we originally attempted to frame this chapter in contrastive rhetoric to compare and contrast the findings with the results of Study 1. However, in the peer review publication process, we were directed to focus on the shifting trend in genre studies more than on contrastive rhetoric; that is, the shift from a view of genre as form and text type to genre as social action and situated process (Coe, 2002; Freedman & Medway, 1994; Miller, 1984; see Johns, 2002, 2003). The emphasis on genre as situated action questions the effectiveness of the explicit teaching of rhetorical form, epitomized by the genre approach promoted by Sydney School in Australia, which emphasizes the teaching of the genre of power and by the teaching of the five-paragraph essay often found in writing instruction in North America. From the perspective that views genre as social action, training students to write essays following a formulaic style is too prescriptive and reductionist. This position parallels practitioners' arguments against using the five-paragraph essay as a model for writing (e.g., Hillocks, 2002; Lewis, 2001; Nunnally, 1991; Wesley, 2000). We framed Study 2 within this discussion and provided a descriptive analysis of how school texts are rhetorically organized. We were also interested in whether the texts differ from the pattern of the five-paragraph theme.

We examined reading materials drawn from selected L1 English language arts textbooks for grades 7 and 8 used in Canada and the U.S.A.—two integrated Canadian textbook series and four American writing and grammar series.[2] We analyzed 25 texts that claim to contain a central opinion of the author and investigated (1) what the general discourse patterns were and (2) whether the main idea or opinion was presented in the introduction section. As in Study 1, our analysis identified a three-part structure consisting of introduction, body, and conclusion in all texts. However, the introductory section of some texts was lengthy with multiple paragraphs (up to ten) and some of these texts placed the main idea at the end of the long introduction, paralleling the notion of delayed introduction of purpose (Hinds, 1990) applied to the introduction. In addition, the opinion or main idea was not necessarily presented in the introduction but rather in the middle or at the end of the essay. Moreover, several texts implied an opinion or main idea only in the conclusion. No textbooks mentioned the five-paragraph theme, although sample essays written by students or commissioned writers roughly followed this pattern. The study suggests a gap between the pattern recommended for school writing and the actual structures that appear in some of the reading materials in school textbooks.

REFLECTION

In order to provide a rough synthesis of our findings, I have created the following table which indicates where the opinion or main idea appears for the first time in the texts we examined.

These findings (see Table 1) among others raise critical questions surrounding the following issues: (1) homogenization of the ideal rhetoric in China and Japan in the era of global communication which is impacted by English, (2) the prescriptive/descriptive gap (i.e., the gap between how a text for writing should be organized and how texts for reading are actually organized), and (3) the relation between the goal of school writing and rhetorical conventions. In retrospect, the two studies appear to follow the framework of ideology critique, as they did find patterns and trends that would challenge common assumptions about essentialized written discourse patterns of Chinese, English, and Japanese which still pervade academic and public discourse. Nevertheless, the three issues raised above go beyond the pursuit of objective counter-truth and problematize aspects of the taken-for-granted assumption from a broader perspective. These issues can indeed be conceptualized and discussed in different ways depending on the political and theoretical orientations of critical inquiry discussed earlier. Below, I will present some reflections on these issues by taking into account these different orientations.

Table 1. The number of essays categorized according to the location of the opinion or main idea.

Location	Introduction	Body	Conclusion	Unidentified
Study 1				
Chinese (N = 9)	3	3	3	0
Japanese (N = 13)	7	0	5	1
Study 2				
Canada (N = 12)*	4	4	6 (3 implicit)	0
USA (N = 13)**	10 (4 long intro)	2 (2 implicit)	1 (1 implicit)	0

* In Study 2, we defined the point of view central to the essay as "main idea" (the most important message in the text) and "opinion" (the author's point of view, belief, or bias), and recorded the location of these two. We identified both "main idea" and "opinion" in two of the Canadian texts, and both are recorded here.
** Four of the ten essays presented an opinion at the end of the introduction with two or more multi-sentence paragraphs.

Homogenization of Rhetoric in Globalization

The emerging pattern we identified in the data suggests a converging trend in rhetoric found in the Chinese, Japanese, and English textbooks. In the case of Japan, researchers have pointed out that the recent L1 academic or school writing instruction tends to promote a deductive pattern with coherence, inclusion of examples, and a clear statement of one's position in the beginning. This indicates the trend in which the ideal rhetorical conventions are converging into the idealized rhetoric of English (Hirose, 2003; Kobayashi & Rinnert, 2002, 2003). In Chinese, a similar trend has been noted (Kirkpatrick, 1997). The findings of our studies parallel this trend.

The liberal pluralist stance or the position of ideology critique would consider this trend to be clear evidence against the traditional assumptions of contrastive rhetoric. It would be argued that there are many ways of organizing texts depending on the purpose and situation or that the concept of cultural uniqueness in rhetoric is a false assumption. The rhetorical genre studies that emphasize rhetoric as social action and process certainly parallels the critique of the static, normative, and essentialized understanding of cultural rhetoric. However, such critiques do not necessarily take into account unequal relations of power in the cultural, political, and historical processes that construct and transform cultural differences (see Kubota, 1997; You, 2005). Ideology critique would pay attention to issues of power, although this position may overlook the cultural difference used as postcolonial resistance as discussed below. Furthermore, underlying both approaches is an assumption that a large corpus of data would reveal an accurate trend of rhetorical structures identified in contemporary texts.

While examining trends taps important aspects of the use of rhetoric as social action, critical contrastive rhetoric would connect the findings with wider political contexts. As I have argued elsewhere about some recent trends in Japanese written discourse patterns (Kubota, 2002a; 2002b), not only has the global spread of English promoted English language teaching in East Asian countries, it has also influenced what is perceived as the ideal way of communicating in the native language. The converging tendency toward the idealized rhetorical pattern of English reflects the trend for standardization of global communication in general, or the establishment of ideal ways of talking and listening, as Cameron (2002) observes. Cameron argues that in the globalization paradigm, the ideal style of communication, not necessarily the language used for communication, is increasingly modeled after the white Anglophone norm. Good oral communication, as promoted in communication skills training to cope with globalizing trends, is often characterized as being direct, articulate, explicit, and yet sympathetic and cooperative. This notion of a global standard in communication is being legitimated in such training, influencing teaching and learning in schools around the globe. For instance, the Japanese textbooks we examined contain sections entitled "group discussion," "panel discussion," and "debate" in which students are instructed to express their opinion clearly at the outset and support their opinion clearly. It seems plain that in the Japanese case, the preference for the Anglophone norm is observed in both oral and written communication, representing a struggle to survive in globalized economy, which in turn homogenizes the ideal ways of speaking and writing.

The above observation indicates the importance of recognizing the shifting nature of rhetorical norms, which is influenced by socioeconomic and political forces. It highlights the dynamic, organic, and political nature of linguistic standards that ruptures cultural stability and neutrality. The converging trend toward the idealized rhetorical pattern of English also reflects the linguistic and cultural relations of power, creating a linguistic and cultural hierarchy. These relations are influenced by politics and international relations of power, which construct discourses about which language should be the model to emulate for effective communication. It is important to note that these power relations are not static but dynamic. The shifting influence of politics on language is demonstrated in the historical shift of language policy in Japan. During World War II, teaching of English was banned because it was the language of the enemy, while the Japanese language was imposed on the Japanese colonies throughout Asia. Sixty years later, the language policy has drastically changed. As a strong military and economic ally of the United States, Japan exhibits a zeal for teaching and learning English, a language regarded as the most important international language. In 2000, the national government even considered making English an official language (see Matsuura, Fujieda, & Mahoney, 2004).

Despite the powerful trend toward convergence into the Anglophone rhetorical norm, there is evidence of resistance. Reporting some key issues discussed at the 4th International Conference on ELT in China, You (2004) comments that presenters such as Andy Kirkpatrick and Shane Xuexin Cao advocated for using Chinese rhetorical tradition in writing English. This signifies postcolonial appropriation of English for resisting assimilation to the Anglophone norm (cf. Canagarajah, 1999). In a critical approach, it is important not to essentialize essentialism as something always negative in terms of its purpose and consequence. Cultural essentialism can be strategically used to fulfill political purposes of solidarity as seen in resistance to (neo)colonial domination, racism, and sexism (see Spivak, 1993). The acknowledgement of multiple meanings and purposes of essentialism broadens the scope of a critical analysis of cross-cultural rhetoric.

In sum, cultural essentialism in rhetoric can be problematized from a stance of liberal pluralism which describes and celebrates rhetorical diversity. It can also be scrutinized from the point of view of ideology critique by seeking objective truth while rejecting false assumptions as ideologies. Yet another critical approach would view power, hegemony, politics, and discourse as major contributors for constructing the idea of what ideal ways of communication should be, while it acknowledges resistance and appropriation that challenges such ideas. In this approach, shifting rhetorical conventions are investigated by situating them in these broader contexts.

The Prescriptive/Descriptive Gap in Rhetorical Organizations

Both Study 1 and Study 2 indicated that the model or sample essays presumably written by students or commissioned authors tended to follow the idealized text structures for opinion writing recommended by the textbooks. However, other opinion texts, either model essays for writing or reading materials drawn from published work and/or commissioned for the textbook, did not necessarily follow this pattern. Although these results come from small-scale studies with limitations, they indicate that the front-loaded pattern for opinion writing is indeed a model for student writing but not necessarily a typical structure in other opinion texts that the students are exposed to.

This observation again confirms the plurality of rhetorical patterns in texts that appear outside of instructional environments. A critique of cultural essentialism would pay attention to this prescriptive/descriptive gap and draw on scholars' observations. For instance, the following comments on a typical deductive pattern for persuasive essays for young writers would support this point:

> In fact, most people will rarely experience persua-
> sive text in this form. Often the most powerful ar-
> guments, the ones that really persuade the listener/
> reader, are narratives, the story of real people's lives
> either depicted through anecdotes . . . If a newspaper
> journalist wants to make a point about the suffering
> of people in a war zone, or the untrustworthiness of
> politicians, we get a news story, not a structured ar-
> gument. (Riley & Reedy, 2000, p. 159)

This comment indicates the existence of diverse patterns used for opinion writing in the real world. Similarly, from the perspective of New Rhetoric, varied writing situations and purposes require different types of writing and a particular text structure per se does not lead to good writing. Coe (2002) states: ". . . there are many academic and professional writing situations in which a thesis statement may not appear in the introduction and/or in which unity of purpose is signified without using a thesis statement; our students need to understand that unity of purpose is what matters" (p. 201). These comments seem to be confirmed by the general findings of the two studies; what is considered to be model or good writing is determined by situated effectiveness which is supported by appropriate rhetorical structures for the particular situation, topic, and purpose rather than a generic prescriptive rhetorical structure for a certain text type. Thus, only teaching how to use prescribed structures might actually restrict students' ability.

The above critique can be taken further to larger political concerns, especially the question of the norm. Issues to address include the following: What political forces construct and perpetuate the norm? How norms influence not only classroom instruction but also the construction of images of certain cultures and languages? Who benefits from the norm and who are disadvantaged by it? Issues of the norm and the prescriptive/descriptive gap indeed indicate an irony in the creation of images of language and culture in cross-cultural contexts. Although there is evidence of an increased influence of idealized English rhetoric in Japanese and Chinese writing instruction in schools and the conventional approach to writing instruction seems to persist, L1 English texts for reading in language arts textbooks are not necessarily organized with this idealized structure. In the age of globalization, East Asian cultures seem to follow the trend of Anglicization of rhetoric on the prescriptive level for instructional purposes, while diverging from the idealized norm on the descriptive level. Conversely, many teachers and general public still seem to believe in the dichotomous cultural differences between the East and the West despite the trend toward cultural homogenization and the observed prescriptive/descriptive gap. The construction and transformation of the images of culture and language are complexly tangled with contradictions and paradoxes.

Clearly, school writing is a type of writing that often differs from everyday written communication, and this seems to be the case in all four cultures in which the textbooks we examined are published. This leads to the question about the goal of school writing.

Goal of School Writing and Rhetorical Conventions—Connection to Testing

If there is a gap between the pattern promoted for school writing and the structures of actual texts that appear in the print culture in everyday life, then for what purpose is writing taught in schools? One answer is testing. In the United States, for example, many states have implemented standardized written assessments for public school students, which tend to reinforce formulaic rhetorical organization for instructional and scoring convenience (Hillocks, 2002). This assessment demand might have to do with the general gap between secondary school and college teachers' perceptions about the usefulness of the five-paragraph essay. From a secondary school teacher's point of view, having a clearly identifiable pattern would be useful for teaching. In real world writing for varied purposes, however, multiple patterns are often available. Thus at a more sophisticated level (i.e., college level writing and beyond), teachers might feel compelled to teach students about the multiplicity of structures available for good writing. Although the field of language testing tends to be focused on scientific inquiry on reliability and validity, social, cultural, and political dimensions of testing are quite relevant to the present discussion of rhetoric in writing instruction. In fact, critical language testing proposed by Shohamy (2001) critically explores how power is implicated in testing and what consequences testing brings forth. In this sense, issues of power, politics, testing, teaching, and rhetoric are meshed in a complex way.

Japan and China have not been affected by student writing assessment to such a degree. However, short L1 essays are increasingly assigned in Japan as part of high school and university entrance examinations. In my observation, formulaic structures are commonly used in commercial handbooks designed to prepare students for taking these exams (Kubota & Shi, 2005). Some handbooks recommend a three-unit style and others recommend a four-unit style which includes introduction of the issue, statement of one's opinion, supporting details, and conclusion (e.g., Higuchi, Ohara, & Yamaguchi, 2003). Here also, tests seem to reinforce formulaic writing. The production, use, and consequences of such a formula in relation to testing require further investigation as part of the cross-cultural puzzle of critical contrastive rhetoric.

The close relation between high-stakes testing and formulaic writing further indicates the disconnection between school writing and real world writing (Dias, Freedman, Medway & Paré, 1999). Such disconnection questions the consequences of teaching the formulaic patterns to ESL students. While it may help them succeed in testing situations, it might not help them develop creative ways of expressing themselves according to the situation and purpose, as many L1 composition specialists worry. Worse yet, without any critical discussion about cultural difference in the writing class, students might perpetuate their preconceived ideas about commonly held cultural differences between English and Asian languages.

Conclusion

The two studies and a reflective analysis indicate that in cross-linguistic and cross-cultural writing, the dichotomy of deductive versus inductive rhetorical patterns often assigned to English and East Asian languages respectively can be critically reevaluated in various ways from different political and theoretical standpoints. While the liberal pluralist position might consider the empirical evidence against the stereotypical cultural images of rhetorical structures sufficient to dismantle such images, neo-Marxist ideology critique might challenge the stereotypes through analyzing a corpus of data to reveal accurate and objective facts about the rhetoric of the self and the other. Critical contrastive rhetoric as problematizing practice would further scrutinize the diverse rhetorical patterns and the converging trend into the Anglicized rhetoric by making connection to broader issues of politics, power, discourses, and resistance. This perspective questions the role that the prescriptive norm plays in the construction of the images of cultural rhetoric as well as the relationship between the perpetuation of the prescriptive norm and the politics of testing. In this way, the dynamic, diverse, disaporic, and hybrid nature of cultural rhetoric found in the two studies can be not only confirmed but also problematized in critical contrastive rhetoric. Furthermore, there is a possibility of appropriating specific rhetorical features as a means of resistance. The diverse and dynamic nature of rhetoric can be continuously explored in relation to various factors such as the process of text production for school textbooks, the politics of testing and assessment, discourses on global communication, and so on. As Study 2 indicates, making a study align with a framework of critical contrastive rhetoric in a peer review process of publication may not always be straightforward. Moreover, with many theoretical and political orientations within a critical framework makes critical scholarship complex. Constant reflection is essential for articulating the theoretical and political framework used in research that seeks non-essentialist understandings of culture and language in cross-cultural writing research and teaching practice.

Notes

1. We focused on all genres because unlike the Chinese textbooks, the Japanese textbooks presented instruction on various text types in a generic manner rather than focusing specifically on opinion/argumentative writing.

2. We first analyzed "essays" in the Canadian textbooks because "essay" was defined as a form of writing in which an author presents an opinion about a topic. When we tried to find comparable texts in American literature (reading) textbooks, we found that texts labeled as "essays" were generally nonfiction narratives and much longer than Canadian essays. Thus, we decided to examine persuasive texts in writing and grammar textbooks.

References

Atkinson, D. (1997). A critical approach to critical thinking in TESOL. *TESOL Quarterly, 31,* 71–94.

Atkinson, D. (2004). Contrasting rhetorics/contrasting cultures: Why contrastive rhetoric needs a better conceptualization of culture. *Journal of English for Academic Purposes, 3,* 277–389.

Benesch, S. (2001). *Critical English for academic purposes: Theory, politics, and practice.* Mahwah, NJ: Erlbaum.

Cahill, D. (2003). The myth of the "turn" in contrastive rhetoric. *Written Communication, 20,* 170–194.

Cameron, D. (2002). Globalization and the teaching of 'communication skills.' In D. Block & D. Cameron (Eds.), *Globalization and language teaching* (pp. 67–82). London, UK: Routledge.

Canagarajah, A. S. (1999). Resisting linguistic imperialism in English teaching. Oxford: Oxford University Press.

Canagarajah, A. S. (2006). TESOL at forty: What are the issues? *TESOL Quarterly, 40,* 9–34.

Coe, R. M. (2002). The new rhetoric of genre: Writing political beliefs. In A. M. Johns (Ed.), *Genre in the classroom: Multiple perspectives* (pp. 197–207). Mahwah, NJ: Erlbaum.

Connor, U. (2002). New directions in contrastive rhetoric. *TESOL Quarterly, 36,* 493–510.

Connor, U. (2004). Intercultural rhetoric research: Beyond texts. *Journal of English for Academic Purposes, 3,* 291–304.

Dias, P., Freedman, A., Medway, P., & Paré, A. (1999). *Worlds apart: Acting and writing in academic and workplace contexts.* Mahwah, NJ: Erlbaum.

Fairclough, N. (1995). *Critical discourse analysis.* London: Longman.

Freedman, A., & Medway, P. (1994). Introduction: New views of genre and their implications for education. In A. Freedman & P. Medway (Eds.), *Learning and teaching genre* (pp. 1–24). Portsmouth, NH: Boynton/Cook Publishers.

Fulkerson, R. (2005). Composition at the turn of the twenty-first century. *College Composition and Communication, 56,* 654–687.

Higuchi, Y., Ohara, M., & Yamaguchi, M. (2003). *Shin "kata" gaki shōronbun: Sōgō hen* (New "form" writing short essays: Comprehensive volume). Tokyo: Gakushû Kenkyû Sha.

Hillocks, G. (2002). *The testing trap: How state writing assessments control learning.* New York: Teachers College Press.

Hinds, J. (1983). Contrastive rhetoric: Japanese and English. *Text, 3,* 183–195.

Hinds, J. (1990). Inductive, deductive, quasi-inductive: Expository writing in Japanese, Korean, Chinese, and Thai. In U. Connor, & A. M. Johns (Eds.), *Coherence in writing: Research and pedagogical perspectives* (pp. 87–109). Alexandria, VA: TESOL.

Hirose, K. (2003). Comparing L1 and L2 organizational patterns in the argumentative writing of Japanese EFL students. *Journal of Second Language Writing, 12,* 181–209.

Johns, A. M. (2002). Introduction: Genre in the classroom. In A. M. Johns (Ed.), *Genre in the classroom; Multiple perspectives* (pp. 3–13). Mahwah, NJ: Erlbaum.

Johns, A. M. (2003). Genre and ESL/EFL composition instruction. In B. Kroll (Ed.), *Exploring the dynamics of second language writing* (pp. 195–217). Cambridge, UK: Cambridge University Press.

Kaplan, R. B. (1966). Cultural thought patterns in Inter-cultural Education. *Language Learning, 16,* 1–20.

Kirkpatrick, A. (1997). Traditional Chinese text structures and their influences on the writing in Chinese and English of contemporary Mainland Chinese students. *Journal of Second Language Writing, 6,* 223–244.

Kobayashi, H., & Rinnert, C. (2002). High school student perceptions of first language literacy instruction: Implications for second language writing. *Journal of Second Language Writing, 11,* 91–116.

Kobayashi, H., & Rinnert, C. (2003). Composing competence: How L1 and L2 writing experience interact. In M. Baynham, A. Deignan, & G. White (Eds.), *Applied linguistics at the interface* (pp. 105–118). London, UK: Equinox.

Kress, G. (1990). Critical discourse analysis. In W. Grabe (Ed.), *Annual Review of Applied Linguistics* (pp. 84–99). Rowley, MA: Newbury House.

Kubota, R. (1997). Reevaluation of the uniqueness of Japanese written discourse: Implications to contrastive rhetoric. *Written Communication, 14,* 460–480.

Kubota, R. (2002a). Japanese identities in written communication: Politics and discourses. In R. T. Donahue (Ed.), *Exploring Japaneseness: On Japanese enactments of culture and consciousness* (pp. 293–315). Westport, CT: Ablex.

Kubota, R. (2002b). Impact of globalization on language teaching in Japan. In D. Block, & D. Cameron (Eds.), *Globalization and language teaching* (pp. 13–28). London, UK: Routledge.

Kubota, R. & Lehner, A. (2004). Toward critical contrastive rhetoric. *Journal of Second Language Writing, 13,* 7–27.

Kubota, R., & Shi, L. (2005). Instruction and reading samples for opinion and argumentative writing in L1 junior high school textbooks in China and Japan. *Journal of Asian Pacific Communication, 15,* 97–127.

Kumaravadivelu, B. (2006). TESOL methods: Changing tracks, challenging trends. *TESOL Quarterly, 40,* 59–81.

Lewis, S. (2001). Ten years of puzzling about audience awareness. *Clearing House, 74* (4), 191–197.

Luke, A. (2004). Two takes on the critical. In B. Norton, & K. Toohey (Eds.), *Critical pedagogies and language learning* (pp. 21–29). Cambridge, UK: Cambridge University Press.

Matsuura, H., Fujieda, M., & Mahoney, S. (2004). The officialization of English and ELT in Japan: 2000. *World Englishes, 23,* 471–487.

Maynard, S. (1998). *Principles of Japanese discourse: A handbook.* Cambridge, NY: Cambridge University Press.

Miller, C. (1984). Genre as social action. *Quarterly Journal of Speech, 70,* 151–167.

Nunnally, T. E. (1991). Breaking the five paragraph theme barrier. *English Journal, 80* (1), 67–71.

Pennycook, A. (2001). *Critical applied linguistics: A critical introduction.* Mahwah, NJ: Erlbaum.

Pennycook, A. (2004). Critical applied linguistics. In A. Davies, & C. Elder (Eds.), *The handbook of applied linguistics* (pp. 784–807). Malden, MA: Blackwell.

Riley, J., & Reedy, D. (2000). Developing writing for different purposes: Teaching about genre in the early years. London: Paul Chapman Publishing.

Shi, L. (2002). How Western-trained Chinese TESOL professionals publish in their home environment. *TESOL Quarterly, 36,* 625–634.

Shi, L., & Kubota, R. (2007). Patterns of rhetorical organizations in Canadian and American language arts textbooks: An exploratory study. *English for Specific Purposes, 26,* 180–202.

Shohamy, E. (2001). *The power of tests: A critical perspective on the uses of language tests.* London: Longman.

Spack, R. (1997). The rhetorical construction of multilingual students. *TESOL Quarterly, 31,* 765–774.

Spivak, G. (1993). *Outside in the teaching machine.* New York: Routledge.

Tsao, F-F. (1983). Linguistics and written discourse in particular languages: English and Mandarin. *Annual Review of Applied Linguistics, 3,* 99–117.

You, X. (2004). New directions in EFL writing: A report from China. *Journal of Second Language Writing, 13,* 253–256.

You, X. (2005). Conflation of rhetorical tradition: The formation of modern Chinese writing instruction. *Rhetoric Review, 24,* 150–169.

Wesley, K. (2000). The ill effects of the five paragraph theme. *English Journal, 90* (1), 57–60.

Wodak, R. (1996). *Disorders of discourse.* London: Longman.

11 Theory and Practice in Second Language Writing: How and Where Do They Meet?

Wei Zhu

Theory development and instructional practice constitute the core activities in the field of second language writing. That they are essential to our field and are also seen as connected is reflected in how they are treated in various discourse forums of the field. Discussions addressing theory and instruction occupy significant space in monographs or edited volumes dealing with various aspects of second language writing (e.g., Connor & Johns, 1990; Grabe & Kaplan, 1996; Hyland, 2004; Johns, 1997, 2002a), and sections or chapters on theoretical perspectives and frameworks are often followed by those on instructional practice. Journal articles and academic presentations focusing on theoretical/research issues in second language writing are likely to conclude with discussions of the implications of the theory or research for classroom instruction, and those focusing on instruction are likely to begin with explanations of relevant theoretical perspectives and/or research findings to provide support for the discussion of instructional practices that ensues. It may be argued that much effort has been devoted to connecting theory and practice in second language writing, with more emphasis given to the insight that theory has to offer for instructional practice.

Continued effort to connect theory and practice and to explore the relationship between theory and practice in second language writing is essential for the sustained growth of the field. Exploration of the theory-practice relationship will offer us a valuable opportunity for a reflection on the purpose and direction of our field as well as on the contributions of theoretical and instructional activities as sources of knowledge for our field. The importance of addressing the interrelationship between theory and practice in second language writing has long been recognized. Silva (1990), in a historical review of instructional approaches in second language writing, argued for the need for a "coherent model of the interrelationship of ESL writing theory, research, and practice" (p. 19) for the development and evaluation of instructional approaches. More recently, Kroll (2003) treated the theory-practice relationship in second language writing in her introduction to an edited volume prepared for future second language writing teachers. That theory-practice relationship received such attention in the introduction to a book prepared for future second language writing teachers is perhaps no accident. It reflects the significance of the topic for our field.

In this chapter, I explore the relationship between theory and practice in second language writing. I begin by defining the types of theory that are relevant to second language writing and then proceed to a brief discussion of the situated nature of second language writing instructional practice. I then turn to a discussion of the relationship between theory and practice in second language writing, emphasizing the bi-directional, interdependent, and mediated nature of this relationship. I conclude the chapter with a discussion of the implications of this conception of theory-practice relationship for second language writing teacher development.

THEORY IN SECOND LANGUAGE WRITING

Before a discussion on the relationship between second language writing theory and practice is attempted, it is useful to first ponder on what constitutes the "theory" in the theory-practice relationship. The term "theory" can take on multiple meanings. Stern (1983), for example, differentiated among three meanings of theory.[1] According to Stern (1983), theory in the broadest sense, T1, "refers to the systematic study of the thought related to a topic or activity" (p.25). Theory in this sense "offers a system of thought, a method of analysis and synthesis, or a conceptual framework in which to place different observations, phenomena, or activities" (p. 25–26). T2 refers to the "different schools of thought" under T1, "each with their own assumptions, postulates, principles, models, and concepts" (p. 26). T3 refers to theory used in the narrower sense in natural and human sciences, namely as hypotheses which have been tested or as hypotheses postulated for the explanation of behaviors and phenomena in the subject area. Stern's T3 seems to encompass the two forms of theory discussed by Larsen-Freeman and Long (1991): the "set-of-laws form" and the "causal-process form." Theory in the set-of-laws form "typically consists of a collection of (often unrelated) statements recording what is (thought to be) known about the phenomenon" (Larsen-Freeman & Long, 1991, p. 223; parentheses original). The statements are presented as generalizations and are based on repeated observations of a phenomenon or behavior. Theory in this sense is data driven and is developed through research. Theory in the set-of-laws form, however, does not offer explanations for the observations made. Theories in the causal-process form are "consistent with existing knowledge about the matters they treat, but unlike theories of the set-of-laws form, also attempt to explain those phenomena" (Larsen-Freeman & Long, 1991, p. 224). Theory in this sense contains not only statements of facts and observations but also claims about causal relationships. That is, these theories are formal theories in the scientific sense, attempting to offer explanations as to why/how a phenomenon or process occurs and to predict future observations. Theories in the T3 sense could be "micro" or "macro," depending on what a theory is trying to account for (McLaughlin, 1987).

The various meanings of theory presented above are relevant to a discussion of theory in the context of second language writing. A theory in the T1 sense may refer to a comprehensive theory of second language writing which offers a conceptual framework for a synthesis and analysis of our understanding of second language writing. Theories in the T2 sense may refer to the various views and postulations of, orientations towards, and approaches to language, text, composing, and learning. Theories in the T3 sense may refer to statements/generalizations made of second language writing based on empirical research or to formal theories/models which have explanatory and predictive power and which can generate specific hypothesis to be tested by the scientific method.

Significant progress has been made in theorizing second language writing since the 1990s, particularly in the sense of T2 and the "set-of-laws" form of T3 (i.e., theory as statements about what has been learned about a phenomenon).[2] Various views of and approaches to language, text, composing, writer, culture, literacy and other aspects germane to L2 writing have entered and guided discussions of L2 writing and writing development (e.g., Atkinson, 2003; Benesch, 2001; Connor, 1996; Cumming, 1998; Kubota, 2003; Prior, 1998; Swales, 1990), allowing L2 writing to be approached and explored from a multitude of theoretical perspectives. In the meantime, a body of empirical research on second language writing has accumulated, making it possible to develop research-based statements about different facets of L2 writing (for two recent overviews of L2 writing research, see Polio, 2003; Silva & Brice, 2004). Several important foci of empirical research in the L2 writing context include L2 students' composing processes (e.g., Raimes, 1985, 1987; Zamel, 1982, 1983; Sasaki, 2000); L2 reading and writing connections (e.g., Eisterhold, 1990; Carson, Carrell, Silberstein, Kroll & Kuehn, 1990); features of L2 texts (e.g., Reynolds, 1995; Simpson, 2000; Hirose, 2003); writing tasks and contexts (e.g., Carson, 2001; Leki & Carson, 1997; Zhu, 2004); the nature and impact of teacher and peer feedback on student writing (e.g., Ferris, 1997; Ferris & Roberts, 2001; Lockhart & Ng, 1995; Villamil & Guerrero, 1998), and more recently, the role of the computer in second language writing development (for a synthesis of this research, see Pennington, 2003).

However, a T1 for second language writing, a broad theory which integrates different elements of L2 writing, is yet to be developed. Although a comprehensive theory is not yet available, several elements that need to be addressed in a comprehensive theory of L2 writing have been proposed. Silva (1990), for example, suggested that a comprehensive theory of L2 writing address the elements of the writer, the reader, the text, the context, and the interaction of these factors. Johns (1990) proposed that besides factors related to the reader and the writer, "a view of reality and truth" (p. 31) and a view of language be included in a complete theory of L2 writing. Besides a T1, a theory of second language writing in the sense of an explanatory and predictive theory of T3, a theory that "would make strong specific predictions about how given individuals and groups will perform under a range of conditions and a specific set of tasks" (Grabe, 2001, p. 40) is not currently available either.

Efforts to theorize second language writing have been influenced by theories from several related fields. Given the interdisciplinary nature of second language writing as a field of inquiry and practice (Matsuda, 1998, 2003a; Silva & Leki, 2004), it is not surprising that theories from the parent disciplines of second language writing, composition studies and applied linguistics (Silva & Leki, 2004), and related fields such as linguistics, education, and psychology, to name a few, have influenced the development of theory in L2 writing. Theoretical views of writing, of learning, and of the nature and source of language and knowledge originated in various disciplines have been applied to second language writing. Sociocultural theory and activity theory, for example, have guided much of the recent research examining student interaction and learning in L2 writing contexts (Guerrero & Villamil, 1994, 2000; Storch 2002, 2004; Swain, Brooks, & Tocalli-Beller, 2002; Thorne, 2004; Villamil & Guerrero, 1996, 1998). While it is important to be open to possible applications of theories from related fields to L2 writing, it is also essential for L2 writing to develop theories that can address the uniqueness and specificity of L2 writing.

PRACTICE IN SECOND LANGUAGE WRITING

Practice as used in this chapter refers to all facets of second language writing instruction and assessment. As such, it encompasses activities related to the design and development of the curriculum, the selection and development of instructional materials and tools, and the planning and implementation of teaching and feedback activities. In addition, it includes assessment; assessment provides information concerning the effectiveness of instruction but also can exert a powerful influence on instruction through positive or negative backwash. Effective practice entails a mutually enhancing relationship between instruction and assessment.

Second language writing instructional practices are multi-dimensional and multifaceted, addressing a full spectrum of affective, cognitive, and social issues involving the writer, the writing process, the written text, and the context for writing. They include all activities which support and engage the students in the process of L2 writing, such as those which motivate students to learn, which raise student writers' awareness of texts, the composing process, and the writing context, which assist student writers to develop a variety of strategies, which help students to practice skills needed for different writing purposes and rhetorical modes, which provide feedback on student writing through feedback activities or formal means of assessment, and which help student writers develop the ability to reflect on their own writing needs, goals, experiences, and skills. Like educational practices in general, instructional practices in the context of second language writing entail extensive decision making. Decisions need to be made about what skills to teach, how to organize a course, what teaching/ learning activities to implement, what materials and tools to use to support learning, what writing tasks to assign, and when and how to provide feedback and to perform assessment.

While it is possible to discuss practice in abstract terms, practice by nature is socially, culturally, and institutionally situated. Because of this, factors related to the broad education system, institutional philosophy and theoretical and pedagogical orientations, institutional resources (i.e., financial, technological, personnel, facilities), and established organizational and reward structures can have a powerful influence on instructional practices. Teachers constitute a particularly important element in instructional practice. They are the ones who implement the curriculum, who design, select, and implement instructional activities, who adapt or create instructional materials, and who select or develop specific assessment tools and techniques. Teachers are responsible for making and carrying out instructional decisions on a daily basis and are directly involved in instructional practice. It may not be an overstatement that teachers constitute the most important element in instructional practice.

The situatedness of instructional practice indicates that practice in each instructional context is somewhat unique. Not only does practice occur in specific contexts but effective practice should respond to the unique needs of the instructional context in which it occurs. No two contexts are identical, and no context is static. The situatedness of instructional practice means that practice in different contexts has different features, and this has important implications for a discussion of theory-practice relationship in second language writing.

THE RELATIONSHIP BETWEEN THEORY AND PRACTICE IN SECOND LANGUAGE WRITING

Discussions addressing the connection between theory and practice in second language writing seem to have focused more on "theory to practice," with practice at the receiving end. A more complete picture of the theory and practice relationship in second language writing emphasizes the bi-directional, interdependent, dynamic, and mediated nature of this relationship. Practice often motivates theory development by raising questions about various aspects of second language writing and serves as the site in which theory is tested. Theory, in turn, influences practice by providing views of and approaches to writing and writing development to inform the development of teaching methods, by providing research-based evidence to support the formulation of instructional principles to guide practice, and by providing frameworks and tools for the examination and understanding of instructional practice. The relationship between theory and practice in second language writing is also mediated, with the teacher as the critical human element mediating theory and practice.

The influence of practice on theory development in L2 writing should not be underestimated. Practice raises questions for theory and motivates the development of theoretical views and perspectives on writing (theory in the T2 sense) as well as of theory in the T3 sense through empirical research. As reflected in the two recent comprehensive reviews of L2 writing research (Polio, 2003; Silva & Brice, 2004), many issues examined in L2 writing research which contributes to the development of theory in the T3 "set-of-laws" sense are rooted in practice. Practice drives theoretical development in the sense that questions encountered in practice which cannot be accounted for by existing theory provide impetus for the development of new theory. Practice also plays an important role in testing theory. Thus, theory development in second language writing does not occur independently of practice.

Practice is also influenced by theory and benefits from theoretical insights, but the influence of theory on practice needs to be examined more closely. Theory may constitute a major contributor to changes in practice; that is, practices in professions change because "the process of knowledge growth, criticism, and development in the academy leads to the achievement of new understandings, new perspectives, or new ways of interpreting the world" (Shulman, 2004, p. 531). That changes in theoretical perspectives contribute to changes in instructional practices can be seen in the broader field of second language learning and teaching and in the field of second language writing specifically. Changes in theory, particularly in the sense of T2 (i.e., different schools of thought, perspectives, and views) have provided momentum for the development of instructional approaches needed to address changes in the educational context, in goals of language learning, and in students' needs. In the field of second language learning and teaching, the development of instructional approaches such as the Audiolingual Method and Communicative Language Teaching was strongly influenced by changes in theoretical views of language and of learning (Richards & Rogers, 2001). In second language writing, theory in the T2 sense has offered different views and perspectives on writing and written texts, which in turn has impacted instructional practice. Different views of writing and written texts have supported the development and implementation of instructional approaches emphasizing different dimensions of writing in the second language writing context. For example, cognitive views and models of the writing process (Flower & Hayes, 1980, 1981, 1984; Bereiter & Scardamalia, 1987) lent support to a set of instructional practices embodied in the cognitive process approach to writing, which was introduced to L2 writing instruction in the late 1970s and early 1980s. A theory of language, a social view of meaning and meaning making, on the other hand, has supported the development of genre approaches to second language writing instruction (Hyland, 2003).[3] Within the process or the genre approaches, instructional practices are aligned with the underlying theoretical views of writing or text. The cognitive process pedagogy underscores the cognitive dimension of the writing process, focusing in particular on intervention and strategy development. The genre pedagogy, on the other hand, highlights the writing context, the social functions of writing, and the features of written discourse. As can be observed in these examples, instructional practices are influenced by changing or alternative views of learning, writing, language, and text.

While theory in the T2 sense influences L2 writing practice through supporting the development of instructional approaches, theory in the sense of T3 (research-based statements about what has been learned about a phenomenon) contributes to changes in practice by providing additional support concerning the relevance or efficacy of the instructional approaches under examination.[4] For example, some of the research on L2 writing processes in the early 1980s indicated similarities between L1 and L2 writing processes and lent empirical support for the introduction of the process pedagogy to the L2 writing context. Theory in the T3 sense, in addition, constitutes an especially important source of information for the formulation of instructional principles which may be applied to guide more effective instructional practices. Research on peer response offers a case in point. Since the 1980s, peer response in which students exchange drafts and provide feedback on one another's writing has entered the second language writing classroom. Peer response in the L2 context can have cognitive, social, linguistic and practical benefits, yet it is not without difficulties and criticism (Ferris & Hedgcock, 2005; Liu & Hansen, 2002). How to utilize peer response effectively has become an important issue. A significant body of research has been conducted on L2 peer response, and this research has deepened our understanding of the factors that influence L2 peer response. Research on L2 peer response has examined students' views and perceptions of peer response (Mangelsdorf, 1992; Nelson & Carson, 1998), student interaction during peer response (Guerrero & Villamil, 1994; Lockhart & Ng, 1995; Villamil & Guerrero, 1996), and the effect of training students for peer response (Stanley, 1992; Berg, 1999). This body of L2 peer response research has offered significant insight into peer response processes and contributed to the formulation of instructional principles which can be applied to guide more effective use of peer response groups in the L2 writing classroom (e.g., Ferris & Hedgcock, 2005).

Theory in the T2 and T3 sense influences practice; the influence, nevertheless, is not absolute, uniform, or direct. Rather, it is relative and mediated. Instructional approaches and practices supported by changing theoretical views may not be adopted or implemented in all instructional contexts. Even in the heyday of the process movement, process-oriented pedagogies were not enthusiastically implemented by all second language teachers in all L2 contexts (Matsuda, 2003b). Even if an approach or a set of theory-based practices is adopted, it may be implemented in ways inconsistent with its underlying theory. Educational research has indicated that "teachers' personal theories and beliefs serve as the basis for classroom practice and curriculum decision making" (Ross, Cornett, & McCutcheon, 1992).[5] A teacher's theory "consists of sets of beliefs, images, and constructs about such matters as what constitutes an educated person, the nature of knowledge, the society and the psychology of student learning, motivation, and discipline" (McCutcheon, 1992, p. 191). Teachers' theories are personal in nature, are not always articulated but are reflected in practice (McCutcheon, 1992), and differ among teachers due to different personal experiences and differences in teaching contexts. Educational research has shown that teachers mediate curriculum invention and implementation (Parker & McDaniel, 1992; Tobin & LaMaster, 1992) and that teachers implement instructional changes according to their own beliefs (Tobin & LaMaster, 1992). Similar observations have been made in the context of second language writing. Shi and Cumming (1995) examined five teachers' conceptions of L2 writing instruction, and their findings pointed to the role teachers play in mediating changes in instructional practice. Shi and Cumming (1995) pointed out that "curriculum change in second language writing—even if only considered as the introduction of a simple, minor pedagogical innovation—is not a uniform process but rather is construed uniquely by individual instructors, who may accommodate or resist it in terms of their personal beliefs, founded on years of previous experience, reflection, and information" (p. 104). This suggests that changes in instructional practices are mediated through the teachers, specifically their beliefs.

Second language writing instructional practices occur in very diverse contexts and are influenced by numerous contextual variables such as instructional setting, program goals, available resources and materials, and student characteristics. This means that application of instructional principles derived from theory to specific teaching contexts is far from an automatic, straightforward, and linear process. Because theory itself is developed in specific contexts, meaningful application of theory to instruction in the classroom first entails an understanding and evaluation of the relevance and appropriateness of a particular theory to the specific teaching context in which instruction takes place. Theory developed out of some contexts may not be appropriate or even relevant to practice in others; therefore, the application of theory and research findings to the classroom needs to be approached cautiously (Lightbown, 2000, 2002). Second language writing specialists have long cautioned against unquestionably applying theories from L1 contexts to the L2 writing contexts (Silva, 1993). Because of the very diverse contexts for L2 writing instruction, we also need to be cautious about applying L2 writing theories across L2 writing contexts.

Successful application of theory to practice requires teachers to make instructional decisions based on an assessment of the teaching/learning situation and an evaluation of relevant research. Let's again use peer response as an example. As we often see in the research literature, sociocultural theory supports student interaction during the learning process and offers strong theoretical justification for peer response. L2 writing research has yielded principles for effective L2 peer response in the classroom (Ferris & Hedgcock, 2005). However, sociocultural theory and research-based instructional principles still do not supply ready answers to the many questions about peer response that may arise in practice. Teachers need to make decisions concerning group formation, group size, peer response procedures, the role of L1 in peer response, etc. based on an understanding of the relevant theoretical principles and research findings and an assessment of contextual variables such as the nature of the writing task, student familiarity with peer response, the specific purpose(s) of the peer response task at hand, and students' language proficiency levels, writing skills, and educational experience. And there is no guarantee that first attempts at implementing peer response would be successful. Teachers perhaps need to apply, observe, analyze, adapt, reflect and reapply. It is through this recursive process that application of theory to practice may become successful, and the teacher is the key mediator in this process.

As discussed above, the relationship between theory and practice in second language writing is bi-directional, interdependent, and mediated. This relationship is also dynamic and is perhaps more accurately described as a process in which practice and theory motivate and enhance the development of each other. Odell (1993) pinpoints the nature of this relationship when he asserts that "theory needs practice and practice needs theory; each continually challenges and refines the other" (p. 6). Questions encountered or phenomena observed in practice motivate research and the development of new theoretical views, and theory in turn is used to guide and inform practice. New questions encountered in practice may raise additional questions, leading to further research and refinement of theory, which in turn influences practice. This dynamic, interactive, and reciprocal relationship between theory and practice allows advancement in both theory and practice in our field. In the L2 writing classroom, this mutually motivating relationship between theory and practice enables teachers/researchers to seek answers to questions encountered in practice by conducting research and using research findings to inform instructional practices.

Kramsch (2002) offers an excellent example of how observations made in her classroom led to research, and how her research findings shed light on the phenomena observed in practice. In Kramsch's example, observations made of students' written summaries of a story discussed in class—that students had different points of view as to what the story was about and that they reconstructed the story in different ways—raised questions for Kramsch and led her to theories about identity and writing, about genre, and about schema. The theories provided constructs that helped Kramsch frame questions for a more systematic examination of the phenomena observed. In her study, Kramsch investigated how student writers "constructed themselves and the character" (p. 202) of the story by asking two groups of learners of German (American and French) as well as three groups of native speakers of German to write summaries of the same story. She also interviewed some American students. Kramsch found that 1) summary is "a culturally marked genre" (p. 202); and 2) that students, as authors, were able to make conscious decisions about their texts at both macro and micro levels. Kramsch noted several ways in which the research findings would influence her classroom practice.[6] Kramsch's example illustrates the dynamic and interactive relationship between theory and practice in which observations made during/about practice led to research, and findings of research were examined to guide practice. Note that in Kramsch's example the teacher/researcher served as the agent in the practice-theory-practice process.

Kramsch's example also indicated another role theory plays in the theory-practice relationship. In addition to guiding practice, theoretical frameworks, concepts, and constructs serve as community tools and resources to scaffold the examination of problems or phenomena observed in practice. In Kramsch's (2002) example, theoretical constructs and frameworks assisted the framing of research questions for empirical inquiry and provided disciplinary tools to describe and discuss practice, to contemplate and reflect on practice, and to structure and share instructional experiences, all of which enabled a better understanding of practice.

Practice in second language writing contexts is complex, multifaceted and multidimensional. Effective second language writing instruction needs to address many different factors, and it is highly unlikely that any one single theory can inform all aspects of practice even in one instructional context. Second language writing research has indicated that L2 writing instructors draw on different theoretical constructs and orientations in their practices (Cumming, 1992, 2003). Second language writing instructional practices are also situated and constantly face new challenges. Because of this and of the tentative nature of theory, we cannot expect theory to provide us with "unchanging universally applicable principles" (Odell, 1993, p. 2) nor can we expect theory alone to provide answers to all questions encountered in practice. While we recognize the role of theory in informing practice, we should also value practical knowledge as a source of information for practice and as a source of learning for teachers (Shulman, 2004). Collective reflection in which teachers reflect on and share information about what they do and what they have learned from practice with other members of the "community of practice" (Lave & Wenger, 1991) can contribute significantly to a deepened understanding of practice in second language writing and help broaden teachers' repertoire of instructional practices.

CONCLUSION

In this chapter, the relationship between theory and practice in second language writing is described as bi-directional, interdependent, dynamic, and reciprocal. Theory and practice motivate the development of each other, and each is "capable of informing and remaking the other" (Odell, 1993, p. 2). This conception of the relationship between theory and practice means that as our field moves forward we need to give full attention to the interaction between theory and practice. After all, "our understanding of our discipline is not simply knowledge of theory or knowledge of practice. Our knowledge of composing consists of the claims we can make as the result of the ongoing interaction between theory and practice" (Odell, 1993, p. 6). The relationship between theory and practice is also mediated, with the teachers as the most important element mediating theory and practice.

Different conceptions of the relationship between second language writing theory and practice have different implications for the preparation of future second language writing teachers, particularly in terms of defining the roles of second language writing teachers and the knowledge bases and skills needed by future second language writing teachers. While there is no doubt that "theory to practice" constitutes an important facet of the relationship between theory and practice, conceptualizing the relationship between theory and practice predominantly in this term likely casts teachers in the limited role of the consumers of theory. On the other hand, a conception of the theory and practice relationship as bi-directional, mutually informing, and mediated by teachers sees the teachers as participants in the practice-theory-practice process and as contributors to the development of theory as well as practice in our field. This conception requires an expansion of traditional teacher roles to include those of the reflective thinker (Richards, 1998; Richards & Lockhart, 1994) as well as the researcher involved in theorizing second language writing. Preparing teachers who can contribute to the development of both theory and practice and who can successfully mediate the theory and practice relationship will contribute significantly to the sustained growth of second language writing as a field of inquiry and practice.

Teacher preparation programs need to address more explicitly the dynamic, interactive, and reciprocal relationship between theory and practice and help teachers develop the skills and knowledge bases needed to understand and enhance the interaction between theory and practice. Effective teaching does not simply result from the mastery of a set of pedagogical techniques, and teachers need to develop an understanding of theory (in both the T2 and T3 sense) relevant to second language writing. Teachers also need to develop an ability to apply theory and research to practice critically and judiciously and to understand the complex, recursive, adaptive, and reflective process of applying theory to practice. At the same time, teacher preparation programs need to help teachers understand that they also have a role to play in contributing to the development of theory in L2 writing and assist teachers to develop an ability to make this contribution. Teachers are in a unique position to identify questions for empirical inquiry and to test theory, and bringing teachers into the process of theorizing L2 writing will help broaden the base for theory development in L2 writing. Preparing teachers to become participants in the process of connecting L2 writing theory and practice promotes the development of both L2 writing theory and practice and is essential to the development of our field.

ACKNOWLEDGMENTS

I would like to thank Jane Harvey for her assistance with library research and locating some of the sources used in this chapter.

NOTES

1. Stern discussed the various meanings of theory in the context of second language teaching theory. An example of T1 given by Stern is a theory of second language teaching. Examples of T2 provided by Stern included different approaches to second language teaching such as the audiolingual approach and the direct method as well as cognitive theory. Examples provided by Stern for T3 included learning and personality theories from psychology.

2. Olson (1999), taking a postmodern perspective, distinguished between "theorizing" and "theory." According to Olson, while theory can be "dangerous" from a postmodern perspective, theorizing "can be productive" (p. 8). Such a distinction between theory and theorizing is not made in the present essay.

3. Three approaches to genre are discussed in the literature: English for Specific Purposes, New Rhetoric, and the Australian systemic and functional approach (Hyon, 1996; Johns, 2002b).

4. Empirical research on the efficacy of L2 writing instructional approaches and techniques often yields mixed results, and research that systematically examines the impact of instructional approaches on student writing development is still much needed.

5. Teachers' theories are also referred to as teachers' "personal theories" (Pape, 1992), "theories of practice" or "theories of action" (McCutcheon, 1992).

6. Implications of the research findings for classroom practice discussed by Kramsch include 1) focusing on how students use semiotic resources to express meaning in the classroom, 2) supporting and raising students' awareness of their authorial voices, 3) providing opportunities for students to compare and contrast their writing to "enhance students' discoursal selves" (p. 207), and 4) helping students learn ways to analyze their own writing.

REFERENCES

Atkinson, D. (2003). Writing and culture in the post-process era. *Journal of Second Language Writing, 12,* 49–63.

Benesch, S. (2001). *Critical English for academic purposes: Theory, politics, and practice.* Mahwah, NJ: Erlbaum.

Bereiter, C., & Scardamalia, M. (1987). *The psychology of written composition.* Hillsdale, NJ: Erlbaum.

Berg, E. C. (1999). The effects of trained peer response on ESL students' revision types and writing quality. *Journal of Second Language Writing, 8,* 215–241.

Carson, J. (2001). A task analysis of reading and writing in academic contexts. In D. Belcher and A. Hirvela (Eds.), *Linking literacies: Perspectives on L2 reading-writing connections* (pp. 48–83). Ann Arbor, MI: University of Michigan Press.

Carson, J., Carrell, P., Silberstein, S., Kroll, B., & Kuehn, P. (1990). Reading-writing relationships in first and second languages. *TESOL Quarterly, 24,* 245–266.

Connor, U. (1996). *Contrastive rhetoric: Cross-cultural aspects of second-language writing.* Cambridge: Cambridge University Press.

Connor, U., & Johns, A. (Eds.). (1990). *Coherence in writing: Research and pedagogical perspectives.* Alexandria, Virginia: Teachers of English to Speakers of Other languages.

Cumming, A. (1992). Instructional routines in ESL composition teaching. *Journal of Second Language Writing, 1,* 17–35.

Cumming, A. (1998). Theoretical perspectives on writing. *Annual Review of Applied Linguistics, 18,* 61–78.

Cumming, A. (2003). Experienced ESL/EFL writing instructors' conceptualizations of their teaching: Curriculum options and implications. In B. Kroll (Ed.), *Exploring the dynamics of second language writing* (pp. 71–92). Cambridge: Cambridge University Press.

Eisterhold, J. C. (1990). Reading-writing connections: Toward a description for second language learners. In B. Kroll (Ed.), *Second language writing: Research insights for the classroom* (pp. 88–101). Cambridge: Cambridge University Press.

Ferris, D. R. (1997). The influence of teacher commentary on student revision. *TESOL Quarterly, 31,* 315–339.

Ferris, D. R., & Roberts, B. (2001). Error feedback in L2 writing classes: How explicit does it need to be? *Journal of Second Language Writing, 10,* 161–184.

Ferris, D. R., & Hedgcock, J. S. (2005). *Teaching ESL composition: Purpose, process and practice* (2nd edition). Mahwah, NJ: Erlbaum.

Flower, L., & Hayes, J. (1980). The cognition of discovery: Defining a rhetorical problem. *College Composition and Communication, 31,* 21–32.

Flower, L., & Hayes, J. (1981). A cognitive process theory of writing. *College Composition and Communication, 32,* 365–387.

Flower, L., & Hayes, J. (1984). Images, plans and prose: The representation of meaning in writing. *Written Communication, 1,* 120–160.

Grabe, W. (2001). Notes toward a theory of second language writing. In T. Silva & P. Matsuda (Eds.), *On second language writing* (pp. 39–57). Mahwah, NJ: Erlbaum.

Grabe, W., & Kaplan, R. (1996). *Theory and practice of writing.* New York: Longman.

Guerrero, M.C.M. de, & Villamil, O.S. (1994). Social-cognitive dimensions of interaction in L2 peer revision. *Modern Language Journal, 78,* 484–496.

Guerrero, M.C.M. de, & Villamil, O. S. (2000). Activating the ZPD: Mutual scaffolding in L2 peer revision. *Modern Language Journal, 84,* 51–68.

Hirose, K. (2003). Comparing L1 and L2 organizational patterns in the argumentative writing of Japanese EFL students. *Journal of Second Language Writing, 12,* 181–209.

Hyland, K. (2003). Genre-based pedagogies: A social response to process. *Journal of Second Language Writing, 12,* 17–29.

Hyland, K. (2004). *Genre and second language writing*. Ann Arbor, MI: University of Michigan Press.

Hyon, S. (1996). Genre in three traditions: Implications for ESL. *TESOL Quarterly, 30,* 693–722.

Johns, A, M. (1990). L1 composition theories: Implications for developing theories of L2 composition. In B. Kroll (Ed.), *Second language writing: Research insights for the classroom* (pp. 24–36). Cambridge: Cambridge University Press.

Johns, A. (1997). *Text, role, and context*. Cambridge: Cambridge University Press.

Johns, A. (Ed.) (2002a). *Genre in the classroom: Multiple perspectives*. Mahwah, NJ: Erlbaum.

Johns, A. (2002b). Introduction. In A. Johns (Ed.), *Genre in the classroom: Multiple perspectives* (pp. 3–13). Mahwah, NJ: Erlbaum.

Kramsch, C. (2002). From practice to theory and back again. *Language, Culture and Curriculum, 15,* 196–209

Kroll, B. (2003). Introduction: Teaching the next generation of second language writers. In B. Kroll (Ed.), *Exploring the dynamics of second language writing* (pp. 1–10). Cambridge: Cambridge University Press.

Kubota, R. (2003). New approaches to gender, class, and race in second language writing. *Journal of Second Language Writing, 12,* 31–47.

Larsen-Freeman, D., & Long, M. (1991). *An introduction in second language acquisition research.* New York: Longman.

Lave, J., & Wenger, E. (1991). *Situated learning: Legitimate peripheral participation.* Cambridge: Cambridge University Press.

Leki, I., & Carson, J. (1997). "Completely different worlds": EAP and the writing experiences of ESL students in university courses. *TESOL Quarterly, 31,* 39–69.

Lightbown, P. (2000). Classroom SLA research and second language teaching. *Applied Linguistics, 21,* 431–462.

Lightbown, P. (2002). The role of SLA research in L2 teaching: Reply to Sheen. *Applied Linguistics, 23,* 529–535.

Liu, J., & Hansen, J. G. (2002). *Peer response in second language writing classrooms.* Ann Arbor, MI: University of Michigan Press.

Lockhart, C., & Ng, P. (1995). Analyzing talk in ESL peer response groups: Stances, functions, and content. *Language Learning, 45,* 605–655.

Mangelsdorf, K (1992). Peer reviews in the ESL composition classroom: What do the students think? *ELT Journal, 46,* 274–284.

Matsuda, P. K. (1998). Situating ESL writing in a cross-disciplinary context. *Written Communication, 15,* 99–121.

Matsuda, P.K. (2003a). Second language writing in the twentieth century: A situated historical perspective. In B. Kroll (Ed), *Exploring the dynamics of second language writing* (pp. 15–34). Cambridge: Cambridge University Press.

Matsuda, P.K. (2003b). Process and post-process: A discursive history. *Journal of Second Language Writing, 12*, 65–83.

McCutcheon, G. (1992). Facilitating teacher personal theorizing. In E.W. Ross, J.W. Cornett, & G. McCutcheon (Eds.), *Teacher personal theorizing* (pp. 191–205). Albany, NY: State University of New York Press.

McLaughlin, B. (1987). *Theories of second-language learning.* New York: Edward Arnold.

Nelson, G. L., & Carson, J., G. (1998). ESL students' perceptions of effectiveness in peer response groups. *Journal of Second Language Writing, 7,* 113–132.

Odell, L. (1993). Introduction: Theory and practice. In L. Odell (Ed.), *Theory and practice in the teaching of writing: Rethinking the discipline* (pp. 1–8). Carbondale: Southern Illinois University Press.

Olson, G. (1999). Toward a post-process composition: Abandoning the rhetoric of assertion. In T. Kent (Ed.), *Post-process theory: Beyond the writing-process paradigm* (pp. 7–15). Carbondale: Southern Illinois University Press.

Pape, S. (1992). Personal theorizing of an intern teacher. In E.W. Ross, J.W. Cornett, & G. McCutcheon (Eds.), *Teacher personal theorizing* (pp. 67–81). Albany, NY: State University of New York Press.

Parker, W.C., & McDaniel, J. E. (1992). Bricolage: Teachers do it daily. In E.W. Ross, J.W. Cornett, & G. McCutcheon (Eds.), *Teacher personal theorizing* (pp. 97–114). Albany, NY: State University of New York Press.

Pennington, M. (2003). The impact of the computer in second language writing. In B. Kroll (Ed.), *Exploring the dynamics of second language writing* (pp. 287–310). Cambridge: Cambridge University Press.

Prior, P.A. (1998). *Writing/Disciplinarity: A sociohistoric account of literate activity in the academy.* Mahwah, NJ: Erlbaum.

Polio, C. (2003). Research on second language writing: An overview of what we investigate and how. In B. Kroll (Ed.), *Exploring the dynamics of second language writing* (pp. 35–65). Cambridge: Cambridge University Press.

Raimes, A. (1985). What unskilled ESL students do as they write: A classroom study of composing. *TESOL Quarterly, 19,* 229–258.

Raimes, A. (1987). Language proficiency, writing ability, and composing strategies: A study of ESL college student writers. *Language Learning, 37,* 439–468.

Reynolds, D. (1995). Repetition in nonnative speaker writing: More than quantity. *Studies in Second Language Acquisition, 17,* 185–210.

Richards, J. C. (1998). *Beyond training.* Cambridge: Cambridge University Press.

Richards, J., & Lockhart, C. (1994). *Reflective teaching in second language classrooms.* Cambridge: Cambridge University Press.

Richards, J., & Rodgers, T. (2001). *Approaches and methods in language teaching.* Cambridge: Cambridge University Press.

Ross, E. W., Cornett, J. W., & McCutcheon, G. (1992). Teacher personal theorizing and research on curriculum and teaching. In E.W. Ross, J.W. Cornett, & G. McCutcheon (Eds.), *Teacher personal theorizing* (pp. 3–18). Albany, New York: State University of New York Press.

Sasaki, M. (2000). Toward an empirical model for EFL writing processes: An exploratory study. *Journal of Second Language Writing, 9,* 259–291.

Shi, L., & Cumming, A. (1995). Teachers' conceptions of second language writing instruction: Five case studies. *Journal of Second Language Writing, 4,* 87–111.

Shulman, L. (2004). *The wisdom of practice: Essays on teaching, learning, and learning to teach.* San Francisco, CA: Jossey-Bass.

Silva, T. (1990). Second language composition instruction: developments, issues, and directions in ESL. In B. Kroll (Ed.), *Second language writing: Research insights for the classroom* (pp. 11–23). Cambridge: Cambridge University Press.

Silva, T. (1993). Toward an understanding of the distinct nature of L2 writing: The ESL research and its implication. *TESOL Quarterly, 27,* 657–675.

Silva, T., & Brice, C. (2004). Research in teaching writing. *Annual Review of Applied Linguistics, 24,* 70–106.

Silva, T., & Leki, I (2004). Family matters: The influence of applied linguistics and composition studies on second language writing studies—past, present, and future. *Modern Language Journal, 88,* 1–13.

Simpson, J. (2000). Topical structure analysis of academic paragraphs in English and Spanish. *Journal of Second Language Writing, 9,* 293–309.

Stanley, J. (1992). Coaching student writers to be effective peer evaluators. *Journal of Second Language Writing, 1,* 217–233.

Stern, H. H. (1983). *Fundamental concepts of language teaching.* Oxford, UK: Oxford University Press.

Storch, N. (2002). Patterns of interaction in ESL pair work. *Language Learning, 52,* 119–158.

Storch, N. (2004). Using activity theory to explain differences in patterns of dyadic interactions in an ESL class. *The Canadian Modern Language Review, 60* (4), 457–480.

Swain, M., Brooks, L., & Tocalli-Beller, A. (2002). Peer-peer dialogue as a means of second language learning. *Annual Review of Applied Linguistics, 22,* 171–185.

Swales, J. (1990). *Genre analysis.* Cambridge: Cambridge University Press.

Thorne, S. (2004). Cultural historical activity theory and the object of innovation. In K. van Esch & O. St. John (Eds.), *New insights into foreign language learning and teaching* (pp. 51–70). New York: Peter Lang.

Tobin, K., & LaMaster, S. U. (1992). An interpretation of high school science teaching based on metaphors and beliefs for specific roles. In E.W. Ross, J.W. Cornett, & G. McCutcheon (Eds.), *Teacher personal theorizing* (pp. 115–136). Albany, New York: State University of New York Press.

Villamil, O.S., & Guerrero, M.C.M. de (1996). Peer revision in the L2 classroom: Social-cognitive activities, mediating strategies, and aspects of social behavior. *Journal of Second Language Writing, 5,* 51–75.

Villamil, O.S., & Guerrero, M.C.M.de (1998). Assessing the impact of peer revision on L2 writing. *Applied Linguistics, 19,* 491–514.

Zamel, V. (1982). Writing: The process of discovering meaning. *TESOL Quarterly, 16,* 195–209.

Zamel, V. (1983). The composing processes of advanced ESL students: Six case studies. *TESOL Quarterly, 17,* 165–187.

Zhu, W. (2004). Writing in business courses: An analysis of assignment types, their characteristics, and required skills. *English for Specific Purposes, 23,* 111–135.

12 Theory-and-Practice and Other Questionable Dualisms in L2 Writing

John Hedgcock

Theory/Practice? Theory TO Practice? Theory AND Practice?

When I was invited to explore the topic of practice and theory in second language (L2) writing, in my positivist naiveté, I thought, "That shouldn't be too hard." After all, the disciplinary boundaries for a long time have seemed clear: *Theory* is mainly the work of scholars and empirical researchers, and *practice* is what teachers "do" in classrooms with their learners (cf. Matsuda, 1999). If only such convenient distinctions were that simple.

"Theory" often refers to an abstract "thing" (e.g., a principle, precept, or prediction) generated by "experts" or "theorists" and ideally reshaped by researchers. "Practice" frequently refers to a concrete and more pedestrian "thing" or activity that involves classroom teachers "doing" the work of teaching and student writers learning to write. In this dualistic system, labor is distributed according to the nature of the mission, the content of each constituency's output, and the stakeholders who see to it that the teaching and development of L2 writing skills somehow "happen." The diagram in Figure 1 attempts to illustrate these *perceived* relationships.

The distribution of labor, of course, is not truly dichotomous. Writing about preparing L1 composition teachers, Stenberg and Lee (2002), claimed that "theory and practice . . . function in interplay," with pedagogy encompassing both (p. 328). The spheres of thought, work, and action actually overlap or at least intersect (Olson, 2002). I call this intersection an application metaphor. The public discourse in our field tends to reify the separability of practice and theory through the application metaphor. Let me offer an example or two: Valdés, Haro, and Echevarriarza (1992) wrote that " . . . an adequate theory of second language writing is needed that can *guide* both the teaching and the assessment of written language production" (p. 347, emphasis added). We should note which constituency shapes the practical agenda.

In *Theory and Practice of Writing,* Grabe and Kaplan (1996) laid out a comprehensive theoretical model, an "ethnography of writing," in which they portrayed a theory-*to*-practice perspective that hints strongly at the top-down hierarchy illustrated in Figure 1. Although they were cautious about implementation, the application metaphor is explicit: For them, a chief question for the field revolves around

> the pedagogical implications that follow from a theo-
> ry of writing: 'How does one develop writing instruc-
> tion from a theory of writing?' The most realistic an-
> swer is that the movement from theory to practice is
> not necessarily direct, nor is it necessarily straight-
> forward. One does not simply 'apply' a theory and
> thereby produce a means of instruction. At the same
> time . . . discussion of theory . . . makes a number
> of strong suggestions for designing writing curricula.
> (Grabe & Kaplan, 1996, p. 235)

Thus, the theory-*to*-practice relationship, though not necessarily tidy, is often seen as essentially *unidirectional,* a feature that my diagram simplistically illustrates. In characterizing a theory of practice, de Beaugrande (1997) went some distance toward bidirectionality by asserting that a main criterion for establishing any theory's validity should be the "applicability" of that theory to actual practice, and Rajagopalan (2004) claimed that applied linguistics is undergoing an irreversible "neo-empiricist swing" (p. 412). Nonetheless, I believe that domains of activity sometimes operate autonomously. Instructional practice has been going on for centuries, sometimes quite indepen-dent of any formalized theory or philosophy (Musumeci, 1997), and traditional and current-traditional rhetoric are still practiced in quite a few educational institutions (Fulkerson, 2005). Empirical research moves forward without being "guided," "driven," or necessarily "in-

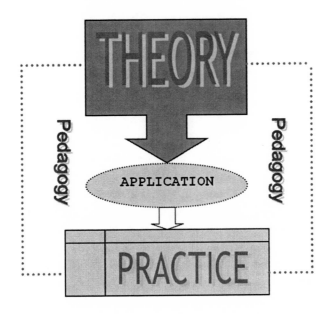

Figure 1. Perceived relationships between theory and practice.

spired" by a single theory, irrespective of whether that theory is formally articulated or quite implicit (de Beaugrande, 1997; Olson, 1994; Rajagopalan, 2004).

We can find evidence of practice-theory separation and status differentials not only in the content of the literature, but also in the rhetorical structures of our field's canonical texts. For instance, we can observe the division of thematic headings in recent issues of *TESOL Quarterly:*

ARTICLES

FORUM

BRIEF REPORTS AND SUMMARIES

TEACHING ISSUES

REVIEWS

This distribution conveys the implicit message that theory and research articles belong in a distinct category from teaching-related contributions. Similar distributions abound, but it is striking that the dualistic scheme—whether or not it is actually dialectic (Evensen, 1997)—has not been more widely challenged until recently.

When we thoughtfully consider who generates "theory," who participates in "practice," and how all of this work connects, things get very messy, very fast. Roles, responsibilities, and privileges get tangled and very difficult to parse and sort. We see the theory/practice "divide" obscured. I have always thought the dichotomy represented an easy but misleading dualism (Hedgcock, 2002). Nonetheless, it is extremely difficult to develop a full picture of the range of dynamic activities in L2 writing because it is so complex to map these connections meaningfully, as my drawing in Figure 2 clearly shows.

A discovery that I made in trying to map out the epistemological and pedagogical territory was that *practice* was, in fact, pervasive. For that reason, I placed it in a central position to signify that *theory-building, empirical research,* and *writing instruction* are all activities that we *practice.* Most of us might just agree on that feature of my schema, although we would probably never agree on the labels, conduits, or configurations—and perhaps we don't need to, if we submit to a kind of simplistic post-modernism in which claiming or professing an ideological view is optional (Fulkerson, 2005).

Among the hard questions that emerged as I reviewed sources on practice, research, and theory concerns our operational definitions of these domains of activity. It occurred to me that perhaps our public discourse (including talk and writing about "theory") has not actually caught up to what we really *do* in the day-to-day work of professionals who work with multilingual writers. I wonder if there might be alternatives to the dualistic, or dialectic, scheme that seems so intractable and pervasive. Lawrence Berlin (2005) made a strong appeal for shifting toward a Freirian *praxis* model in ESL teaching. Along similar lines, David Block (2003) called for a "sociocultural turn" in L2 acquisition, as did Karen Johnson (2006) in teacher education. Before we consider *praxis* and sociocultural turns, though, I suggest that we take stock of current conceptualizations of practice and theory.

What Do We Mean by Theory? What Do We Mean by Practice?

I had originally envisioned exploring the theory-practice interface and the application metaphor (or fallacy). I ended up getting tied up (if not mummified) in the web of Figure 2 and stuck on how disparately the experts characterize theories, models, and methods. Also nagging at me was the question of why we assume a strong need for "theory" to begin with: On what grounds do we insist on a formalized theoretical foundation for our many activities? Grabe (2001) cautioned that "theories of writing, as all-encompassing views, can lead researchers and teachers away from the real examination of writing performances in well-recognized contexts and can lead to vague generalizations and confusion" (p. 39). I concur with Grabe, as my current understanding of writing processes is vague, general, and confused.

Still, I cannot seem to shake Kurt Lewin's (1951) oft-cited dictum that "there is nothing so practical as good theory" (p. 7). Indeed, Grabe (2001) outlined eight specific, pragmatic, *practical* benefits of a modest descriptive theory, which would "describe what writing is; how it is carried out as a set of mental processes; how it varies (both cognitively and functionally) across tasks, settings, groups, cultures, and so forth; how it is learned (and why it is not learned); and how it leads to individual differences in performance" (p. 41). Grabe and Kaplan (1996) encapsulated the aims of such a theory in the form of this incisive question: "*Who writes what to whom, for what purpose, why, when, where, and how?*" (p. 203). I would insert an addendum: "*. . . and in what (linguistic) medium?*" A theory that can fully address this question (to paraphrase Grabe, 2001) would supply us with:

1. An account of how writers generate texts and why readers deem texts effective;
2. An explanation of why writing quality varies when context, topic, and task are held constant;
3. An understanding of why some writers produce unsuccessful texts under certain conditions and when assigned specific composing tasks;
4. A characterization of how developmental paths vary under divergent conditions;
5. Criteria for evaluating curricula, instructional methods, and educational outcomes;
6. Frameworks for constructing effective, construct-appropriate writing curricula;
7. Tools for devising productive teaching practices and response methods;

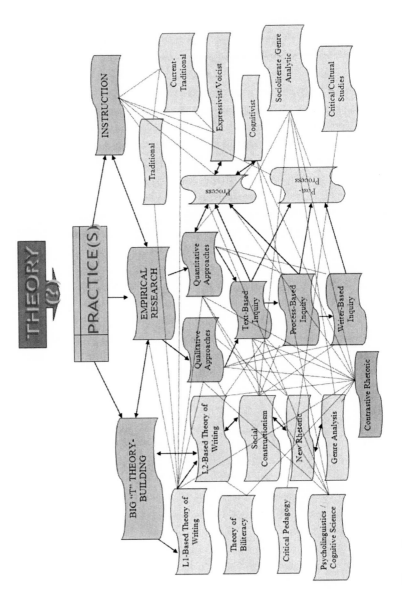

Figure 2.

8. Reliable, valid, and fair procedures for assessing written products and writers' skills.

In appraising the state of the art, Barbara Kroll (2003) echoed leading researchers (e.g., Cumming, 1998; Cumming & Riazi, 2000; Gebhard, 1998; Grabe, 2001; Hyland, 2002), who observed that what we know about composing and learning to write is essentially descriptive, "thus making theory-building difficult" (p. 6). We may still be a long way from achieving theoretical maturity, which would entail a knowledge base that provides both explanatory and predictive power. And circumvention probably won't help much: As Kroll (2003) pointed out, "substituting the notion of 'models' for theories does not resolve the dilemma" (p. 6). Furthermore, "no matter how much we help student writers 'improve' their composing process(es), we are still talking about *methods* and not *theory*" (p. 7, my emphasis).

A Survey of Surveys

Based on my review of expert sources on L1 and L2 writing, I couldn't agree more. Surveys of the epistemological landscape chart the territory with very different measurement tools, resulting in a bewildering range of theoretical catalogues and methodological taxonomies. I would like to share an entirely non-scientific survey of surveys to illustrate the interesting and contradictory ways in which theoretical, ideological, and disciplinary boundaries are drawn.

Bräuer (2000) accounted for what he called a paradigm shift (cf. Kuhn, 1962) by classifying theories of product, process, and writer by decade:

- Writing in the 1960s and 1970s (Cognitivism)
- Writing in the 1970s and 1980s (the "Literacy Crisis")
- Writing in the 1990s (Genre Analysis)

Nice and tidy, to say the least, but the boundaries and labels are confined to L1 composition and rhetoric. Even if viewed as complementary, Bräuer's scheme would probably not sufficiently address the core question posed by Grabe and Kaplan (1996).

In the same volume, Homstad and Thorson (2000) presented a survey of what they called "theories" of "writing and language pedagogy," also tidily compartmentalizing shifts in practice:

- Grammar-Translation
- Audiolingualism
- The Proficiency Movement
- Writing Research Today
  - Writing Across the Curriculum (WAC)

  · Foreign Language (in contrast to ESL) Writing Instruction
  · Process-Oriented FL/L2 Writing Instruction
  · Genre-Oriented FL/L2 Writing Instruction

It is encouraging to see explicit reference to multilingual learners, but
the authors' survey is a catalogue of methods, rather than theories
(though, here again, boundaries are blurred).

More recently, in a 568-page tome subtitled *Theory and Practice in
the Teaching of Writing,* Clark and colleagues (2003) also divided the
theory-research-practice landscape diachronically:

- The Writing Process Movement
  · Stages of Writing
  · Observational Studies
  · Cognitive and Developmental Models (e.g., Flower & Hayes,
    1981)
- Expressivism and Voicism
- Social Constructionism
- Post-Process Theory

Clark's taxonomy is more comprehensive and ideologically informed
than that of Bräuer (2000), and categories veer into familiar L2 writing territory, similar to that covered in comparable books on L2 writing (e.g., Ferris & Hedgcock, 2005; Hyland, 2003). Topics related to
the teaching and learning of multilingual writers, however, are covered
in a single chapter that provides a disturbingly lopsided and outdated
perspective on L2 acquisition while overlooking a great deal of L2
writing literature (Hedgcock, 2004).

More recently, Hayes (2006) postulated three "new directions" in
writing theory: (1) Research on working memory in writing; (2) studies of freewriting and its effect on writing skills; (3) Activity Theory as
a framework for understanding contexts for writing. Not surprisingly,
Hayes's orientation is distinctly psycholinguistic, but taken together,
these directions might address the *who, what, why, where, when,* and
how laid out by Grabe and Kaplan (1996). However, the textual, or
linguistic, dimension—the *what*—is not explored extensively, and
pedagogy is essentially absent from the discussion.

In the same volume, Paul Prior (2006) proclaimed with surprising
boldness that "sociocultural theories represent the dominant paradigm

for writing research today" (p. 54). This social turn came as news to me, and I suspect that many of my colleagues would be equally surprised to learn that this paradigm shift had taken hold without their having noticed. Prior's bulletin about this social turn is not bad news, necessarily, but I am not convinced that we have actually witnessed an epistemological tsunami. According to Prior, "it would be difficult to find situated studies of writing that do not at least gesture toward some sociocultural theory or cite the many writing researchers who have drawn on sociocultural theory and methodology in their own research" (p. 64). Unlike Hayes (2006), Prior mindfully included the activities of theory-building, research, *teaching*, and *learning* in his survey:

> Mapping Sociocultural Theory: A History of Three Entangled Traditions
>
> • A Sociocultural Theory of Writing
> • Redrawing the Oral-Literate Divide
> • Emerging Schooled Literacies
> • Writing in College and Beyond: Disciplinary and Workplace Discourse Practices

Influenced as I am by post-modernism, I shiver at the hint of epistemological absolutism, as well as the striking absence of reference to writing in multilingual contexts.

I will conclude my meanderings with a look at Richard Fulkerson's (2005) ambitious state-of-the-art essay, "Composition at the Turn of the 21st Century," published in *College Composition and Communication*. In "Mapping Comp-landia" (p. 655), Fulkerson took an axiological perspective in assessing the implications of three dominant approaches to composition: "(1) critical/cultural studies, (2) expressivism, and (3) procedural rhetoric," (p. 655). He acknowledged that current-traditional rhetoric is widely practiced but claimed that it no longer dominates. He also considered process and post-process movements to be digressive, with "procedural rhetoric" branching into three subcategories, as we see in this breakdown:

• Current-Traditional Rhetoric
• Critical/Cultural Studies {1}
• Expressivism—still "going strong" (p. 666) {2}

- Process and Post-Process [Fulkerson called this subhead a "digression"]
- Procedural Rhetoric (Three Emphases) {3}:
  · Composition as Argumentation
  · Genre-Based Composition
  · Composition as Introduction to an Academic Discourse Community (à la Bartholomae, 1985)

Fulkerson intriguingly asserted that " . . . virtually no one in contemporary composition theory assumes any epistemology other than a vaguely interactionist constructivism" (p. 662). I am not convinced that his analysis grapples with genuine theoretical concerns; his synthesis takes on epistemological questions from a decidedly pedagogical perspective. Fulkerson provocatively concluded that, in college composition, "the major divide is . . . between a postmodern, cultural studies, reading-based program, and a broadly conceived rhetoric of genres and discourse forums . . ." (p. 679). Fulkerson's L1 composition survey portrayed a world that is very different from the world of L2 writing as I perceive it. At the same time, we see that the questions of L1 compositionists intersect with our own (Hedgcock, 2005; Kroll, 2003) and that social-constructionist trends in the two domains may parallel one another but not necessarily converge.

So, Where Are We, Theoretically and Practically Speaking?

If there is a constant across these taxonomies, it would involve the interdependent connections among theory-building, research, and instructional *practices* in first and L2 writing. My modest sampling of theoretical and pedagogical surveys bears out Barbara Kroll's (2003) observation that "what can pass for theory is sometimes better labeled a methodology or a widely held belief" (p. 6). Practice pervades theory, research, and teaching, and it seems to me that the theory-practice duality and its corollary application model are convenient but outdated labels for what composition professionals actually do (and have been doing all along).

Candlin and Hyland (1999) claimed that diverse approaches to text analysis, views of composing processes, and methods for investigating writing "can be integrated and made to inform distinctive approaches to the practice of writing and writing instruction. In this way, theory and practice in writing inform each other in a reflective praxis" (p. 1). This view hints at a contradiction: On the one hand, the assertion that "perspectives" on writing "can be integrated and made to inform" instruction reflects a unidirectional application model, yet it also holds that "theory and practice" can "inform *each other*" reflexively. They can, but I am not sure they do in the way that Candlin and Hyland intend, partly because it could be naïve to aim for practice-to-theory movement, which could even be seen as contradictory to a strictly positivist axiology and model of knowledge construction.

PRAXIS? MAYBE, BUT HANDLE WITH CARE

I would like to suggest that the L2 writing community and its public discourse may have, operationally speaking, abandoned positivist dualisms to a degree, gravitating toward a theory of practice (Bourdieu, 2003; Dubetz, 2005) or *praxis* orientation (Freire, 1970, 1998) in the course of a complex, nuanced sociocultural turn (Durst, 1999).

To pick up on the "reflective praxis" mentioned by Candlin and Hyland (1999), I would posit that our discipline has engaged in reflective praxis for quite some time. Drawing on Freire (1998), Berlin (2005) defined *praxis* as "the nexus of theory and practice," which "works from a standpoint where each element informs the other" (p. 22). Unlike the dualistic view where practitioners "apply" theory, in praxis, "theory and practice cannot simply *inform,* but must also *transform* one another" (Berlin, 2005, p. 22). Praxis may also require rethinking our operational definition of theory. In a recent apologia recasting the role of theory, DiPardo and Sperling (2005), co-editors of *Research in the Teaching of English,* wrote that, "when fully embraced, theory becomes more than the far-out hunch that popular usage would have it, more than the blue-sky imaginings of academics who seldom venture into schools" (p. 138). de Beaugrande (1997) argued that a theory's applicability to clinical practice should be a chief criterion for judging a theory's validity (cf. Bruthiaux, 2005; Rajagopalan, 2004; Widdowson, 2005). Moreover, Freire (1998) maintained that, rather than molding practice from theory (in other words, enacting the application metaphor), theory should emerge "soaked in well-carried-out practice" (p. 21). Although practices such as teaching and investigating writing should unquestionably be informed by theory, no theory "should . . . be created in a vacuum, devoid of the environmental and contextual influences that inform it" (Berlin, 2005, p. 22).

These are not uncontroversial visions of how the activities laid out in Figure 2 might be undertaken, but they seem to align reasonably well with Prior's (2006) appraisal of the state of the art. A *praxis* orientation might precipitate an equalizing effect among our diverse spheres of activity, such that theory is no longer perceived as the engine driving composition teaching and research (as it tends to be in a positivist frame of reference). Instead, we might do well to evolve more modest yet ecologically flexible expectations of our theoretical sources, as Olson (1994) proposed:

> If we think of a theory as a machine to think with, a device for organizing and interpreting events with the aim of bringing other questions and other forms of evidence into conjunction, then it is not at all unreasonable to aspire to a theory of how writing contributes not only to our understanding of the world but also of ourselves. (p. xvii)

Some might say that our profession has already advanced in this direction, which points toward developing theories of how learning to write is inextricably intertwined with culture, ideology, ethics, sociopolitical structures, and identity construction. A *praxis* orientation might thus propel the field forward from binary reasoning and the limitations of the application metaphor. However, I would offer one bit of caution: Like any shift in thought, action, or orientation motivated by a novel principle or ideology, praxis can be interpreted (or misinterpreted) prescriptively, if not dogmatically—a fine line walked by strong praxis proponents (e.g., Berlin, 2005; Edge & Richards, 1998; Simon, 1992).

SUMMATIVE THOUGHTS AND FURTHER QUESTIONS

Rather than leaving readers with the mess that we started out with in Figure 2, I decided to conclude with a list of my preliminary discoveries and ruminations. I hope they stimulate productive conversations about praxis.

1. The theory/practice dualism is reductive and has been misleading all along, as very little that we do by way of planning and delivering L2 writing instruction or assessing writing can be fairly classified as "atheoretical." All that we do as L2 writing

professionals is driven by some theory (a folk theory, a covert theory in the guise of intuition) or a theory of practice.

1. Clearly, we find little congruence in portrayals of theory-building, research, and models of practice in L1, L2, or sources that address biliteracy.

2. Do we have ongoing consensus that a singular or unifying "theory" of L2 writing is achievable, given the disparate nature of our thinking and knowledge construction processes? If we settle on the need for a coherent theory or framework, isn't that a positivist objective? Not that there's anything inherently wrong with positivism (Berlin, 2005, and Johnson, 2006, notwithstanding), but to what degree is a coherent epistemology truly necessary?

3. If we had a unified theory, would we "use" it? (See Point 1, above: Don't our practices already guide our "theory"-building? Consider the shift from current-traditional to process-oriented instruction to post-process: Haven't pedagogical paradigm shifts coincided with (or propelled) our questions, frameworks, and methods of inquiry?)

4. In L2 writing, we seem to operate productively thanks to "intersections" between L1 and L2 composition and rhetoric, but it is difficult to find evidence of consistent mutuality or equality of exchange. The influence of trends in L1 composition theory on the L2 writing community has been profound, but is that relationship reciprocal?

5. The praxis construct may be a useful name for the ways in which capital "T" theory, empirical research, and instructional practice have influenced one another as our field has emerged and evolved. However, the L2 writing community of practice has characterized much of its work retrospectively through a positivist lens, perpetuating unproductive dualisms in our work (e.g., theory/practice, process/product) and in our public discourse.

REFERENCES

Bartholomae, D. (1985). Inventing the university. In M. Rose (Ed.), *When a writer can't write: Studies in writer's block and other composing process problems* (pp. 134–165). New York: Guilford Press.

Berlin, L. N. (2005). *Contextualizing college ESL classroom praxis: A participatory approach to effective instruction.* Mahwah, NJ: Erlbaum.

Block, D. (2003). *The social turn in second language acquisition.* Washington: Georgetown University Press.

Bourdieu, P. (2003). *Outline of a theory of practice.* New York: Cambridge University Press.

Bräuer, G. (2000). Product, process, and the writer within: History of a paradigm shift. In G. Bräuer (Ed.), *Writing across languages* (pp. 15–22). Stamford, CT: Ablex.

Bruthiaux, P. (2005). Introduction. In P. Bruthiaux, D. Atkinson, W. G. Eggington, W. Grabe, & V. Ramanathan (Eds.), *Directions in applied linguistics: Essays in honor of Robert B. Kaplan* (pp. 3–11). Clevedon, UK: Multilingual Matters.

Candlin, C. N., & Hyland, K. (Ed.). (1999). *Writing: Texts, processes, and practices.* London: Longman.

Clark, I. L. (with Bamberg, B., Bowden, D., Edlund, J. R., Gerrard, L., Klein, S., Neff Lippman, J., & Williams, J. D.). (2003). *Concepts in composition: Theory and practice in the teaching of writing.* Mahwah, NJ: Erlbaum.

Cumming, A. (1998). Theoretical perspectives on writing. *Annual Review of Applied Linguistics, 18,* 61–78.

Cumming, A., & Riazi, A. (2000). Building models of adult second-language writing instruction. *Learning and Instruction, 10,* 55–71.

de Beaugrande, R. (1997). Theory and practice in applied linguistics: Disconnection, conflict, or dialectic? *Applied Linguistics, 18,* 279–313.

DiPardo, A., & Sperling, M. (2005). Theories we live by: Editors' introduction. *Research in the Teaching of English, 40,* 137–139.

Dubetz, N. E. (2005). Improving ESL instruction in a bilingual program through collaborative, inquiry-based professional development. In D. Tedick (Ed.), *Second language teacher education: International perspectives* (pp. 231–255). Mahwah, NJ: Erlbaum.

Durst, R. K. (1999). *Collision course: Conflict, negotiation, and learning in college composition.* Urbana, IL: NCTE.

Edge, J., & Richards, J. (1998). Why best practice is not good enough. *TESOL Quarterly, 32,* 569–576.

Evensen, L. (1997). Applied linguistics within a principled framework for characterizing disciplines and transdisciplines. *AILA Review, 12,* 31–41.

Ferris, D., & Hedgcock, J. S. (2005). *Teaching ESL composition: Purpose, process, and practice* (2nd ed.). Mahwah, NJ: Erlbaum.

Flower, L. S., & Hayes, J. R. (1981). A cognitive process theory of writing. *College Composition and Communication, 32,* 365–387.

Freire, P. (1970). *Pedagogy of the oppressed* (M. B. Ramos, Trans.). New York: Continuum.

Freire, P. (1998). *Teachers as cultural workers: Letters to those who dare teach* (D. Macedo, D., Koike, & A. Oliveira, Trans.). Boulder, CO: Westview Press.

Fulkerson, R. (2005). Composition at the turn of the 21st century. *College Composition and Communication, 56,* 654–687.

Gebhard, M. (1998). Second language writing theory. In M. L. Kennedy (Ed.), *Theorizing composition: A critical sourcebook of theory and scholarship in contemporary composition studies* (pp. 277–280). Westport, CT: Greenwood Press.

Grabe, W. (2001). Notes toward a theory of second language writing. In T. Silva & P. K. Matsuda (Eds.), *On second language writing* (pp. 39–57). Mahwah, NJ: Erlbaum.

Grabe, W., & Kaplan, R. B. (1996). *Theory and practice of writing.* Harlow, UK: Longman.

Hayes, J. R. (2006). New directions in writing theory. In C. A. MacArthur, S. Graham, & J. Fitzgerald (Eds.), *Handbook of writing research* (pp. 28–40). New York: Guilford.

Hedgcock, J. (2002). Toward a socioliterate approach to language teacher education. *Modern Language Journal, 86,* 299–317.

Hedgcock, J. (2004). Composition studies expanded. [Review of the book *Concepts in composition: Theory and practice in the teaching of writing*]. *American Journal of Psychology, 117,* 145–155.

Hedgcock, J. (2005). Taking stock of research and pedagogy in L2 writing. In E. Hinkel (Ed.), *Handbook of research in second language teaching and learning* (pp. 597–614). Mahwah, NJ: Erlbaum.

Homstad, T., & Thorson, H. (2000). Writing and foreign language pedagogy: Theories and implications. In G. Bräuer (Ed.), *Writing across languages* (pp. 3–14). Stamford, CT: Ablex.

Hyland, K. (2002). *Teaching and researching writing.* Harlow, England: Longman.

Hyland, K. (2003). *Second language writing.* Cambridge, England: Cambridge University Press.

Johnson, K. E. (2006). The sociocultural turn and its challenges for second language teacher education. *TESOL Quarterly, 40,* 235–257.

Kroll, B. (2003). Introduction: Teaching the next generation of second language writers. In B. Kroll (Ed.), *Exploring the dynamics of second language writing* (pp. 1–10). Cambridge, England: Cambridge University Press.

Kuhn, T. S. (1962). *The structure of scientific revolutions* (2nd ed., enlarged). Chicago: University of Chicago Press.

Lewin, K. (1951). *Field theory in social science: Selected theoretical papers.* New York: Harper Torchbooks.

Matsuda, P. K. (1999). Composition studies and ESL writing: A disciplinary division of labor. *College Composition and Communication, 50,* 699–721.

Musumeci, D. (1997). *Breaking tradition: An exploration of the historical relationship between theory and practice in second language teaching.* New York: McGraw-Hill.

Olson, D. R. (1994). *The world on paper.* Cambridge, England: Cambridge University Press.

Olson, G. A. (Ed.). (2002). *Rhetoric and composition as intellectual work.* Carbondale: Southern Illinois University Press.

Prior, P. (2006). A sociocultural theory of writing. In C. A. MacArthur, S. Graham, & J. Fitzgerald (Eds.), *Handbook of writing research* (pp. 54–66). New York: Guilford.

Rajagopalan, K. (2004). The philosophy of applied linguistics. In A. Davies & C. Elder (Eds.), *Handbook of applied linguistics* (pp. 397–420). Malden, MA: Blackwell.

Simon, R. (1992). *Teaching against the grain: Essays towards a pedagogy of possibility.* London: Bergin & Garvey.

Stenberg, S., & Lee, A. (2002). Developing pedagogies: Learning and the teaching of English. *College English, 64,* 326–347.

Valdés, G., Haro, P., & Echevarriarza, M. P. (1992). The development of writing abilities in a foreign language: Contributions toward a general theory of L2 writing. *Modern Language Journal, 76,* 333–352.

Widdowson, H. (2005). Applied linguistics, interdisciplinarity, and disparate realities. In P. Bruthiaux, D. Atkinson, W. G. Eggington, W. Grabe, & V. Ramanathan (Eds.), *Directions in applied linguistics: Essays in honor of Robert B. Kaplan* (pp. 12–26). Clevedon, UK: Multilingual Matters.

13 Assess Thyself Lest Others Assess Thee

Deborah Crusan

Historically, assessment has been problematic; moreover, most people tend to be very passionate about the subject. For some, testing (of the standardized variety) solves all problems. They admire the reduction-ist elegance intrinsic in a single score on a single test (SAT, TOEFL, GED, Ohio Graduation Test [OGT]) used to sort and categorize peo-ple and, in their eyes, minimize disorder and confusion. To them, a standardized test clearly establishes who has knowledge (albeit a nar-row type of knowledge) and who should graduate, gain admission, get the job, teach a class, or cut their hair. For others, testing is evil in any form, providing little that is beneficial for society. Supporters of both perspectives stand rigidly in their beliefs. It is my hope that as teachers and researchers, we stand in neither camp, but instead appreciate the value of good assessment and use assessment appropriately. We wel-come the questions: What do my students know? What do we teachers need to do to help them?

A division, pointed out by White (1996a), exists between the writ-ing community and the assessment community, and "if this division continues, writing assessment will remain as two separate activities, with no real connection between what we do in our classrooms and the crucial assessment activity that goes on outside these classrooms" (p. 102).

From the perspective of a teacher, writing assessment, like writing, is a continuous process involving both teachers and students. Writ-ing assessment theorists (Hamp-Lyons, 2003; Haswell, 2004a, 2004b; Huot, 2002; White, 1994; White, 1996b) call for assessment closely connected to a classroom syllabus, lessons, and assignments and remind us about the importance of good assessment practices (e.g., the use of multiple genres, fronting of criteria, the use of process-oriented rather than product-oriented pedagogy) (Casanave, 2003; Crusan, 2002; Ferris & Hedgcock, 2005; Hamp-Lyons & Kroll, 1996; Peyton, Staton, Richardson, & Wolfram, 1990). Conversely, large-scale test developers and politicians often call for a kind of testing that has little to do with the way we teach writing in our classrooms because they ascribe to the belief that achievement can be accurately characterized through a one-size-fits-all assessment. At best, this is naïve, and at worst, it puts the entire premise of our education system in jeopardy. However, it is not an intrinsic fault of the test, but rather the hyper-extended uses of the test. The accountability movement, very much alive in the United States today, uses results from standardized tests to trigger labels, sanctions, rewards, and/or interventions for districts, schools, educators, and students; long-range plans propose to extend this accountability process into universities.

In this chapter, I examine this division of writing assessment and discuss how mandated transfer of responsibility from locally developed assessment to homogenized state and federal standards (as the only measure that counts) runs counter to writing assessment theory. My goal in this chapter is to consider the politics at work in assessment and in writing assessment in particular and how these politics affect pedagogy. Finally, I examine a framework for a theory of second language writing assessment based on the work of Huot (2002) and Lynne (2004). While this examination is embryonic and tentative, I hope to offer a basis for enabling further investigation and development.

EXAMINING THE PEDAGOGICAL EFFECTS OF ASSESSMENT

Let us first address the effects large-scale testing has on pedagogy. Of importance to this discussion is the differentiation between testing and assessment. Leung and Lewkowicz (2006) define testing simply as a single instrument; on the other hand, assessment is a broader term for all forms of evaluation. As writing teachers, assessment is intertwined with every aspect of our pedagogy. It should be clear that I am not arguing for the elimination of testing. Instead, I am calling for a careful re-examination of how we use standardized tests scores as the sole criteria upon which to base critical decisions about our students.

First, I examine how large-scale assessments affect teaching practices. Assessment drives instruction. This statement can be interpreted either negatively or positively depending on the context, the type of assessment, and the expected impact of that assessment. Multiple-choice tests assess a relatively narrow range of skills and generally assess surface knowledge and, in the instance of writing, assess the subskills of writing rather than writing for meaning. The test also emphasizes a student's decoding ability. If a multiple-choice, standardized test is driving the curriculum, assessment might have a negative connotation. The score on the test may have little to do with a student's writing ability. Further, a timed writing wherein a student cannot think deeply, read, talk to others about ideas, or revise is equally not a good indication of writing ability.

The consequences of this kind of assessment loom large. Teachers and students are stressed. During these tests, ESL students sit and stare for two hours—a form of abuse, I contend. Nevertheless, if teachers' careers rest on students' scores on standardized tests, what then might be the focus in their classrooms? In all honesty, what does not appear on tests tends to disappear from classrooms in time. Certainly, teachers will place undue weight on preparing for the standardized tests looming over them and their students. If students must write a five-paragraph essay on the test, writing instruction will most probably focus on the five-paragraph essay, sacrificing creativity. "Those who legislate the running of schools prescribe what students should learn, qualifying all learning through the most narrow and fragmented—although statistically manageable—means of assessment available" (Thomas, 2004, p. 77). The bottom line—tests are affecting teachers' pedagogies.

No Child Left Behind (NCLB) holds schools accountable for Average Yearly Progress (AYP). Problems with AYP are numerous. Tests are norm-referenced; that is, "grades or scores are based on a comparison of the test-takers to a 'norming group'" (Bailey, 1998, p. 246). NCLB compares, for instance, the writing of a specific but undefined group of reference third graders in 2006 with the writing of a group of third graders in 2005. It would seem more logical to compare the writing of the same group in progressive years to determine progress in writing rather than indirectly by using a benchmark cohort not matched for even the most obvious variables such as socioeconomic status, second language writing, or developmental issues.

It is crucial that assessment remain in the hands of teachers. Let us examine the rationale of the National Council of Teachers of English

(NCTE). The Writing Study Group of the NCTE Executive Committee published the NCTE Beliefs about the Teaching of Writing (2004). One of these beliefs reads, "Assessment of writing involves complex, informed, human judgment" (NCTE, 2004, Belief 11). The Writing Study Group delineates the various reasons we use writing assessment. Specifically, teachers assess writing to determine either student achievement or what the student does not know. At other times, assessment happens outside the classroom in the form of state- or federally-mandated tests to determine students' educational levels. Sometimes an administration uses writing assessment to encourage the teaching of writing. Finally, even when writing assessment is not the focus—as in content area exams—we still, possibly covertly, evaluate writing. In any of these assessments of writing, assessors form complex judgments. Human beings, not machines, should make these judgments. Moreover, professionals knowledgeable about writing and literacy should make these determinations. (NCTE, 2004). Clearly then "faculty who teach composition courses are in a better position to accurately evaluate what is expected of their students than is the assessment community" (Crusan, 1999, p. 8). Additionally, the Conference on College Composition and Communication's *Standards for the Assessment of Reading and Writing* seventh standard reminds us, "The teacher is the most important agent of assessment" (CCCC, 1994).

As a final point, we need to consider what teachers need to know about writing assessment. I am constantly reminded that "it is essential to develop complex, flexible, conceptual understandings of the landscapes in which you work and to be able to use these understandings flexibly to carry out your teaching practices" (Johnson, 1999, p. 7), and I attempt to transmit this attitude to my students at every opportunity.

Generally, I work with prospective and practicing English as a Second Language teachers at both the master's and undergraduate levels. One of the required courses in our program is *TESOL Assessment*. In my dealings with students in this class, I have found that teachers fear assessment in general and writing assessment in particular; they believe they lack background knowledge in assessment, which is often the case. Even my students who have proven themselves excellent writing teachers, in both L1 and L2, still feel that assessment is something they know nothing about; they do, however, recognize the need to learn about assessment but may judge themselves ill-equipped to learn.

I remind my students that, as teachers, we need to know about assessment, do assessment, and fight for locally developed assessment. It is vital that teachers become involved in the design and implementation of writing assessment at their institutions. They need to know how to create assignments, generate criteria for those assignments, and craft meaningful and fair rubrics to assess their students' writing. They also need to realize that every assignment should have a separate set of criteria and a rubric especially for that assignment. Teachers should be able to encourage student self-awareness and self-critique with a goal of student internalization of the assessment process.

Finally, they should be aware of the difference between formative assessment and summative assessment. By formative, I mean the kind of assessment generally done in the classroom, assessment that is ongoing and helps both the teacher and the student. The teacher can look at the results of formative assessment and modify instruction based on the assessment. Summative assessment commonly makes definitive decisions about students' work.

NCTE (2004) developed a comprehensive list delineating what teachers need to know to be excellent assessors:

- How to find out what student writers can do, informally, on an ongoing basis.
- How to use that assessment in order to decide what and how to teach next.
- How to assess occasionally, less frequently than above, in order to form judgments about the quality of student writing and learning.
- How to assess ability and knowledge across multiple different writing engagements.
- What the features of good writing are, appropriate to the context and purposes of the teaching and learning.
- What the elements of a constructive process of writing are, appropriate to the context and purposes of the teaching and learning.
- What growth in writing looks like, the developmental aspects of writing ability.
- Ways of assessing student metacognitive process of the reading/writing connection.

- How to recognize in student writing (both in their texts and in their actions) the nascent potential for excellence at the features and processes desired.
- How to deliver useful feedback, appropriate for the writer and the situation.
- How to analyze writing situations for their most essential elements, so that assessment is not of everything about writing all at once, but rather is targeted to objectives.
- How to analyze and interpret both qualitative and quantitative writing assessments.
- How to evaluate electronic texts.
- How to use portfolios to assist writers in their development.
- How self-assessment and reflection contribute to a writer's development and ability to move among genres, media, and rhetorical situations.

THE POLITICS OF WRITING ASSESSMENT

We turn now to the political. It is easy to lull ourselves into complacency and think only in the microcosm of our classroom writing assessment, but we can be involved in assessment at a larger level; in fact, we must be passionately involved or assessment will be wrested from us. Frankly, this transfer of responsibility with the result of deskilling teachers is gaining momentum, at least in some states. We must consider perhaps the biggest question regarding the politics of assessment and the glut of testing: why are we testing so much? Everywhere we look today, someone is talking about, writing about, worrying about testing. Testing continues to gain currency especially among politicians who invoke its name to win elections by promising to better our schools through testing. Currently, what had once only been whispered about can now be heard loudly—many contemporary politicians are presently pledging to better our universities by imposing the same kinds of testing, mandating the standardization and homogenization of curriculum. We should not be surprised; if we had been listening carefully, we would have heard the warnings. White (1993), always ahead of his time, cautioned that development of a national test had already started. White (1996a) recounts a story about the first proposal of such a test by the National Education Goals Panel, a panel established by President George Bush with then Governor Bill Clinton as a panel member. According to the panel, they needed a measure of accountability to confirm college graduates' knowledge. The panel rejected White's recommendation of a complex, rich portfolio system, instead trying to reduce intricate notions of literacy into simplistic numerical indicators of achievement—a three-part exam assessing "communication skills, critical thinking, and problem solving skills" (p. 103). The National Assessment of College Student Learning (NACSL) found that information gathered by White's portfolio system would be perhaps unrelated to their purposes, almost admitting that "actual writing is not relevant to a college education" (p. 103). Chilling language taken from the National Center for Educational Statistics website alerts us to what looms in the future: "Activities at the workshop [on the topic of furthering the assessment of national postsecondary outcomes] were designed specifically to address the degree to which state-level assessment initiatives in higher education might aid in the construction of a *national indicator of postsecondary attainment* (italics added) consistent with the National Education Goals, and to determine ways in which NCES (National Center for Educational Statistics) and the states might work more effectively to develop mutually supporting activities and policies in the realm of postsecondary assessment" (NCES, 2006).

White (1996b) cautions us, "If we imagine that in the future, college writing programs will be free from the demands of external assessment, we are ignoring all the signs around us of their increasing importance; they will have more and more effect on what we do. We have only two choices: we can ignore them in the vain hope that they will go away, or we can participate in them in an informed way to make them as good as possible" (p. 103).

Writing assessment specialists (Baron, 2005; Hamp-Lyons & Kroll, 1996; Huot, 2002; White, 1995) have argued that one-shot timed writing tests result in curriculum narrowing and have made a case for multiple measures (Haswell, 2004a, 2004b). Still, standardized tests continue to shape curriculum in the writing classroom, particularly at the high school level, in spite of years of research affirming best practice. Additionally, Thomas (2004) warns us about the "narrow data on student ability and learning and distorted data on school and statewide education quality" (p. 76) standardized tests provide.

For L1 writers, the time constraints of the new SAT essay raises many issues. Writing under the gun, so to speak, causes meteoric rises in affective filters. Students have 25 minutes to write "essays that insightfully develop a point of view with appropriate reasons and examples and use language skillfully" (College Board, 2006). Additionally, the NCTE Task Force (Ball, Christensen, Fleischer, Haswell, Ketter, Yagelski, & Yancey, 2005) fear a narrowing of the curriculum in high school English classes because of the addition of the 25 minute writing test. Teachers will teach the five-paragraph essay, realistically the only writing that can be done in such a short time. However, some might argue that the new SAT writing test will encourage high school teachers to include actual writing in their classes. That may be so. However, as much as the College Board has touted the new SAT for its inclusion of actual writing, a student really does not have to write to score well. Even without writing, a student who "fills in enough correct bubbles with a No. 2 pencil to get a perfect score on the grammar and usage questions can still come away with a respectable 650 points out of a possible 800 on the 'writing' section" of the new SAT (Baron, 2005, p. B14); therefore, the stated intent of the test as a predictor of college success may be compromised by the weighting of the actual writing samples.

Now consider the Next Generation TOEFL iBT, a test required by most American colleges and universities for admission of international students. One part of the test boasts the integration of skills. Specifically, test takers reading a passage, then listening to a lecture, and then responding to a prompt about the material—a highly authentic exercise, albeit timed. However, ETS has also included an independent writing test. Test takers see the following directions: "Read the question below. You have 30 minutes to plan, write, and revise your essay. Typically, an effective response will contain a minimum of 300 words." The example prompt: "Do you agree or disagree with the following statement? Always telling the truth is the most important consideration in any relationship between people. Use specific reasons and examples to support your answer" (TOEFL iBT Sample Test, 2006). Testing of this nature raises multiple red flags. Of course, the test is timed, and timed tests always cause adverse reactions. Since students take the test on the internet, typing speed and accuracy now become an integral component of the assessment. Questions about access, technological sophistication, and affect quickly come to mind. Moreover, the kind of writing a student produces in response to the example prompt would most probably be superficial and even more probably in the form of a five-paragraph essay, reductive at best.

   To be fair, we should consider the other side. Cumming (2002) makes the case that "appeals for assessments of second language writing to involve more than just a single composition in a short period of time" (p. 77), while certainly deserving of consideration, might be unethical when placed in the context of high-stakes, international tests of writing. He claims that three appeals—"to improve the formative value of assessment for students' learning, to correspond more realistically to requirements for performance in educational contexts, and to fulfill an emancipatory function" raise ethical dilemmas impossible to deal with in high-stakes testing. Because of the highly variable nature of writing, "it is difficult to conceive of ways to assess writing, particularly in a second language, that are thoroughly consistent and fair to a population of examinees that, by definition, represents nearly all the variations possible around the world" (p. 79).

   Having considered some of the political implications of testing and assessment, we must now answer the question with which we began. Why so much testing? Emery and Ohanian (2004) retort: "No matter who's talking about education reform (testing usually), look for the footprints of The Business Roundtable" (p. 114). Emery and Ohanian (2004) describe at length what they term "The Business Roundtable (BRT) Power Network" (p. 59), who they are (a group of powerful CEOs like Edward Rust, CEO of State Farm Insurance, who also serves or has served as co-chair of the Business Coalition for Excellence in Education, past chair and member of the board of National Alliance of Business, co-chair of the Subcommittee on Education Policy of the Committee for Economic Development, on the board of McGraw-Hill, the board of Achieve, the board of trustees of the American Enterprise Institute, and then President-elect Bush's Transition Advisory Team Committee on Education), and why they care so much about testing and education. Rust has admitted that "the BRT is committed to beating up on public schools" (Emery and Ohanian, 2004, p. 38). In fact, Rust testified on March 8, 2001, before the Committee on Education and the Workforce. His final recommendation: "States should establish accountability systems with clear consequences for schools, principals, and teachers who persistently fail over time to meet standards. Consequences may include replacing personnel, restructuring or closing schools, and providing options for students to enroll elsewhere" (p. 38).

The short answer to why we have so much testing according to Emery and Ohanian (2004): the ultimate goal of the Business Roundtable is the privatization of our schools through educational reform. Standardized testing and educational materials translate into big dollars for private industry—ETS (among others) is a private industry.

> In 1989 and again in 1995, the national business roundtable put its special brand on education reform, hammering home an agenda that defined reform thusly: state content and performance standards; a state mandated test; rewards and sanctions based on test scores; school site councils composed of administrators, teachers, and parents; professional development focusing on using test scores to drive instructional decisions; and phonics instruction in pre-kindergarten. Not only did the BRT flood the media with this agenda, but since 1989, a network of public and private organizations promoting this beast called systemic reform has developed; it is a network characterized by incestuous partnerships, overlapping, alliances, and common funding sources (Emery & Ohanian, 2004, p. 114).

What has this to do with second language writing assessment? Everything.

FIGHTING THE SYSTEM

Although the temptation to surrender responsibility and submit to the relative ease and low cost of standardized testing is ever present, there are ways in which we can fight and retain our control of assessment at our institutions. One such success story is the creation of Online Directed Self-Placement (ODSP) at Wright State University. Overcoming obstacles of funding, time, territorial concerns, technology, and the threat of a standardized measurement as a placement instrument, we developed an innovative system of placement. "ODSP is a multi-dimensional, uniquely weighted online directed self-placement instrument, which weighs indicators and variables germane to the university student population" (Crusan, 2006, p. 213). Students log onto the ODSP website, complete several demographic questions and then respond either strongly agree, agree, disagree, or strongly disagree to a questionnaire which includes 20 questions for native speakers and 15 questions for nonnative speakers. In the background, an algorithm is weighing data such as test scores (ACT, SAT, SAT writing, TOEFL, TOEFL writing), high school GPA, and high school class rank, information obtained from the university mainframe. The algorithm then reduces all data to one number. This freshman advising team in University College receives scores electronically; students have access to their placement scores through their advisors. While ODSP is not entirely self-placement, it does promote student agency; self-assessment is weighted more heavily than any other piece of information. Further, ODSP includes second language writers, who were omitted from an earlier form of directed self-placement. Finally, while ODSP does not consider actual writing—the financial costs are too high—it does consider multiple variables. We fought very hard to maintain control of writing placement at Wright State; however, it appears that we will soon have an even bigger fight on our hands.

At a meeting recently, the University College at my institution informed me and others at the meeting that the Ohio Legislature was very seriously considering removing developmental writing courses from all but two or three Ohio universities. Only two-year colleges would now offer these courses. Further, universities in Ohio would use a standardized test for placement; the favorite seems to be ACT COMPASS, a multiple-choice test of the subskills of language (punctuation, verb formation and agreement, usage, relationships of clauses, shifts in construction, organization, spelling, and capitalization). "COMPASS offers placement and diagnostic testing in mathematics, reading, and writing—and now includes placement testing for English as a Second Language (ESL) students. ACT has combined COMPASS and ESL measures and advising, course placement, and retention services into one complete package" (ACT, 2006).

It is interesting to note from this quote that ACT offers much more than testing. Like many other American testing giants (i.e., ETS, Harcourt Testing, McGraw Hill), ACT is now in the business of curriculum development as well. Testing companies offer complete testing and teaching packages; the teaching packages contain, among other things, scripts, plans, handouts, and tests. These packages lead to the deskilling of teachers (Shannon, 1992); in other words, teachers surrender control over the goals, methods, materials, and evaluation of instruction to already created materials. With standardization comes the potential for sacrificing student creativity, ignoring the richness of culturally diverse backgrounds, and neglecting the unique problems of students. All of these important educational parameters could be sacrificed at the altar of uniformity if control of assessment is wrested from the hands of teachers and put into the hands of those who know little about teaching.

PROPOSING A THEORY OF SECOND
LANGUAGE WRITING ASSESSMENT

Second language writing researchers (Krapels, 1990; Leki, 1992; Silva, 1993; Silva & Brice, 2004) have established that teachers model much of what they do in the classroom after L1 theories of writing pedagogy. Silva (1993) notes, "There exists, at present, no coherent, comprehensive theory of second language writing" (p. 668) but prodded L2 writing teachers to recognize that there are differences between L1 and L2 writing. Cumming (2001) reminds us that "there is no agreed upon definition" (p. 214) of L2 writing. Ferris and Hedgcock (2005) recognize that "L2 writing lacks a tidy corpus of conclusive theory and research upon which to base a straight-forward introduction to processes of learning and teaching" (p. 3). For that matter, Ferris and Hedgcock (2005) wonder if a comprehensive theory of second language writing is a needed and assert that a wide and varied knowledge base of *theories* (italics added) provides an important foundation for teachers of second language writing.

The same can be said for second language writing *assessment* theory. Much of the theory of first and second language writing assessment is drawn from both measurement theory (Huot, 2002; Bachman & Cohen, 1998) and from L1 assessment theory (Hamp-Lyons, 1996). Hamp-Lyons (2003) claims that assessment researchers, because they are often far-removed from the classroom, often fail to consider the writer.

The assessment of writing has a history rooted in classical measurement theory and was basically the measurement community's domain until the early 70s. The measurement community has been composed of statisticians, administrators, and professional test designers, many of whom are far removed from day to day contact with students and teachers. As a result, they use procedures which are adapted to mass markets and fail to address the specialized needs of the students and teachers (White, 1994). Composition specialists such as White, Lutz,

Lederman, Greenberg, and Donovan found themselves "unwilling to accept the reductive concepts of reading and writing that were dominant in writing testing at that time" (White, 1994, p. 272) and began an ongoing quest for fairness in the assessment of writing.

Even considering this quest by leading writing assessment specialists, the assessment of writing has not enjoyed popularity with composition specialists. Huot (1996a) remarks that, historically, writing assessment has been the domain of measurement experts, and, for the most part, has been "developed, constructed, and privatized by the measurement community as a technological apparatus whose inner workings are known only to those with specialized knowledge" (p. 549). Because of a lack of communication between the composition community and the measurement community, many problems exist in the area of writing assessment. Perhaps part of the problem lies with the fact that the measurement community and the composition community cling to basic theoretical differences in the matter of assessment. Moreover, testing companies often mysticize assessment through the use of statistical and measurement jargon, making assessment a scary proposition for both teachers and students. It is easy to see how the foundational theories undergirding educational psychology and statistics are played out, especially in large-scale assessment of writing where the general focus is on reliability and validity. Bailey (1998) defines reliability as "the extent to which a test measures consistently" (p. 248) and validity as "the extent to which a test measures what it is supposed to measure" (p. 249).

I often wonder if the concepts of reliability and validity as defined above are enough for the writing that our students do in the classroom. Lynne (2004) suggests instead the terms "ethical" for reliability and "meaningful" for validity (p. 117). She continues, "The terms I am proposing have the advantage of looking outward and inward at the same time. Instead of focusing primarily or even exclusively on assessment methodology—as 'validity' and 'reliability' do, at least in the traditional configuration—the criteria of 'meaningfulness' and 'ethics' highlight the context of assessment and the relationships among those involved in the assessment" (p. 117).

Arguments regarding the division present in writing assessment, both in L1 or L2, show us that what we do in our classrooms is very different from the large-scale assessment of writing. Lynne (2004) shows the division between high-stakes assessment and the writing community through her operationalization of terms. Perhaps it is essential to accept that difference and work toward a theory of writing assessment that encompasses the principles we subscribe to as writing teachers and assessors of student writing. Again, my purpose here is not the abolition of standardized testing; instead, my purpose is to protect the kind of writing assessment teachers do in the contexts of their own institutions, preventing the complete intrusion and exclusive use of standardized tests when we assess for placement, for diagnosis, and for achievement. Huot (2002) suggests that we consider any writing assessment theory a work in progress and that we infer principles from existing procedures; he then outlines his "principles for a new theory and practice of writing assessment" (p. 105):

- *Site-Based.* An assessment for writing is developed in response to a specific need that occurs at a specific site. Procedures are based upon the resources and concerns of an institution, department, program, or agency and its administrators, faculty, students, or other constituents.
- *Locally-Controlled.* The individual institution or agency is responsible for managing, revising, updating, and validating the assessment procedures, which should in turn be carefully reviewed according to clearly outlined goals and guidelines on a regular basis to safeguard the concerns of all affected by the assessment process.
- *Context-Sensitive.* The procedures should honor the instructional goals and objectives as well as the cultural and social environment of the institution or agency and its students, teachers, and other stakeholders. It is important to establish and maintain the contextual integrity necessary for the authentic reading and writing of textual communication.
- *Rhetorically-Based.* All writing assignments, scoring criteria, writing environments, and reading procedures should adhere to recognizable and supportable rhetorical principles integral to the thoughtful expression and reflective interpretation of texts.
- *Accessible.* All procedures and rationales for the creation of writing assignments, scoring criteria, and reading procedures, as well as samples of student work and rater judgment, should be available to those whose work is being evaluated.

Clearly, Huot's are principles with which both the L1 and L2 composition communities can live. I argue further for the inclusion of a code of ethics based on the nine principles outlined by the International Language Testing Association:

- respect for humanity,
- confidentiality,
- adherence to ethical principles in research,
- prevention of the misuse of knowledge and skills,
- a commitment to continuing education and sharing of knowledge,
- upholding the integrity of the community,
- improve the quality of language testing,
- mindful of obligations to society, and
- consideration of both the long- and short-term effects of our work.

Both Huot (1996b) and White (1996) call for a theory of writing assessment that will be "accountable to outside forces and public agencies that fund education while helping to ensure that these same programs are true to our philosophies of education, our theories of language, and our pedagogies for productive classrooms" (Huot, 1996b, p. 115). Whatever the case, the second language writing community must realize that this is our fight. It will affect our classrooms at every level sooner rather than later.

REFERENCES

ACT. (2006). *ACT's COMPASS system.* Retrieved May 1, 2006, from http://www.act.org/compass/index.html

Bachman, L. F., & Cohen, A. D. (Eds.). (1998). *Interfaces between second language acquisition and language testing research.* Cambridge, UK: Cambridge University Press.

Bailey, K. M. (1998). *Learning about language assessment: Dilemmas, decisions, and directions.* New York: Heinle & Heinle.

Ball, A., Christensen, L., Fleischer, C., Haswell, R., Ketter, J., Yagelski, R., & Yancey, K. (2005). *The impact of the SAT and ACT timed writing tests* [Electronic version]. Retrieved May 30, 2005 from http://www.ncte.org/about/gov/cgrams/insight/120774.htm?source=gs

Baron, D. (2005, May 6). The college board's new essay reverses decades of progress toward literacy. *The Chronicle of Higher Education,* pp. B14-B15.

Casanave, C. P. (2003). *Controversies in second language writing: Dilemmas and decisions in research and instruction.* Ann Arbor: University of Michigan Press.

CCCC. (1994). *Standards for the assessment of reading and writing* [Electronic Version]. Retrieved March 21, 2006 from http://www.ncte.org/library/NCTEFiles/Resources/Books/Sample/StandardsDoc.pdf

College Board. (2006). *Strategies for success on the SAT essay* [Electronic Version]. Retrieved May 22, 2006 from http://www.collegeboard.com/student/testing/sat/prep_one/sat_essay.html

Cumming, A. (2001). The difficulty of standards, for example in L2 writing. In T. Silva & P. K. Matsuda (Eds.), *On second language writing* (pp. 209–229). Mahwah, NJ: Erlbaum Associates.

Cumming, A. (2002). Assessing L2 writing: Alternative constructs and ethical dilemmas. *Assessing Writing, 8,* 73–83.

Crusan, D. (1999). *Effective assessment for placement of English as a second language writers into composition courses at the university level.* Unpublished doctoral dissertation. University Park, PA: The Pennsylvania State University.

Crusan, D. (2002). An assessment of ESL writing placement assessment. *Assessing Writing: An International Journal, 8,* 17–30.

Crusan, D. (2006). The politics of implementing online directed self-placement for second language writers. In P. K. Matsuda, C. Ortmeier, & X. You (Eds.), *Politics of Second Language Writing: In Search of the Promised Land* (pp.205–221). West Lafayette, IN: Parlor Press.

Educational Testing Services. (2006). *TestLink: Search the test collection database.* Retrieved April 30, 2006 from http://sydneyplus.ets.org

Educational Testing Services. (2006). *TOEFL: Take the iBT tour.* Retrieved May 15, 2006 from http://www.ets.org/toefl/

Emery, K., & Ohanian, S. (2004). *Why is corporate America bashing our public schools?* Portsmouth, NH: Heinemann.

Ferris, D. R., & Hedgcock, J. S. (2005). *Teaching ESL composition: Purpose, process, and practice* (2nd ed.). Mahwah, NJ: Erlbaum.

Krapels, A. R. (1990). An overview of second language writing process research. In B. Kroll (Ed.), *Second language writing: Research insights for the classroom* (pp. 37–56). Cambridge, UK: Cambridge University Press.

Hamp-Lyons, L. (1996). The challenges of second language writing assessment. In E. M. White, W. D. Lutz, & S. Kamusikiri (eds.), *Assessment of writing: Politics, policies, practices* (pp. 226–240). New York: The Modern Language Association of America.

Hamp-Lyons, L. (2003). Writing teachers as assessors of writing. In B. Kroll (Ed.), *Exploring the dynamics of second language writing* (pp. 162–190). Cambridge, UK: Cambridge University Press.

Hamp-Lyons, L., & Kroll, B. (1996). Issues in ESL writing assessment: An overview. *College ESL, 6* (1), pp. 52–72.

Haswell, R. (2004a). *Post-secondary entry writing placement: A brief synopsis of research* [Electronic version]. Retrieved March 3, 2005 from http://comppile.tamucc.edu/writingplacementresearch.htm

Haswell, R. (2004b). *Post-secondary entrance writing placement* [Electronic version]. Retrieved June 21, 2005 from http://comppile.tamucc.edu/placement.doc

Huot, B. (1994). A survey of college and university writing placement practices. *WPA: Writing Program Administration, 17* (3), 49–65.

Huot, B. (1996a). Toward a new theory of writing assessment. *College Composition and Communication, 47* (4), 549–566.

Huot, B. (1996b). The need for a theory of writing assessment. In L. Z. Bloom, D. A. Daiker, & E. M. White (Eds.), *Composition in the twenty-first century: Crisis and Change* (pp. 112–115). Carbondale: Southern Illinois University Press.

Huot, B. (2002). *(Re)Articulating writing assessment for teaching and learning.* Logan UT: Utah State University Press.

International Language Testing Association. (2000). *Code of ethics for language testers.* Retrieved May 14, 2006 from www.iltaonline.com/code.pdf

Johnson, K. E. (1999). *Understanding language teaching: Reasoning in action.* Boston: Heinle & Heinle.

Leung, C., & Lewkowicz, J. (2006). Expanding horizons and unresolved conundrums: Language testing and assessment. *TESOL Quarterly, 40* (1), 211–234.

Lynne, P. (2004). *Coming to terms: Theorizing writing assessment in composition studies.* Logan, UT: Utah State University Press.

National Center for Educational Statistics. (2006). *The national assessment of college student learning: An inventory of state-level assessment activities.* Retrieved May 22, 2006 from http://nces.ed.gov/pubsearch/pubsinfo.asp?pubid=96862

NCTE. (2004). *NCTE beliefs about the teaching of writing* [Electronic Version]. Retrieved February 21, 2005 from http://www.ncte.org/about/over/positions/category/write/118876.htm

Shannon, P. (1992). *Commercial reading materials, a technological ideology, and the deskilling of teachers.* Portsmouth, NH: Heinemann.

Silva, T. (1993). Toward an understanding of the distinct nature of L2 writing: The ESL research and its implications. *TESOL Quarterly, 27* (4), 657–675.

Silva, T. & Brice, C. (2004). Research in teaching writing. *Annual Review of Applied Linguistics, 24,* 70–106.

Thomas, P. (2004). The negative impact of testing writing skills. *Educational Leadership,* October 2004, pp. 76–79.

White, E. M. (1993). Assessing higher order thinking and communication in college graduates through writing. *JGE: The Journal of General Education, 42,* 105–122.

White, E.M. (1994). Issues and problems in writing assessment. *Assessing Writing, 1,* 11–27.

White, E. M. (1995). An apologia for the timed impromptu essay test. *CCC, 46* (1), 30–45.

White, E. M. (1996a). Writing assessment beyond the classroom: Will writing teachers play a role? In L. Z. Bloom, D. A. Daiker, & E. M. White (Eds.), *Composition in the twenty-first century: Crisis and Change* (pp. 101–111). Carbondale: Southern Illinois University Press.

White, E. M. (1996b). Power and agenda setting in writing assessment. In E. M. White, W. D. Lutz, & S. Kamusikiri (Eds.), *Assessment of writing: Politics, policies, practices.* pp. 9–24. New York: Modern Language Association.

14 "Do I Need a Theoretical Framework?" Doctoral Students' Perspectives on the Role of Theory in Dissertation Research and Writing

Diane Belcher and Alan Hirvela

It seems almost commonsensical that decisions about theory would be among the most crucial that doctoral students make in the entire dissertation creation process, as they must decide not only what theories to use but whether or not to use any explicit theory, at what stage/s theory, explicit or implicit, should enter into their project, and even more fundamentally, how to define what they mean by *theory*. Such decisions will shape the research project that becomes a dissertation and its actual writing up (both process and product). Commitment to and use of theory in the dissertation will also serve as a major means by which the dissertation writer will position her/himself within a particular contribution to a field's written knowledge, hence in the field itself.

For experienced researchers, decisions about theory may not be significant obstacles in their research processes, as they may already be committed to a theoretical approach or, because of prior research experience, have a rich repertoire of tried-and-found-helpful theoretical stances from which to choose for particular projects. For novice researchers such as dissertation writers, that is, those generally without prior, well rehearsed theoretical commitments and a wealth of research experience to invoke, the situation is likely to be rather more challenging. If the novice researcher is also in a highly interdisciplinary field in which there is limited consensus on theory use (not uncommon in the social sciences and education), the challenges may be still greater. In this chapter we will consider how doctoral students grapple with theory decision-making in the construction of their dissertations in one interdisciplinary field, namely, second language (L2) writing. Before describing our study itself, we will briefly survey definitions of the term *theory* offered by research methodologists and the current climate for theory in the disciplinary context focused on in our study, the field of L2 writing.

ON UNSTABLE GROUND: THE SLIPPERINESS OF *THEORY*

As Glesne and Peshkin (1992), Lincoln and Guba (1985, 2000), Johnson and Onwuegbuzie (2004) and other research methodologists have noted, there is little agreement among researchers, especially in education and social science fields, on what theory actually is. Glesne and Peshkin (1992) remark that theory may take the shape of sets of individual propositions or of a conceptual framework for reaching understanding; theory, or theory construction, may be seen as what inspires initial research questions, guides and focuses data analysis, or makes the entire research process meaningful; and in research documents, theory may surface as a "tacked on" appendage at the beginning or end, or it may be the unifying force and guiding principle of the entire study (pp. 19–21). For positivists, including many quantitative researchers (though the two are not necessarily isomorphic), theory should be empirically verifiable and able to "explain and predict relationships among phenomena" (Glesne & Peshkin, 1992, p. 19). Universal truths, and, some would add, control of the natural world (Lincoln & Guba, 1985), are the goals of positivistic theory (goals that, while easy to critique in a postmodernist world, we have all obviously been the beneficiaries of, for example, in the form of modern medicine). For post-positivist interpretivists, including many qualitative researchers, theory emerges from "thick description" of "intentions, motives, meanings, contexts, situations, and circumstances of action" and aims at understanding of "lived experience" rather than abstract generalizations and universal truths (Glesne & Peshkin, 1992, p. 19, citing Denzin, 1988, pp. 18, 39). Interpretivists see all theory, in fact, all "reality," as resulting from human construction, hence they reject "naïve realism," preferring to view the world in terms of "constructed realities" rather than as a single out-there, verifiable reality (again, see Glesne & Peshkin, 1992; also Lincoln & Guba, 2000). Interpretivists, thus, readily acknowledge and value the fact that we all create our own reality.

Despite the lack agreement on what constitutes theory (inevitably linked with conceptions of truth and reality), research methodologists have developed taxonomies of theory that can make theory itself somewhat easier to identify and discuss. The following brief typology is derived from a number of other such classification attempts (Denzin, 1988; Glaser & Strauss, 1967; Glesne & Peshkin, 1992; Holliday, 2002; Lincoln and Guba, 1985; Turner, 1985):

1. Causal Theoretical Models: used mainly by quantitative researchers interested in objective, empirically-based generalizations and variables as means of explaining variance in a world that exists outside the human mind (see Glesne & Peshkin, 1992).

2. Locally Grounded Theory: used mainly by qualitative researchers interested in inductive, emergent discovery of patterns, issues, concepts derived from naturalistic inquiry and researcher self-reflexivity (see Lincoln & Guba, 1985).

3. Conceptual Frameworks: used by both quantitative and qualitative researchers as "a broad structure of both explicit and assumed propositions" (Denzin, 1988, p. 49) to inform the entire research process (Glesne & Peshkin, 1992), including the researcher's ideological position (positivist or otherwise) and methodological choices (Holliday, 2002).

We should be careful, however, Johnson and Onwuegbuzie (2004) warn, not to allow recent research "paradigm wars" (p. 14) and the agendas of research methodologists to too rigidly demarcate our view of various types of theory and exaggerate the significance of paradigmatic differences (as items 1 and 2 above appear to do). Johnson and Onwuegbuzie argue that in practice, researchers not infrequently engage in philosophical pragmatism and, as a result, mix paradigms, methodologies, and epistemologies. In other words, practicing researchers may do whatever seems productive as a means of addressing their research questions, including using "mixed-method" approaches (see Creswell, 2003), even if by doing so, they align themselves with seemingly radically different ways of theorizing their research worlds.

THE PROBLEM OF THEORY IN THE FIELD OF L2 WRITING

Leki (2003) has recently pointed out, as she notes others have before her (see Silva, 1990), how "undertheorized" the field of L2 writing appears to be, especially when compared to related fields such as composition and rhetoric, and a fellow subdiscipline of applied linguistics, critical applied linguistics. For Leki, the undertheorized state of L2 writing is evident in its limited reaching to "broader intellectual strands, domains, and dimensions of modern thought and contemporary lived experience" (p. 103). Similarly, Atkinson (2003) has commented on the need to broaden the conceptual scope of L2 writing beyond its usual pedagogical concerns, e.g., teacher feedback, peer response, and treatment of error, and to forge links with "current and emerging areas of local, global, political, intellectual, technological, and sociocognitive concern that are part of the landscape of theory and practice in education, applied linguistics, and social science at the start of the 21st century" (p. 12). Yet, others, such as Matsuda (2003), have warned of the dangers of being too broad and facilely "theoretical" in L2 writing, noting the use of such loosely defined terms denoting theory as "process," which, more realistically speaking, stands for "a set of pedagogical practices," and "post-process," which can easily "mask the complexity of ideas to which it refers" (p. 78). Matsuda's caveats resonate with warnings from educational research methodologists that theory may be as likely to conceal as to reveal (Schutz, 2005; Thomas, 1997).

Silva and Leki's (2004) overview of the "intellectual inheritance" (p. 1) of L2 writing helps us appreciate the challenges involved in efforts to theorize in this field. Its "grandparent" disciplines of rhetoric and theoretical linguistics and its more immediate "parent" disciplines of composition studies and applied linguistics (p. 10) have provided the relatively young field of L2 writing with quite a diverse theoretical legacy. From the parent disciplines in particular, Silva and Leki note, have come what can be viewed as "bipolar disciplinary predilections" (p. 10): both positivist and relativist inquiry paradigms; realist and relativist ontologies; objectivist and subjectivist epistemologies; manipulative empirical and hermeneutical, or interpretivist, methodologies; and explanatory and transformative axiologies. For L2 writing, thus, the challenge of "maturing" as a discipline, Silva and Leki observe, will require "reflecting critically" on these varied inheritances, or even more broadly, "on knowledge of theory and on the results of inquiry from any relevant discipline so that L2 writing professionals can develop their own models and theories" (p. 11). More recently, Silva (2005) has referred to this need for eclectic theory-building, or taking from current research paradigms what seems most likely to serve L2 writing research needs best, as "humble pragmatic rationalism": *"Humble* reflecting the limits of one's knowledge and *pragmatic* in the sense of a pluralistic and eclectic approach that accommodates different worldviews, assumptions, and methods . . . to address . . . specific problems in particular contexts" (p. 8–9). Similarly, Canagarajah (2006), in surveying the current state of the larger umbrella discipline of TESOL, has lauded the "messiness" of practice as one of the productive new metaphors for a field necessarily engaged in "crossing boundaries, mixing identities, and negotiating epistemologies" (p. 30).

For novice disciplinary members still struggling with the meaning and role of theory in their research, and perhaps hoping for guidance, boundary-crossing messiness and critical pragmatic rationalism (for more on *critical* rationalism see Silva & Leki, 2004) may seem somewhat elusive goals, more easily admired in others' work than achieved in one's own. When these novices are doctoral students, achieving such a goal may be an even more complex undertaking. In addition to trying to understand what "theory" means and what role(s) it plays in the dissertation process for their own edification, they must decode and respond to the beliefs and expectations attached to theory not only by their dissertation advisor and committee members—those who will ultimately judge the success of their work—but also by their disciplinary field at large, where they are attempting to establish themselves as contributing members. Faced with, as is not infrequently the case, differences of opinion about theory, doctoral students may find themselves in a sometimes uncomfortable or untenable place as they juggle varied, and perhaps competing, ideas about theory and dissertation writing, including their own emerging perspectives on the contributions theory makes to a quality dissertation. Meloy (2002) observes that "being able to handle ambiguity" (p. 2) is one of the foremost challenges faced by doctoral students, and the domain of theory is a key site of this ambiguity. In the remainder of this chapter we explore how our research participants dealt with these issues.

Methods

In pursuit of our objective, i.e., to better understand how doctoral students handle theory decision-making in the construction of their dissertations in the interdisciplinary field of L2 writing, an effort was made to sample the perspectives of doctoral students on the conceptualization, choice, and application of theory in their dissertations on L2 writing. The number of informants, fourteen, was deliberately kept small to enable more in-depth elicitation of their views than a wider-scale survey would be likely to. It should be noted too that we deliberately selected informants whose dissertation-writing contexts we were fairly familiar with, having been their instructors in graduate courses, served on their doctoral committees, or mentored them as their dissertation advisors.[1] Our familiarity with the informants themselves as dissertation writers, in fact, informed our construction of guiding questions in our open-ended email questionnaire (see appendix) and no doubt played a role in the 100% response rate. In our analysis of the questionnaire responses, each of us, the authors of this study, independently read and constructed lists of major trends in the responses. Upon comparing our findings, we found ourselves to be virtually in complete agreement.

Reflecting on Theory in Dissertations: Fourteen Views

Informant Profiles

The demographic data elicited via our questionnaire did not surprise us, the authors, given, again, our familiarity with the informants, but the data does enable us to present an informant profile that highlights the diversity and commonalities among our informants. The small number of countries represented by the informants' doctoral degree-granting institutions (a result of our convenience sampling), with eleven respondents from universities in the United States and one each from a university in Canada, Hong Kong, and the United Kingdom, belies the cultural diversity among the individual informants, who self-identified as coming from eight different countries (see Table 1). Thus, though the majority of the informants had been doctoral students at US universities, eleven out of the fourteen dissertation writers (almost 80%) were East Asian.

Table 1: Respondents' Countries of Origin and Doctoral Degree-Granting Institutions

		Universities		
		Canadian	HK	UK	US
Native Countries	China (PRC)	I			3
	Hong Kong (PRC)		I		
	Japan				2
	Korea				2
	Russia				I
	Taiwan				I
	Thailand				I
	USA			I	I

Dissertation Topics, Research Paradigms, and Theoretical Orientations

The dissertation topics of the informants can be categorized in six topic areas (see Table 2), with half (7) focused on one area, namely, academic literacy socialization at the college level.[2] The second most popular topic area was technology use (3, or 21 percent).

Table 2: Dissertation Topics: General Categories

Topic Area	Number of Dissertations (N = 14)
Socialization in tertiary L2 academic literacy (mainly writing):	7 focus on undergraduates: I focus on graduate students: 4 focus on both: 2
Technology use for L2 literacy, e.g., Internet, listserv, corpus linguistics	3
Historical study of EFL writing instruction	I
Non-academic L2 literacy practices	I
Theory development for SLA(second language acquisition) /SLL (second language literacy learning) /L2 literacy pedagogy	I
Writing textbook analysis	I

The research paradigms utilized in these dissertations were overwhelmingly qualitative (9, or 64 percent). Almost a third (4) of the dissertations, however, were identified by the informants as mixed method, i.e., with both qualitative and quantitative paradigms, and included such research design components as descriptive statistics, text analysis, interviews, and other methods. One dissertation was labeled by its author as "historical."

When asked to describe the theoretical framework or orientation of their dissertations, the fourteen respondents gave us twenty-one descriptors:

1. academic writing 1
2. case study: 1
3. cultural studies/culture: 2
4. dialectical materialism   1
5. dialogic theory: 1
6. ethnomethodological: 1
7. ethnographic: 1
8. genre theory: 1
9. intercultural rhetoric: 1
10. interpretivism: 1
11. legitimate peripheral participation: 1
12. lexico-grammar/corpus linguistics: 1
13. local enactment: 1
14. NA ("not easy to categorize"): 2
15. naturalistic: 1
16. practical actions: 1
17. revisionary historiography: 1
18. situated learning/situatedness: 2
19. social constructivism: 1
20. social view of literacy: 1
21. socio-cultural/historical theory: 2

Although the number and variety of responses above could suggest respondent uncertainty about what should be considered theoretical, the responses can also be seen as in line with research methodologists' observations that theory can operate on many different levels, including formal, epistemological, methodological, and metatheoretical (see Creswell, 2003; Flinders & Mills, 1993).

Definitions of Theory and Theoretical Framework

When asked to define the term *theory*, the informants' definitions suggested somewhat more uniformity, and could be seen as falling into two large categories. One category was more broadly philosophical, or ontological and epistemological, with respondents referring to the real-world explanatory power of theory: "an assertion describing nature," "ideas, concepts, explanations . . . at some level of abstraction from real events or entities," and "a set of principles to understand the world." Many of the definitions (almost half) explicitly related the meaning-making power of theory to the research process and defined it in such pre- and post-supposition terms as "guiding principle," "specific philosophy to organize information to conduct research," "hypothesis developed to account for . . . ," "conclusions / interpretations about given phenomena, if empirical, based on studies." One respondent connected theory with disciplinary knowledge: "well-recognized philosophical ideas of a discipline or broad intellectual field, i.e., social science." Two responses stood out as rather more anomalous. One of these, from a self-identified ethnomethodologist, resisted the notion of theory, referring to it as "a puzzling social construct: should be defined by use, but used in many different ways." This respondent was more interested in "concepts and exemplars, which serve as an *analytic program*" (respondent's emphasis). Another respondent appeared quite mindful of a power differential among meaning makers, with theory seen as "huge . . . proved, contested, accumulated, and evolved through empirical and conceptual studies" and able to explain "phenomena across contexts, possibly space & time." For this informant, theory was "something that big scholars can generate," not dissertation writers: "I as a junior faculty/scholar would like to build theory . . . in the future."

Ten of the fourteen respondents attempted to distinguish *theoretical framework* from *theory*, and, of these, two saw virtually no difference. In effect then, only eight of the fourteen (57 percent) described what they perceived as some discernible difference between the two terms. The differences identified were fairly evenly divided into scope and function categories, with theoretical frameworks seen as "broader," sometimes based on more than one theory, and as an application to/ for a specific research project, sometimes in the form of a "rationale" or "model." As with theory, two specific definitions of theoretical framework stood out. One, from the same respondent who appeared resistant to the term *theory*, returned to the notion of "analytic program" to define a framework, which was viewed as a "body of resources to serve as a foundation for research interests and methodology." The other response notably unlike the others, especially with respect to amount of elaboration, came from a respondent whose dissertation was focused on theory-building. For this informant, theory was the "core" of a theoretical framework, "its essence," while the framework itself was "a group of mutually interrelated concepts that form a coherent whole; . . . lens to examine phenomena to understand them; epistemological and axiological; an outlook, worldview, conceptual horizon; determines object, goals, method of research." It would perhaps be unrealistic to expect other dissertation writers less focused on theory construction than was this informant to be able to articulate equally comprehensive and complex definitions of theoretical framework.

Placement and Importance of a Theoretical Framework

Several questions were posed about the role of theoretical frameworks in dissertation research and writing. When asked which came first in their own dissertation work, the theoretical framework or the research process, half (7) replied that their development or selection of a theoretical framework preceded their research. The other half saw their framework as more emergent: either as being in place before the research but also shaped by the research process (4) or as emerging during and after the research process (3). Of the latter three, however, one noted: "Telling a good, accurate story with my findings was more important than situating the story in theory." Given that thirteen of the fourteen dissertation writers self-identified their research paradigms as exclusively or partly qualitative, one might have expected far more than half to have had the more locally grounded, emergent theoretical frameworks that many research methodologists (e.g., Lincoln & Guba, 1985) describe as a hallmark of qualitative research. It is easy enough to understand, however, why some novice research writers might prefer the security of launching their projects with a framework in mind rather than waiting (and hoping) for one to "emerge."

The actual placement of the theoretical framework in the text of the dissertations did not necessarily reflect its temporal position in the dissertation writers' cognitive processing. In the documents themselves, the theoretical framework could make an appearance in from one to a total of three chapters (i.e., in the same document). In one respondent's dissertation, the framework was presented in a separate chapter titled "Theory." Interestingly, none of the fourteen informants' mentioned chapters identified as either Discussion or Results as places where their framework was explicitly discussed.

As for perceptions of the importance of a theoretical framework, views ranged from "crucial" and the "basement of constructing research" (which we interpreted as meaning *foundational*) to far less than that. To some, their theoretical framework was an essential "mediating tool" throughout the research process:

> It informed how I needed to proceed with the design of my research, e.g., the procedures, the types of data I was supposed to collect, the types of questions I asked in my interviews and the types of phenomena (textual phenomena and narratives) I needed to analyze and discuss in my thesis.

Another informant observed similarly:

> In my case, my theoretical framework . . . helped me design my study and better understand and organize the enormous amount of data that I collected. . . . I drew on other theories . . . because [one theory] could not fully explain all the incidents or nuances in. . . . [These] theories gave me meta-knowledge and vocabulary to understand and describe. . . .

Some respondents emphasized the role of their theoretical framework in jump-starting their thinking and research process: "I think the most important part was clarifying my thoughts and phrasing my research questions." Others put more emphasis on the cognitive value of theory later in the process: "It was important because it made me think of ways to view my data and explain my findings." Others spoke of the vital role of the theoretical framework in the actual writing up of their research, reporting that it "guided me all the way from proposal to data analysis write-up" or was "very important for consistency in dissertation components." For the respondent primarily focused on theory-building, the framework was more than a means of facilitating research and writing processes: "The construction of a theoretical framework was one of the main objectives of my research." Clearly the majority of the informants, however, had a more utilitarian view of their frameworks and were more content with finding, or cobbling together, and fine-tuning frameworks that would serve their research purposes.

Table 3: Placement of Theoretical Framework in Specific Dissertation Chapters

Dissertation Chapter/s with Theoretical Framework	Number of Dissertations
Introduction	1
Literature Review	4
Introduction and Literature Review	5
Introduction, Literature Review, and Conclusion	1
Introduction and Methods	1
Conclusion	1
Theory	1

For a minority (4) of the respondents, a theoretical framework was not seen as an important part of their dissertation, though their reasons for this view varied considerably. One noted that she never found or developed what she had hoped for: "I still feel that my dissertation needed a theory." Another remarked that because of the novelty of her research: "Honestly I didn't know what kinds of very 'specific' theories I would draw upon for my study." Still another, the respondent cited earlier as concerned about the accuracy of her "story," was glad that her work was ultimately not constrained by a theoretical framework:

> From beginning to end I actively tried to find points of contact between my work and existing theoretical perspectives. . . . In the end, I felt that the most important story in my findings would be diminished if I tried to ground the telling of them in a firmly recognizable, established theoretical framework. . . .

The informant self-identified as an ethnomethodologist also felt that a framework could be less than helpful:

> My goal was to collect naturally occurring phenomena in a normal context, so imposing an *a priori* framework would have been counterproductive. I thought it was important to look at what my students were

> doing under normal, usual classroom conditions. I
> believe that this understanding must come first be-
> fore we can begin to understand how students learn
> to write—and . . . too often researchers impose theo-
> ry . . . before they have enough materials. . . .

This informant did note, however, that "it was *very* [respondent's em-
phasis] important . . . to have a well-formed perspective on the character of the social world and its organization" and that "this came
from readings in sociology, anthropology, education, naturalistic inquiry. . . ." From this informant's perspective, research methodology
trumped theoretical framework, as "ethnomethodology has a notori-
ously insolent view of theory." Of course, in this case, one could argue
that research methodology took the place of a theoretical framework,
and, in fact, the informant volunteered a similar observation, "that
[educational] research methodologies have within them implicit theories of language, learning, instruction, and how social worlds are organized."

What role the dissertation advisors played in the dissertation writers' perceptions of the importance of a theoretical framework is far
from clear. Almost half (6) of the informants reported that they and
their advisors were in agreement on the importance of a theoretical
framework to dissertation research and writing, but a substantial percentage (5, or 36%), reported never having discussed the matter with
their advisor. We could interpret this silence on the issue as suggesting
unspoken agreement, a laissez faire approach to advising, or even a lack
of interest in theory on the advisor's part. There was another smaller
group of informants (3) who mentioned not being in agreement. One
of these informants was initially at odds with the dissertation advisor:

> At first, I didn't take it seriously to have a framework
> for my study. I thought reviewing the previous stud-
> ies was enough. . . . However, my advisor empha-
> sized that I need to have a theoretical framework that
> would guide my study, and later when I wrote up
> my dissertation, I realized what [was] meant. I can't
> imagine how I can deal with the huge data of my re-
> search without the framework.

Another informant, whose primary dissertation objective, as noted above, was theory construction, felt that the advisor never quite appreciated what was being attempted:

> Probably due to the theoretical and, therefore, unconventional nature of my research, the theoretical framework I came up with in the last chapter was understood by my advisor as merely a conclusion or summary of the main discussion.

Only one informant spoke of coming close to serious disagreement:

> Well, we had a bumpy ride. . . . Both of us were newcomers in learning and working on this type of . . . studies. . . . However, the . . . framework seemed to be way too messy for [the advisor] . . . although [s/he] did try [his/her] best to help. . . .

Again, however, for most of the informants, the advisors were either in agreement or silent (not explicitly in disagreement) about the role of a theoretical framework.

Far more likely than a dissertation advisor to change the writers' thinking about their theoretical framework and its importance was, as suggested above by a respondent, the actual engagement in the dissertation research and writing processes (sometimes seen as concurrent). One informant spoke of the writing process clarifying the role of theory, just as theory clarified the data being written about:

> While the framework seems important for all the stages of dissertation research, I realized its importance at the time of my dissertation writing. A theory is like a lens, through which the researcher sees their data. The interpretation of the data may be different depending on what kind of lenses they use.

The data itself, however, sometimes became a lens through which to see theories differently:

> I basically got stuck at some parts and wasn't happy about my findings. Of course, I talked to people and read a lot of literature and came to learn more about the theories/framework I developed in the initial stage of my work. However, as I gained better under-

> standing of them [the theories] . . . I wanted to expand
> and revise my understanding . . . and . . . to find out
> other frameworks. . . . My findings also suggested that
> I needed to do the same.

Another informant observed that writing about the data revealed limitations in the framework, or at least in how the writer was interpreting it, and that reinterpretation could have an impact on the outcome:

> Even though I began to write it following a certain
> framework, I was puzzled when facing with some contradiction with it. So what I did was reinterpreting the
> framework in order to adjust the output of my study.

Still another informant referred to "constantly revising my theoretical framework." Others mentioned not revising their frameworks *per se* but bringing in additional theories "for enriching my understanding" and even taking additional courses to understand what else "should also be importantly factored in." Only one informant, who, as noted earlier, was concerned about the accuracy of the story of the findings, observed that the research and writing processes led to the realization that a theoretical framework was not essential:

> So I started . . . with a fairly conscious intention to
> find a framework for my research, and the assumption
> that if I read enough and thought enough, I'd find it.
> Ultimately I didn't, but by the time I got to the end of
> the dissertation process I'd stopped worrying about it;
> I had findings, I thought they were important. . . . So
> essentially I did a 180-degree turn over the course of
> writing my dissertation.

Clearly, for some writers, having a theoretical framework explicitly in mind is not essential to their research and writing processes, and the "commonsensical" observation that began this chapter, that theory decision-making is likely to be crucial for dissertation writing, may make less sense in the case of some writers.

THE DIFFICULTY OF THEORY DECISION-MAKING

For most of the informants, however, developing (or finding) a suitable theoretical framework for their dissertation work was seen as critical to its success and a particularly arduous undertaking. More than half of the informants (9) described the task as "difficult," including several who saw it as extraordinarily daunting: "It was *very very very* difficult. The most difficult among all parts of the [doctoral] thesis" [informant's emphasis]. Another similarly described it as "one of the most challenging parts despite the guidance from mentors." Some pointed to reasons for the difficulty, not least of which was uncertainty about the construct, *theoretical framework:* "I was lost at the start of thinking about my dissertation because I didn't really understand what the theoretical framework was and how to set it up." Finding a good fit for the dissertation topic was also seen as part of the challenge: "After I chose my topic, I came to consider where my study stood in terms of the theoretical framework, and it was not an easy task." Another commented on the problem of a "theory first" belief: " . . . my initial belief in a 'theory first' approach caused me to search for something that I ultimately concluded didn't exist." Several pointed to the need to go beyond prior training and comfort level: "Definitely difficult—with a strong background in Applied Linguistics, it was a real adventure for me to explore such new areas as [those needed to develop the framework]. . . ." Another, though, found all stages of dissertation to be challenging in that they all "are different and call for different types of thinking, planning." Interestingly, working with the framework in the later stages of the dissertation was seen by some as no less challenging than the initial development and application of the framework: "I think it was very difficult for me . . . connecting [the findings] to the theoretical framework. Since my time was very limited . . . I just gave up doing it."

The minority of informants (5) who did not find development of their theoretical framework especially difficult also pointed to a variety of reasons for this relative ease. For one, it seemed simply a matter of choosing a framework others had developed:

> Well, the framework is an already established item. The pioneers established the orientation based on strong research. So I believed that I had to follow the perspectives correctly, not changing or adding anything.

Another informant had spent years developing an "analytic program" that was thus "well-formed before I got to the dissertation." One informant credited prolonged engagement with theory in the doctoral program: "It was not quite difficult for me . . . because this framework came from my engagement in . . . over the past four years of my studies . . ." Another pointed to wide-ranging relevant reading of the research literature, enabling the informant to "draw upon many . . . studies which included very specific, clear, and well-developed theoretical frameworks." One respondent gave a very philosophically "qualitative" response, observing that the framework was just "a natural product of the quest for the answer to my research question." We should note that there is not necessarily any correlation between perceptions of ease or difficulty and the sophistication or effectiveness of the theoretical framework that writers develop.

Advice for Future Dissertation Writers

Given the accounts of their experience with theory in their own dissertations, the advice that the informants offered future dissertation writers regarding theory was not entirely surprising. Most frequently mentioned was the need to be careful not to commit too prematurely or exclusively to any theory. One informant very explicitly warned of initial commitment to the "wrong" theory: "If I had initially grounded my study within certain theoretical frameworks, I hadn't been able to produce a kind of study that I have done." Another stressed the importance of trying out various theories/frameworks, staying critical, and consulting with more knowledgeable others:

> Don't expect that you can find a perfect theory or theoretical framework . . . ready for application in your thesis. Do a bit of data collection. . . . Critique it [the theory] . . . allow it to interact with your own data. . . . Talk to your supervisor. . . . Report your views [to the supervisor] . . . at some fixed stages of your thesis development. . . . Discuss your work with an expert(s) in the field who also uses the theories/ frameworks.

The advantages of early selection of a theoretical framework were touted, though, by those who had benefited from it in their own work:

> It is helpful to have a theoretical framework at the beginning stage . . . because the theoretical framework

can help shape the design of the study and predict what the researcher may experience in the fieldwork.

Yet this informant too warned of being too reliant on a particular framework:

> On the other hand, it is also important for the researcher not to be constrained by the theoretical framework, which should primarily function as a general guideline. The researcher should be open to any relevant theories in the process of data collection and analysis.

Pragmatism was salient in much of the advice offered: "Never slavishly follow a theory or framework unless it is well-established or you need it to advance some claims. . . ." This informant also noted the need to be realistic and view one's theoretical commitment in a dissertation as just that, not a lifetime commitment: "You may change your mind about the theory or the theoretical framework after you've completed your thesis. This is normal, I think." Still more pragmatically-oriented was the recommendation to simply follow one's advisor's lead, bearing in mind that there could be a price to pay:

> If you are the practical type, and if your work is closely related to your advisor's, find out the theoretical framework/theories your supervisor uses and develop yours along that line. This can save time, but it may also prevent you from learning other equally powerful theories.

Several emphasized the value of extensive reading and willingness to revise:

> Start early and read widely on the topic of your dissertation; identify important works in the literature (with the help of your advisor and/or committee members, if necessary); let your research questions lead you to the theoretical framework, and leave the framework open to revision.

Even a "sloppy" framework was not seen as a problem if one keeps reading:

> It is Ok to have a sloppy theoretical framework at
> first, but you need to keep up your reading in order to
> construct a theoretical framework that will best suit
> the goal of your study.

Two informants advised wariness about theory in general. One of these cautioned against "incorporat[ing] theory for the sake of doing it," which could "lead to findings that fall outside the scope of the framework being neglected." Another theory-wary respondent, the ethnomethodologist, advised that the best theory is no theory, yet even avid theory advocates, especially proponents of grounded theory, might find much to agree with in this recommendation of situated-ness:

> I have little confidence in the utility of theory for. . . .
> I would encourage students to look closely at local
> settings and actions and to build good descriptions
> of them. To me, such accounts are more instructive
> than theory. I worked very hard to find a way to live
> with my materials.

CONCLUSION

Theory as seen in the descriptions of its use (or nonuse) in the dissertation research and writing of the fourteen informants focused on in this study appears in a multitude of guises, just as the educational research methodologists cited earlier in this chapter have suggested it typically does (e.g., Creswell, 2003). Theory for our informants was implicit and explicit, heuristic and explanatory, tied to precise research methodologies and grandly conceptual, what motivated their research and guided their writing, a lens that sometimes clarified and sometimes constrained thought. With respect to the disciplinary context of L2 writing, the pluralistic eclecticism that Leki and Silva (2004) and Silva (2005) have called for in L2 writing was in abundant evidence in the informants' reflections on their use of theory. The dissertation writers were obviously eager to take advantage of the types of "broader intellectual strands" that Leki (2003, p. 103), Atkinson (2003), and others have seen as much needed in L2 writing as a field. None of our informants could be described as narrowly focused on exclusively pedagogical concerns.

Perhaps much of the credit for encouraging junior researchers to consider theory, or engage in reflective meaning-making, should go to the dissertation task itself. The dissertation project gives doctoral students both reason to think about theorizing and the time and space (in the document itself) to theorize. While the refereed research article is a much more privileged genre in professional academia, seen as essential to advancement of professional knowledge and professional careers, the more expansive genre of the dissertation is far more likely to invite and even compel exploration of theory. When looking for advances in theorizing in L2 writing or any field, we would do well to take a close look at dissertations. Dissertation writers themselves, through their written research products and self-revelations about their research and writing, problem-solving, and meaning-making processes, may have much to tell the rest of us, including those of us who have researched and published extensively but may not have seriously considered the role of theory in our work since the writing of our own dissertations.

Notes

1. Many of the informants for this study had also participated in our earlier study of dissertation writers' research paradigm commitments (see Belcher & Hirvela, 2005).

2. Please note that in order to maintain the anonymity of the dissertation writers, the specific topics of their dissertations are not revealed, and in all subsequent discussion of their work, many other details that might enable identification of the writers have been removed.

References

Atkinson, D. (2003). L2 writing in the post-process era: Introduction. *Journal of Second Language Writing, 12,* 3–15.

Belcher, D., & Hirvela, A. (2005). Writing the qualitative dissertation: What motivates and sustains commitment to a fuzzy genre? *Journal of English for Academic Purposes, 4,* 187–205.

Creswell, J. W. (2003). *Research design: Qualitative, quantitative, and mixed methods approaches.* Thousand Oaks, CA: Sage.

Flinders, D. J., & Mills, G. E. (1993). *Theory and concepts in qualitative research.* New York: Teachers College Press.

Glaser, B., & Strauss, A. (1967). *The discovery of grounded theory: Strategies for qualitative research.* Chicago, IL: Aldine.

Glesne, C., & Peshkin, A. (1992). *Becoming qualitative researchers: An introduction.* London: Longman.

Holliday, A. (2002). *Doing and writing qualitative research.* London: Sage.

Johnson, R. B., & Onwuegbuzie, A. (2004). Mixed methods research: A research paradigm whose time has come. *Educational Researcher, 33*(7), 14–26.

Leki, I. (2003). Coda: Pushing L2 writing research. *Journal of Second Language Writing, 12,* 103–105.

Lincoln, Y., & Guba, E. (1985). *Naturalistic inquiry.* Newbury Park, CA: Sage.

Lincoln, Y., & Guba, E. (2000). Introduction: The discipline and practice of qualitative research. In N. Denzin & Y. Lincoln (Eds.), *Handbook of qualitative research,* Second edition (pp. 1–28). Thousand Oaks, CA: Sage.

Matsuda, P. K. (2003). Process and post-process: A discursive history. *Journal of Second Language Writing, 12,* 65–83.

Meloy, J. (2002). *Writing the qualitative dissertation: Understanding by doing.* Mahwah, NJ: Erlbaum.

Schutz, A. (2005). Theory illuminates (and conceals): A response to the critique of Samantha Caughlan. *Educational Researcher, 34* (2), 17–18.

Silva, T. (2005). On the philosophical bases of inquiry in second language writing: Metaphysics, inquiry paradigms, and the intellectual zeitgeist. In P. Matsuda & T. Silva (Eds.), *Second language writing research: Perspectives on the process of knowledge construction* (pp. 3–16). Mahwah, NJ: Erlbaum.

Silva, T., & Leki, I. (2004). Family matters: The influence of applied linguistics and composition studies on second language writing studies—past, present, and future. *Modern Language Journal, 88,* 1–13.

Thomas, G. (1997). What's the use of theory? *Harvard Educational Review, 67,* 75–104.

APPENDIX

Questionnaire

Directions: Please answer the questions below in the context of your dissertation research and writing experiences.

Background information:

1) Title of dissertation:
2) Research paradigm employed (quantitative, qualitative, mixed methods):
3) Key terms describing theoretical framework or orientation of your study (e.g. "New London Group Orientation," "Eth-

nomethodological Inquiry," "Genre Theory," "Critical Theory,"
"Critical Contrastive Rhetoric"):

4) Institution where doctoral degree was granted or is being pur-
sued:

5) Native Country:

Questions

6) How do you define the terms "theory" and "theoretical framework"?

7) How important was the construction of a suitable theoretical
framework in the development of your dissertation? That is,
how much importance did you place on the theoretical framework relative to the various components of a dissertation? Also,
were you in agreement with your advisor on the relative importance of this framework in your research and the writing up of
it?

8) There are different schools of thought on when and how a theoretical framework should be developed. Some maintain that
theory must come first and thus shape the design of a dissertation, while others feel that the research process shapes the theoretical framework. Which school of thought did you follow in
your dissertation experience?

9) As you worked on your dissertation, did you adjust or revise
your theoretical framework or your thoughts on the importance
of theory in dissertation writing? If so, how and why?

10) Where in your dissertation did you place your theoretical
framework (e.g, in the introduction, in the literature review, or
in a separate "Theoretical Framework" chapter)? Why?

11) To what extent, and in what ways (if any), did your theoretical
framework impact on your writing about the results of your dissertation research? For example, did you consider your theoretical framework as you reported and/or discussed your results?

12) How difficult, relative to other aspects of the dissertation
(writing the methods chapter, reporting results, etc.), was the
development of your theoretical framework?

13) What role(s), if any, do you feel dissertation advisors should
play in assisting advisees in constructing their theoretical
framework?

14) What advice concerning theoretical frameworks would you
give to future dissertation writers in the field of L2 writing?

Contributors

Dwight Atkinson is an applied linguist and second language educator who specializes in writing, qualitative research approaches, and second language acquisition. Current projects include developing a "sociocognitive" approach to second language acquisition and research on the experiences of vernacular language-schooled students in English-language universities in India. Atkinson's past work has ranged widely, from the history of medical and scientific research writing in English, to critiques of concepts in writing instruction such as critical thinking and voice, to explorations of the concept of culture, to writings on qualitative research methods. Atkinson teaches courses in qualitative research, postmodernism, and second language acquisition at Purdue University.

Diane Belcher, Professor of Applied Linguistics at Georgia State University, is former co-editor of the journal *English for Specific Purposes* and incoming co-editor of *TESOL Quarterly*. She also co-edits the teacher reference series *Michigan Series on Teaching Multilingual Writers*. She has guest-edited the *Journal of Second Language Writing* three times, authored a number of articles on advanced academic literacy, and edited five books, the most recent being *English for Specific Purposes in Theory and Practice*.

Suresh Canagarajah is the Kirby Professor in Language Learning and Director of the Migration Studies Project at Pennsylvania State University. He teaches World Englishes, Teaching and Research in Second Language Writing, Postcolonial Studies, and Theories of Rhetoric and Composition in the departments of English and Applied Linguistics. He has taught before in the University of Jaffna, Sri Lanka, and the City University of New York (Baruch College and the Graduate Center). He has published on bilingual communication, learning of writing, and English language teaching in professional journals.

Joan Carson is Professor Emerita in the Department of Applied Linguistics and ESL at Georgia State University. Her research interests include second language literacy and sociolinguistic aspects of second language acquisition. She has published widely in journals such as *Applied Linguistics, Journal of Second Language Writing, Language Learning, TESOL Quarterly,* and *Written Communication.*

Deborah Crusan is Associate Professor of TESOL/Applied Linguistics at Wright State University, Dayton, Ohio, where she teaches grammar, linguistics, and assessment courses in the MATESOL program and graduate seminars concerning the politics of assessment and writing assessment. She has published about writing assessment in recognized journals in the field such as *Assessing Writing* and *English for Specific Purposes* and has published chapters in *The Norton Field Guide* and edited collections about second language writing. She has served as chair of the Second Language Writing Interest Section at TESOL and is a member of the CCCC Committee on Second Language Writing. Her research interests include writing assessment particularly for placement of second language writers, directed/guided self-placement and its consequences for second language writers, and the politics of assessment.

Alister Cumming is Professor and Head of the Modern Language Centre at the Ontario Institute for Studies in Education, University of Toronto. His research and teaching focus on writing in second languages, literacy and assessment in classroom and formal testing contexts, and curriculum evaluation, particularly of programs for English as a second or foreign language. Alister has published extensively on these topics as well as conducting various research and evaluation projects in Canada and internationally. He currently serves as Executive Director for the journal *Language Learning* and as Chair of the TOEFL Committee of Examiners at Educational Testing Service.

Doug Flahive is the Coordinator of the Graduate Program in TESOL at Colorado State University where he teaches courses in Second Language Acquisition, Statistics and Research Design for Applied Linguistics, and the Development of Second language Literacy Skills. His research interest in Second Language Writing began over 3 decades ago when he tallied T-units in a corpus of 300 essays. This interest continues today with his research and publications in the L2 writing areas of error correction, metadiscourse and metaphor usage, reading/writing relationships and, most recently, meta-analyses of selected areas of research.

Lynn M. Goldstein is Professor and program chair, TESOL and applied linguistics, at the Monterey Institute of International Studies, where she teaches graduate courses in the teaching of writing, sociolinguistics, methods, pedagogical grammar, research, professional writing, and web design for language professionals. Her research focuses on folklinguistics and on composition, particularly feedback and revision. She has published in *TESOL Quarterly, Journal of Second Language Writing, Studies in Second Language Acquisition* and in edited anthologies. She is the author of *Teacher Written Commentary in Second Language Writing Classrooms* (University of Michigan Press). She has received the TESOL/Newbury Distinguished Research Award for her work on the acquisition of nonstandard dialects of English, and honorable mention for the best article published in the *Journal of Second Language Writing* for her and Susan Conrad's work on feedback and revision.

Linda Harklau (PhD, University of California, Berkeley) is a Professor in the Teaching Additional Languages program and Linguistics program at the University of Georgia. Her research and teaching focus on second language literacy development and qualitative research on adolescent and young adult immigrants. Her work has appeared in *TESOL Quarterly, Linguistics and Education, Educational Policy, Journal of Literacy Research, Journal of Second Language Writing,* and *Anthropology and Education Quarterly.* She was lead editor of the volume, *Generation 1.5 Meets College Composition* (Erlbaum, 1999).

John Hedgcock is Professor of Applied Linguistics at the Monterey Institute of International Studies in Monterey, California, USA, where he teaches in the MATESOL/MATFL Program. His research interests include second language reading and writing, second language acquisition, and teacher preparation. He is co-author of *Teaching ESL Composition: Purpose, Process, and Practice* (2nd ed.) and *Teaching Readers of English: Students, Texts, and Contexts.* His recent publications have appeared in the *Journal of Language, Identity, and Education, The Modern Language Journal,* and *Applied Language Learning.*

Alan Hirvela is an Associate Professor of foreign and second language education at Ohio State University. He taught previously at the Chinese University of Hong Kong. He is the author of *Connecting Reading and Writing in Second Language Writing Instruction*, and co-editor (with Diane Belcher) of *Linking Literacies: Perspectives on L2 Reading-Writing Connections*, and *The Oral-Literate Connection: Perspectives on L2 Speaking, Writing and Other Media Interactions*.

Ryuko Kubota is a Professor in the Department of Language and Literacy Education at the University of British Columbia. She has taught English and Japanese as foreign languages and has engaged in ESL and foreign language teacher education in the U.S. and Canada. Her research interests include: second language writing, critical pedagogies, and issues of culture and politics in second language education. Her articles have appeared in such journals as: *Canadian Modern Language Review, Critical Inquiry in Language Studies, English Journal, Foreign Language Annals, Journal of Second Language Writing, TESOL Quarterly, Written Communication*, and *World Englishes*.

Lourdes Ortega is Associate Professor of Second Language Studies at the University of Hawai'i at Mānoa. Her research interests include L2 writing, second language acquisition, and the use of research methods in applied linguistics. Recent books are *Synthesizing Research on Language Learning and Teaching* (co-edited with John Norris, Benjamins), *The Longitudinal Study of Advanced L2 Capacities* (co-edited with Heidi Byrnes, Routledge), and *Understanding Second Language Acquisition* (Arnold).

Dudley W. Reynolds is an Associate Teaching Professor and Director of Research in English Language Learning at Carnegie Mellon University in Qatar. His research addresses the development and assessment of second language literacy by both adult and adolescent learners. The author of *One on One with Second Language Writers: A Guide for Writing Tutors, Teachers, and Consultants*, he currently serves on the editorial board of the *Journal of Second Language Writing* and the Board of Directors of Teachers of English to Speakers of Other Languages (TESOL).

Christine Tardy is an Assistant Professor in the Department of Writing, Rhetoric, and Discourse at DePaul University, where she teaches courses in writing, applied linguistics, and TESOL. Her research interests include second language writing, genre and discourse studies, TESOL teacher education, and the politics of English. Her work appears in journals such as *Journal of Second Language Writing, Journal of English for Academic Purposes*, and *English for Specific Purposes*, and in numerous edited collections. Her book, *Building Genre Knowledge* (Parlor Press, 2009), explores the process of multilingual genre learning in academic contexts.

Gwendolyn Williams (PhD, University of Georgia) is an Assistant Professor in the Teaching English to Speakers of Other Languages program at the University of Nevada, Reno. Her research focuses on teacher identity as part of teacher development for ESL teachers and international teaching assistants. She also is interested in the influences of culture and identity on English language teaching and learning. Dr. Williams teaches courses in second language curriculum development, theory and practice in ELL reading and writing, TESOL practicum, TESOL professional development, and World Englishes.

Wei Zhu teaches in the MA program in Applied Linguistics and the interdisciplinary Ph.D program in Second Language Acquisition and Instructional Technology at the University of South Florida. Her research interests include writing needs analysis, peer feedback, the role of computer-mediated communication in student writing development, and academic literacy. Her work has appeared in journals such as *Written Communication, Language Learning, TESL Canada Journal, English for Specific Purposes,* and the *Journal of Second Language Writing.*

Index

Committee on Education and the
   Workforce, 253
Communicative Language Teaching, 215
communism, 7, 11
community of practice, 98, 99,
   104, 221, 241
complex social settings, 94
composing: competence, 59; processes, 28, 32, 33, 39, 47, 212,
   228, 238
composition studies, 71, 97, 100,
   102, 111, 161, 167, 175, 191,
   227, 243, 261, 266, 283
computer, 40, 121, 129, 155, 212,
   226
Comte, A., 96
concrete examples, 13, 191
conference abstract, 118
conference feedback, 76
Conference on College Composition and Communication, 248
confidence intervals, 139, 156
confidentiality, 259
Connelly, M., 19, 42
Connor, U., 59, 60, 66, 67, 99,
   100, 107, 147, 153, 194, 206,
   209, 212, 224
Connor-Linton, J., 60, 67
Conrad, S., 76, 77, 78, 82, 85, 86,
   88, 89, 153
conscious noticing, 9
constant comparative method,
   103, 104
constructed realities, 264
constructivism, 192, 238
constructs, 35, 42, 50, 135, 144,
   155, 156, 160, 170, 171, 189,
   217, 220, 260
consumers of theory, 221
contact zone: 185, 186, 187, 190;
   model, 186
content: 42, 57, 58, 85, 87, 114,
   115, 118, 120, 121, 144, 152,

165, 196, 225, 229, 254; area
   exams, 248; knowledge, 115;
   validity, 57
context: 12, 32, 43, 44, 50, 51, 52,
   57, 58, 61, 65, 68, 69, 71, 76, 95,
   99, 100, 105, 114, 118, 120, 133,
   136, 138, 146, 184, 190, 192,
   211, 212, 213, 214, 215, 217,
   218, 220, 222, 225, 233, 247,
   249, 253, 257, 264, 274, 281,
   283; ecological, 61; historical,
   27, 51; local, 95, 185; macro,
   51; micro, 51; of situation, 100;
   social, 39, 48, 49, 50, 51, 52, 62,
   63, 65, 66, 100, 105, 178, 187,
   189, 192
context-sensitive assessment, 258
continua of biliteracy, 19
contrastive rhetoric, 17, 54, 59, 67,
   68, 99, 100, 107, 186, 191, 193,
   194, 196, 199, 204, 205, 206,
   207
Cook, V., 50, 53, 67, 206
Corbin, J., 38, 47
Cornett, J.W., 217, 226, 227, 228
correlation, 134, 157, 279
counter opinions, 195
cover notes, 75
covert theory, 241
creativity, 51, 181, 247, 256
criterion measure, 130
critical: applied linguistics, 10,
   191, 192, 193, 266; consciousness, 10; contrastive rhetoric,
   68, 186, 191, 194, 195, 199,
   204, 205, 207, 284; decisions,
   246; discourse analysis, 101,
   186, 192; EAP, 186; language
   testing, 191, 203; linguistics,
   186; literacy, 10; paradigms,
   96; pedagogy, 9, 11, 17, 18, 110,
   190, 191; pragmatic rationalism, 267; rationalism, 116, 267;
   thinking, 178, 180, 182, 192,

310

About the Editors

Paul Kei Matsuda is Associate Professor of English at Arizona State University, where he works closely with doctoral and master's students in applied linguistics, composition, rhetoric and TESOL. Founding co-chair of the Symposium on Second Language Writing and Series Editor of the Parlor Press Series on Second Language Writing, Paul has published widely on second language writing in a wide variety of edited collections as well as journals such as *College Composition and Communication, Composition Studies, Computers and Composition, College English, English for Specific Purposes, International Journal of Applied Linguistics, Journal of Basic Writing, Journal of Second Language Writing,* and *Written Communication.* URL: http://matsuda.jslw.org/.

Tony Silva is a Professor in the Department of English at Purdue University, where he directs and teaches courses in the Graduate Program in ESL and the ESL Writing Program. To date, he has directed or served on the graduate committees of more than one hundred MA and PhD students and has received eight Excellence in Teaching Awards. He co-edited the *Journal of Second Language Writing* from 1992 to 2007 and has served as the co-host of the Symposium on Second Language Writing since 1998. He has co-edited four books, co-authored another, and published his work in such journals as the *Annual Review of Applied Linguistics, College Composition and Communication, ELT Journal, Modern Language Journal, TESOL Quarterly,* and *Written Communication.*

CPSIA information can be obtained at www.ICGtesting.com
Printed in the USA
LVOW101201271211

261050LV00001B/58/P

9 781602 351387